IN TRUE

FACE

IN TRUE

FACE

A WOMAN'S LIFE
IN THE CIA, UNMASKED

JONNA MENDEZ

WITH WYNDHAM WOOD

PUBLICAFFAIRS

New York

PublicAffairs
Hachette Book Group
1290 Avenue of the Americas, New York, NY 10104
www.publicaffairsbooks.com
@Public_Affairs

Printed in the United States of America
First Edition: March 2024

Published by PublicAffairs, an imprint of Hachette Book Group, Inc. The
PublicAffairs name and logo is a registered trademark of the Hachette Book Group.

The Hachette Speakers Bureau provides a wide range of authors for speaking
events. To find out more, go to hachettespeakersbureau.com or email
HachetteSpeakers@hbgusa.com.

PublicAffairs books may be purchased in bulk for business, educational, or
promotional use. For more information, please contact your local bookseller or the
Hachette Book Group Special Markets Department at special.markets@hbgusa.com.

The publisher is not responsible for websites (or their content) that are not owned
by the publisher.

Print book interior design by Sheryl Kober

Library of Congress Cataloging-in-Publication Data

Names: Mendez, Jonna, author.
Title: In true face : a woman's life in the CIA, unmasked / Jonna Mendez With
    Wyndham Wood.
Description: First edition. | New York, NY : Hachette Book Group, Inc., 2024. |
    Includes index.
Identifiers: LCCN 2023039156 | ISBN 9781541703124 (hardcover) |
    ISBN 9781541703148 (ebook)
Subjects: LCSH: Mendez, Jonna. | United States. Central Intelligence
    Agency—Officials and employees—Biography. | Women spies—United
    States—Biography. | Espionage, American—History. | Undercover
    operations—United States.
Classification: LCC JK468.I6 M466 2024 | DDC 327.12730092 [B]—dc23/
    eng/20231122
LC record available at https://lccn.loc.gov/2023039156

ISBNs: 9781541703124 (hardcover), 9781541703148 (ebook)
LSC-C

Printing 1, 2023

To Ruth Bader Ginsburg and Eloise Page, whose work and dedication have changed the lives of countless women who came after them, inside the CIA and far beyond. Your legacies inspire us to reach higher, shatter ceilings, and forge ahead. Thank you for paving the way.

CONTENTS

CONTENTS

I ask no favor for my sex. All I ask of our brethren is that they take their feet off our necks.

—Ruth Bader Ginsburg

CHAPTER 1

Close Call

I'd been told to wait at the airport for an official car to arrive. There were always detailed, specific instructions in case the car was late or didn't show up at all. *Under no circumstance* was I, a single, unescorted woman, to get into a "taxi." That would be "provocative" behavior, marking me as a woman looking for trouble, so instead I sat on an airport bench and waited. All too aware of the leering stares of men walking by, I unzipped my bag and retrieved the large shawl packed by Maggie, our housekeeper and lifelong friend. I draped it over my bare arms, eager to cover my pale skin.

The next morning, I was to report to the field office. I was in my mid-twenties but already I'd grown accustomed to this routine, stopping in first thing to meet the local Chief of Station at the start of each new assignment abroad. I also looked forward to seeing an old friend, Judi.

When I arrived at the Chief's office the next morning, he was waving a flimsy sheet of paper in the air. It was an incoming cable from headquarters, and he held it between thumb and forefinger as if it were smoking hot. As his staff settled into nearby chairs, he read it aloud, his eyebrows rising and falling as he spoke: a terrorist group member whom the Chief had previously met in another country, on another assignment, was now attempting to make contact. The terrorist wanted to meet with him. Here. Now. According to this FLASH cable, which was the highest priority level of CIA communications, this terrorist was a rogue, and the lethal, razor-sharp edge of an emerging radical Islamist jihadi group. He'd already helped to bring down an American plane and was running from Interpol and the local intelligence service. He was also only a single step ahead of his own terrorist organization, which sought to assassinate him; he had gone rogue and now posed a danger to them as well. He was seeking safe harbor, and the Chief knew, as we did, that the meeting would have to take place soon. The terrorist claimed to have information about a planned hijacking of another American airline: Pan Am. That last line was the bait. This was urgent.

The Chief immediately informed us—three case officers, an intel analyst, and one support person—that he would not attend the meeting alone. We would be there with him to keep our eyes on the bad dude who was summoning him. Above all, our job was to ensure that our boss did not leave the meeting with the terrorist under any circumstances. This guy was desperate. And dangerous. Capable of anything.

I'd been flown in to direct a photo-training operation, but in the blink of an eye my assignment had changed. As a Disguise officer, I now had only hours to disguise our Chief, but I had brought no disguise materials with me.

The Chief was tall with a scarred face and a noticeable Southern drawl. I asked a case officer to buy the largest shalwar kameez available and a pair of everyday sandals from the nearest market. I needed to make the Chief look local, understated. After coloring his blond hair black and adding a custom mustache from a disguise kit left behind by a recently departed case officer, I found a pair of outdated dark horn-rimmed glasses. I then applied a touch of Judi's makeup to darken his complexion. I also gave him a cigar and a leather portfolio, suggesting he light the cigar and enter the lobby of the hotel like he owned the place. Once he was in disguise, the Chief transformed. He was a natural actor whose sheer size commanded respect. The goal was for him to be able to evaluate the situation, incognito, before deciding to make the meeting and reveal himself. The Chief was scared of this terrorist. So was I.

The other officers and I then got busy de-Americanizing ourselves. We removed wedding rings, got rid of American cigarettes, and changed into locally bought clothes and shoes; items we each had in our closets for moments like this, when we needed to melt into the crowd. Separately, we made our way to the hotel, a glitzy American chain festooned with crystal chandeliers, miles of marble, and a small jungle of tropical palms in the lobby. I entered the lobby as the affluent tourist I was impersonating, maintaining a confident, slightly aloof demeanor as I silently catalogued the next several steps of our operational plan. "Hope you know what the hell you're doing," the nervous young guy in our group murmured as we went through the door together. I was a woman, which perhaps to him meant a weak link in the operational chain. Field work had long been considered the agency's "real" work—men's work. I said nothing but shot him a look.

We'd arrived early to find observation points around the enormous, light-filled atrium lobby. We were all a bit jittery, a little charged

3

up, and that was a good thing. My extensive training had taught me how to stay focused in these kinds of high-stakes circumstances; the nerves would ensure we stayed on point. It wasn't just the Chief's life on the line; it was potentially also a planeful of American passengers who would be at risk if this operation failed.

The initial goal was for the Chief to see the terrorist first, which would allow him to abort if the meeting did not look or feel right. The guys in our group spread out among the other casuals, some sitting and others standing at different points in the lobby and bar, some reading newspapers while others ordered drinks. I chose a rug shop just off the lobby that had glass walls on three sides. I'd have a direct line of sight into the lobby, where the meeting would take place. As I entered the shop, nodding hello to the proprietor, I felt a bead of sweat trickle down my back, even as my hands felt cold from the hotel's excessive air conditioning.

Our housekeeper, Maggie, always ensured I had a supply of long-sleeved, ankle-length clothing in dark colors, plus numerous shawls, whenever I traveled to this part of the world, where female modesty rules, even as the heat smothers. I'd been able to put together a costume from my own suitcase: dark blue loose pants, a matching long-sleeved tunic with gold buttons, and a deep green and navy Varanasi dupatta, or stole. Still looking foreign, but, I hoped, not American, my brick-red lipstick allowed me to fit in with the hotel's well-heeled, international clientele.

The merchant offered me tea and I began looking at his inventory of Iranian carpets—Afshar and Shiraz in particular, which were rugs I already collected and knew enough about to sound like a serious customer. While the proprietor rolled out samples from his inventory, I kept a close eye on the lobby. As the meeting time approached, I got up and walked across the vibrantly colored spread of carpets. I then kneeled on the floor to appear to be examining them while also getting a better view of the meeting site.

My heart was pounding when the Chief strode into the lobby with a larger-than-life demeanor. He sat down on a white sofa littered with silk cushions and casually began the elaborate ceremony of cutting and lighting his cigar as he scanned the lobby. That's when I looked up—through the glass wall of the rug shop, across the hallway, and through another glass wall. Standing there, inside the newsstand, was the terrorist. He was short, about 5'4", and dressed in a typical beige shalwar kameez. He was flanked by two huge, turbaned guards—Pashtuns, I guessed—each with a Kalashnikov slung unapologetically over his shoulder. This terrorist was being hunted, yet here he was, boldly announcing his presence with his heavily armed companions. It was a shocking sight, and the hotel staff clearly knew enough not to object to this open display of power.

As I stared across the hallway, the terrorist suddenly looked at me. We made eye contact. Eye contact is connection, recognition. It is personal. It's also something CIA operatives are trained not to do. As our eyes locked on one another, I suddenly felt trapped inside an invisible, almost electric circuit. His gaze remained fixed on me, like a laser beam cutting right through my disguise, for what felt like an eternity. He wanted me to know that he knew. *This is it. They're going to shoot me.* I was exposed, with no easy way out.

Frozen in place on my hands and knees, my mind flashed back to the Wall of Stars in the lobby of CIA Headquarters in Langley. Made of white Alabama marble, each star is carved with care and precision, each one representing a CIA employee who died in the line of duty. Some are named, but many are not. Their identities will never be known. They died in faraway places, serving their country, often under cover. Even their families may never know the real story. They remain unseen, even in death.

With each passing second that the terrorist held my stare I felt increasingly sure I was about to die. No one would ever know what had happened to me. I was traveling incognito; officially I was not there. Then suddenly, he hesitated. He looked down and turned away. With his bodyguards in tow, he walked into the lobby and toward the Chief.

He'd made me, then moved on. As he receded down the hallway, my blood ran cold. I had never encountered what felt like pure evil before. I was stunned by its power. I felt chilled, my breathing shallow, my pulse pounding in my ears, deafening.

Lucky. This is what luck looks like.

Once the Chief's meeting with the terrorist concluded, we dispersed, exiting the hotel one by one at different times. That evening I went to Judi's place to have a drink. If the men were gathering to celebrate, I was certainly not invited. Nor was she.

The next day the local English language newspaper reported the terrorist's arrest by local police. True, but only after the Chief had debriefed him on the hijacking threat. He told the Chief that he had identified four of his people in the hotel; I was one of them. Those details did not appear in the news the next morning.

Decades later I still vividly remember the rush of cold terror that ran through me as my eyes locked with the terrorist's. It is one thing to read classified, internal reports about terrorism as part of your job; it is entirely another to be face-to-face with a man known for his ruthless brutality. Still, it was these types of ops that kept me hooked to a career that was as exciting as it was challenging. As often happened, the final outcome remained a mystery. Sometimes I would learn the result of an operation weeks after I'd played my part, but oftentimes I knew only details related to my specific contributions. Inside the CIA information is currency, both precious and potentially dangerous. At nearly all levels of the food chain, information is siloed on a need-to-know basis. I had to trust that the role I was playing was important, a necessary component of a bigger picture I would probably never see. Success earned no applause, and none was expected. That was the nature of the work, and of the job.

It was a career I loved. I was doing work that mattered, work that made a difference—making history in some small way. It wasn't a path I'd ever imagined for myself. I was, after all, just a girl from Wichita, Kansas, seeking adventure, never dreaming that would translate into a life that was both covert and trailblazing.

CHAPTER 2

A First-Time Expat

A t twenty years old I landed in Europe as a civilian, somewhat by luck, thanks to Sherrie, my best friend from Wichita. When she did what every good Kansas girl should—get engaged—she chose a military man who'd been assigned to Europe. When I received my invitation to her nuptials in Fulda, Germany, I hesitated. At the time I was dating Don, my first love. He was an upperclassman at Wichita State University, an English lit major like me, and we were happily immersed in our world of books, jazz, and romance. When I decided to attend the wedding, I told myself that I would be back. I told Don that too. But deep down, part of me knew it was a breaking free that would be hard to reverse.

Prior to attending WSU, I'd spent most of my childhood in a large house on twenty acres that butted up against the Wichita city line. The property was owned by an elderly woman who had asked my parents to live there and take care of it for her, which we did for nearly twenty years, rent-free. Throughout my childhood, my sister Jennifer, who was fifteen months older than I, was my near constant companion. Our two younger sisters, Holly and Heidi, were eleven and seventeen years younger than I, an age gap that felt so large that we sometimes seemed like two families.

One of my most distinct early childhood memories occurred during a game of hide-and-seek with the neighborhood kids. After searching for the best hiding spot, I crawled inside the kitchen cabinet beneath the sink and asked Jennifer to close the door, which she did. I hovered inside that small, dark space, waiting. I would surely be the last one found! Making sure not to move a muscle or make a noise, I continued waiting, anticipating being discovered. Then more time passed, and no one found me. The house had gone completely silent, I realized. Where were they? I tried forcing the door open, but it wouldn't budge; Jennifer had locked the door. Beginning to feel afraid, I yelled out Jennifer's name repeatedly, but no one came. Time passed and I stayed stuck inside that space, which seemed to shrink the longer I was in there. Eventually, someone heard my shouting and let me out. For years afterward, I would awaken in the middle of the night in a cold sweat after yet another nightmare about being confined inside a small space. Claustrophobia would haunt me for decades.

My parents both worked throughout my childhood, my mother in computers back when they were enormous reel-to-reel units, and my father as a flight-line mechanic. Both were employed by the airplane manufacturers—Boeing, Learjet, Cessna, and others—that dominated the local economy. My dad often worked night shifts and would usually cook for me and Jennifer when we made the short walk home from school at lunchtime. He, not my mother, was the better cook in the house.

Growing up, I'd been best known as Jennifer's bookish little sister. She was the pretty, magnetic, popular one, the sister everyone remembered from the moment they laid eyes on her. I never got the attention she did, but I'd always had a daredevil streak that occasionally placed me in the spotlight, however briefly. One summer during our annual trip to Kentucky to visit our paternal grandfather, who was the proud patriarch of an enormous family—my father was one of eleven children—I'd jumped from the second-story hay loft in his barn down to the ground floor. Hoping to impress the local kids who claimed to perform this neat little trick often, I sprained both ankles instead. My grandfather, Dr. Hiestand, the county doctor and at one point the local mayor too, promptly bandaged my legs and prescribed several weeks of bed rest. Years later, my good friend Skaye and I climbed to the top of the air traffic control tower to watch planes take off, but we were soon waved down by the men who worked inside the tower. During the drive home, we laughed so hard about our little adventure that I scraped the side of my car against a concrete guardrail, briefly generating a noticeable array of sparks, and stripped a large amount of paint off that side of my car. I don't remember how I explained that to my parents, but I'm pretty sure I omitted a few key details from my retelling. At the end of my senior year in high school, I pushed the limits even farther, leading a walkout that lasted several days. Those of us who participated weren't allowed to make up the work we'd missed, which meant that anyone with an average below a B+ was at risk of failing to graduate that year. I was a good enough student to qualify for graduation, but barely. This time I'd almost pushed my luck too far.

By the time I received Sherrie's wedding invitation, Jennifer had bolted from our home for Aspen and the soaring vistas of the Colorado Rockies. As much as I was enjoying my college life with Don, part of me also knew that I, too, was ready to seek out new adventures. The tall grass prairies of Kansas were enchanting in their own way, but no match for the lure of faraway places I longed to explore.

Soon after Sherrie and Dave's wedding I felt that yearning more keenly than ever. I simply couldn't yet leave the rolling green hills and forested landscape. Within a matter of days, I'd fallen in love with Germany, its landscape and its people. My family has German roots, and I felt what seemed like a subliminal recognition, a genealogical awakening. Eager to continue my overseas exploring but with little money on hand, I boarded a train to Frankfurt and checked into a cheap hotel overlooking the Hauptbahnhof, or central train station.

Jennifer and I had both held jobs throughout high school, paying our way and buying our own cars. One of my jobs had been in the surgical wing at the hospital in Wichita. That job, more than any others, had given me my first taste of true independence. No one at the hospital knew Jennifer, so the moment I walked inside those doors, I was Jonna Hiestand, a valued employee. That experience gave me the confidence to know that I could support myself, even on a faraway continent I'd barely begun to explore.

After I woke up in my first hotel room in Frankfurt that first morning, I walked back to the station and settled inside a phone booth, where I began cold-calling American organizations with local offices. The American consulate? No, they provided visas, not jobs. American Express? No. Bank of America? Another no. The call to Chase Manhattan Bank, my fourth call, gave me a flutter. Did I speak German? No. Did I have a work permit? No. Bank experience? No. In the first of a lifetime of mysteriously lucky breaks, they asked me to come in for an interview and then, inexplicably, offered me a job. I broke the news to Don and to my parents, who didn't seem especially surprised. Perhaps they'd expected me to follow in Jennifer's footsteps.

I was twenty years old, and now a *gastarbeiter*, or foreign worker, with barely any German under my belt. I promptly enrolled in evening German classes at Berlitz. Every Friday I would take my new-found vocabulary into the bank and try it out on my colleagues. Carol, another American employee who was already fluent, never failed to correct my errors, somewhat imperiously.

My first job at Chase was in the accounting office and was devastatingly boring. Once my superiors discovered that I wasn't especially useful in that department, I was moved to work for the President of the bank, doing his English correspondence. That job suited me far better. Before long I rented a top-floor room in a tiny town called Eschborn from Herr and Frau Pilarski, who were friends of a new colleague at the bank. House rules allowed me two showers per week, which was typical for Germans. After explaining that Americans prefer to bathe daily, I was endlessly grateful when they agreed to relax our agreement.

I spent frequent evenings with my new bank friends and colleagues, learning German and tasting local beers and wines. I especially loved *volksmarching*, organized hiking, on weekends. Being a self-supporting young female expat felt exhilarating. Not only was I no longer known as Jennifer's little sister, but I was also a novelty, an attractive, young American woman who was in demand. I could finally be myself, and the experience was far more exciting than even I'd imagined.

As time wore on, I began noticing a group of loud and somewhat rowdy—by German standards—young Americans that came into the bank every few weeks. They were not US military, they told me;

they were civilians. It was the mid-sixties and Frankfurt seemed to be owned by the US Army's V Corps, a holdover since after WWII, when the US military moved in to monitor the postwar transition. The huge hospital at the city's center was US Army. The soldiers that appeared nearly everywhere were US Army. Being American, and looking American, often led people to assume you were affiliated with the military.

John Goeser was one of the Americans in that group. Tall, trim, and handsome, he stood out effortlessly. Both well traveled and well educated, he had a finely honed mastery of the German language. As I began spending more time with my new American expat friends, our mutual interest grew. John had grown up mostly in Europe but had attended American University in Washington, DC. With him at my side, I felt both the comfort of being with a fellow American and the exhilaration of knowing that his European upbringing made the continent infinitely more accessible. We went to festivals and visited vineyards, and his language skills often gained us entry through gates and into wine cellars where most Americans could not go. Simple weekend road trips became unpredictable adventures with the perfect dash of the forbidden. I loved every moment.

Early in our relationship I joined an international ski club and went on a weekend ski trip to Andermatt, Switzerland. After waking up on Saturday morning, snuggled in the snowy embrace of the Swiss Alps, I was amazed to find John sipping coffee in the hotel's breakfast room. He told me that he had been "driving by" and thought he would stop in. You'd have to google a video of "driving to Andermatt in the snow" to understand what a wry, ridiculous comment this was, and why I was quickly falling for him.

As John and I grew closer, I also got to know his roommate, Gary, with whom he shared a large apartment in the city's center. During my first visit I noticed an enormous pile of dirty dishes in the kitchen, which they never washed. When they ran out of clean dishes, they simply bought more. This same philosophy applied to laundry. When John ran out of clean, pressed shirts, he purchased new ones. On one visit I counted seventy(!) shirts in his closet. Their *putzfrau*, or housekeeper, came frequently, but it seemed apparent to me that her visits weren't frequent enough.

Nearly a year after we'd begun dating, he and I were sitting at a café table in the Vienna U-Bahn when he scribbled a poem onto a napkin and slid it across the table to me. It read:

Beautiful Jonna
With your blue eyes looking at me
What would your answer be
If I asked you to marry me?
Yes I will
No I won't
or just wait and see?

I said yes—I was having the time of my life and we were a good match in many ways—and soon afterward his parents happily welcomed me into their family. In their grand Vienna apartment, I first experienced the dynamic social life of America's overseas diplomats—the parties, the martinis, the elegant entertaining, and the odd Hollywood actor or famous musician who might drop in.

At the age of twenty-one, less than two years after becoming an expat, my life was changing once again, this time in more ways than I yet knew.

A couple of days after John read me his proposal poem, he took me aside. There was something he needed to tell me: his original story about being just a civilian was a cover. In fact, he was a civil servant working for the CIA. His roommate, Gary? CIA. Several of the well-heeled martini drinkers he'd introduced me to in Vienna? Also CIA. Without knowing it, I'd been neck-deep in America's overseas intelligence-gathering community.

We would need to live under cover, which would include obfuscating the details of our lives and his career with friends and family outside of the CIA. People from my past could not know where he worked, what he was doing, or even where he was at certain times. Much of the life I'd known would have to come to an end. After taking some time to think it over, I decided those sacrifices felt worthwhile. Being head over heels made the decision feel easy. While I had no idea what being the wife of a CIA officer would feel like, what I did know—that we would likely be assigned to live in different parts of the world together —sounded like the adventure of a lifetime. I wasn't wrong about that.

CHAPTER 3

Contract Wife

John and I were married on Memorial Day weekend at the town hall in Bern, Switzerland, where he'd lived as a child. I spent my last night as a young single woman at the historic Hotel Schweizerhof with Sherrie and Jeanne, two friends from home. We shared a room, pushing two twin beds together so we could all sleep together. We filled the crack with pillows, and I got the middle spot—and very little sleep.

My parents couldn't attend our wedding—the trip would stretch their budget too far—but John's parents drove in from Vienna. I wore a short white wedding dress with a huge bow on the back, and after we got hitched, an Italian couple scheduled to marry after us took our wedding photo. Once they'd been married, we returned the favor and took theirs. Our reception consisted of a small luncheon. It was

entirely unlike the formal, formulaic traditions most girls from Wichita adhered to when they married. There were no long invitation lists to agonize over, no meetings with cake bakers or caterers, no fretting about which band or photographer to choose. Instead, we simply arrived at the appointed time and happily began our new life. The elegant ease of the day suited me perfectly; I'd always prioritized adventure over tradition. It was a characteristic that would serve me well in ways I couldn't yet imagine.

After lunch, I changed into my wedding-day outfit, which featured an enormous pink wide-brimmed hat. Without a single hotel reservation in hand—there were always rooms available back then—we got into our "deluxe" model Volkswagen Beetle, which at the time cost around $1,500, and set out for Italy.

The drive from Bern into the Alps was a revelation. We passed through Grindelwald, and with ski season over, we took the lift to the top and walked back down. It felt like Shangri-la, complete with cows in the meadows, each one wearing a bell. Many times over the years that followed, John and I returned to Grindelwald, never tiring of its dramatic natural beauty. As we navigated the Alps, we made a point of driving over the Gotthard Pass. There is a Gotthard tunnel now, but who would drive through it when you can drive over the top? It's a series of rounded hairpin turns that snake up and down the mountain, all at a precarious angle that will quickly make you feel grateful for the grounding forces of gravity.

We then wound our way through Bolzano, Italy, eventually ending up on the Lido, an island across the lagoon from Venice—both places where John's father had once lived. By the time we reached Pisa we were running low on money, so we pointed our Volkswagen Beetle north, climbed back up over the Alps, at only about 30 mph, and slithered down the other side into Germany and back to Frankfurt. Cutting our honeymoon short hardly fazed us; the trip hadn't disappointed in the least.

———

Some months before John and I married, I'd bidden farewell to Chase Manhattan Bank to begin a new job at the US Army's 97th General Hospital in the Dornbusch area of Frankfurt. On a whim I'd taken a civil service exam before leaving the US that made me eligible for clerical positions with the military and other branches of government. I'd also worked at Wesley Hospital in Wichita while at WSU. In this new job I was being paid in American currency, with a favorable exchange rate of four marks to the dollar. After being paid in deutsche marks at Chase, my new salary seemed like a huge amount of money. In the space of one year, I'd become a married woman supervising two dozen secretaries and making more money than I could spend. I'd somehow tumbled into a life of international intrigue that now included financial freedom, too.

As Mrs. John Goeser, I was eligible to be hired as an entry-level CIA contract employee—a "contract wife," as we were then called. It seemed like a great opportunity to work all around the world. Not working never crossed my mind. I'd had at least a part-time job since I was seventeen, including working two or three different jobs in college—one at a bookstore, which I enjoyed thoroughly—and paying my own tuition the entire time. Although more women were entering the workforce, being a full-time homemaker and wife remained a pervasive cultural norm. However, that option wasn't on my radar. John and I would be partners, and we would both work. It was our tacit agreement, and one we honored throughout our twenty-three-year marriage.

With an eye on our long-term future, I embraced my new opportunities at the CIA, but was quickly dismayed to learn that being a "dependent," as I was called in US government parlance, was a deep dive into second-class citizenship. There was little I could do without John's written permission or physical presence, including purchasing a movie ticket at the American theater. When I opened my own bank account, John was automatically given full access to it. But when I needed to deposit or withdraw money from his account, I had to bring a signed form granting me permission. The military officials would sometimes talk to him while I stood at his side, referring to me as "she," as in "Tell her she needs to get you to sign the permission form for purchasing cigarettes at the PX." Misogyny reigned. I fumed.

At the time I assumed these requirements reflected arcane US military policy. They may have, but decades later I would open Michelle Obama's book *The Light We Carry* and learn about the Equal Credit Opportunity Act. Passed in 1974, it was the first time that women and other minorities in the United States were protected from discrimination when applying for loans and lines of credit. Prior to the passage of that law, even widows and divorced women had to bring a man with them to open a bank account. Before this law, women's incomes were typically discounted by 50 percent when financial institutions calculated credit maximums. These are the kinds of limitations I would have expected in the Middle East, but even in the 1960s, I would have been shocked to learn that I was unable to conduct my own financial affairs in my native country. The United States, it turned out, may have allowed women more freedom than in some other parts of the world, but there was no denying that women remained second-class citizens there, too, in more ways than I realized at the time.

As I endured treatment that seemed unsuited to a grown woman, my new job at the CIA also felt a lot like a demotion. After supervising a large group of secretaries at the hospital, I had dropped to the bottom of the rung, an entry-level secretary whose prior experience, skills, and potential were invalidated the moment I signed on with the CIA. At the time this was simply how women entered the agency; with or without advanced skills, most women started in the typing pool, where we were assigned a very low GS grade.

The GS system was, in theory, a way to organize and structure the agency's enormous workforce. As a CIA employee, your General Schedule (GS) grade determined which positions and salary level you qualified for. In practice, however, the system was undeniably biased against women, who almost universally began at the CIA with a far lower GS grade than men, perhaps a GS-03 or GS-04. The agency's "crème de la crème," all of whom were men, might eventually get to the highest level, GS-18, and then qualify for a Senior Intelligence Service level, which was doled out to a relatively small group of men at the tippy top of the food chain. While none of these grades were easy to attain, entering the agency as, say, a GS-07, as men might typically do, provided a substantial advantage; even after years of service, many women never attained that GS grade.

In *Circle of Treason*, the book she cowrote with Sandra Grimes about traitor Aldrich Ames, CIA veteran Jeanne Vertefeuille noted the GS system's partiality toward men. After being offered a second assignment in Africa, she turned down the post. "It was the African component's policy (freely expressed in those days)," she wrote, "not to promote women above GS-07. I had attained that grade long ago. Looking for advancement, I sought a job outside of Africa, and found one—in Helsinki, Finland. Not only would this give me the opportunity to see a different part of the world, the job was rated as GS-09, one of the few such slots available to women then."

I would soon discover that there were other ways the GS system worked against women. Each tour abroad, which typically lasted two years, was followed by a home tour, where you were assigned to a job in Washington, DC. Upon returning from each post, a contract wife's GS grade was automatically bumped down, sometimes to the GS grade she was given upon first signing on with the CIA. The same adjustment occurred if she earned a higher GS level during a home tour and was then assigned abroad; upon leaving DC, as a contract wife her GS level was typically bumped down by several levels. If this sounds harsh, it was, and even more so because this practice typically applied to women accompanying their spouses. It also meant that any hard-earned promotions, which were granted only during the annual review, were rendered null and void the moment you returned to or departed from DC. It was yet another reality faced only by women. Men were often promoted during their tours and rewarded for their service abroad and at home.

As a twenty-two-year-old newly married CIA employee, I was noticing some of this but didn't yet give any of it too much thought. There was, after all, a lot of adjusting to do. Nearly overnight, much of my life began to center around obfuscation and deception. I always had to be aware of to whom I was speaking or writing, what I was revealing, how they did or didn't know me. Even my best friends and family didn't know what I did or who I worked for. It could get confusing, but of course, the system worked well because it had to—field officers' and foreign assets' lives depended on its efficacy.

Fortunately, I had John at my side to answer questions no one else could. I was also getting to know new people inside the CIA, some of whom would become lifelong friends. There were now insiders and outsiders, and to most people, I had to lie, inventing clever cover stories to explain our stays abroad. I grew inevitably closer to the insiders.

No one really knew who I was anymore. I quickly discovered that I didn't mind it that way. I didn't realize it at the time, but I was doing what every aspiring intelligence officer must do—cut cords that connected me to my extended family and most of my friends from home. Without warning or expectation, I opened a door and walked into the shadows. Many who'd once known me would never hear from the real me again.

Like John, I too now worked in the city center. My office was near the IG Farben building, which was also the original headquarters of the notorious IG Farben chemical company. They had amassed their incredible fortune partly from producing Zyklon B, the cyanide-based gas that was used in Auschwitz and other concentration camps to kill over one million people. That history rattled around in my brain each time I walked by the building's massive bronze doors on my way to work.

We were fortunate to have Frau Schmidt, our first *putzfrau*, to keep our apartment clean and tidy. Remembering how much time and energy my mother had had to dedicate to caring for our home, as well as me and my three sisters, I felt horribly guilty that I wasn't doing that work myself. Perhaps to even that score, Frau Schmidt's signature was rearranging the furniture—every single week. Inevitably, you'd arrive home after a long day and have to spend your first several minutes dragging furniture back into its rightful place.

In our free time John and I visited vineyards and attended wine festivals, shopping in local stores and enjoying our life in Europe. By train Paris was only four hours away, and the Netherlands, Italy, and other parts of France were accessible within a day's journey. To ski or hike in Switzerland or stroll down the Champs-Élysées—these were some of the many choices we faced on weekends. During one weekend trip I took with two women friends to Amsterdam in 1968, we paused at a newsstand, curious about several cover photos that showed rioting. Soon after we realized the images were from back home, and a reporter approached to inquire about our reaction to the Martin Luther King assassination. We'd not yet heard that news and were sickened to learn he'd been killed.

When John and I did stay closer to home, we set out on local adventures, including exploring the Taunus Mountains just north of the city. I photographed hang gliders as they launched from its mountaintops. That is, until John and I went up in gliders ourselves. Those views are still with me today.

Inspired by Europe's scenery and culture, I began using my cameras on weekends in a more serious way, documenting the winemaking cellars and vineyards. It was an easy, engaging way of getting to know the local culture and people. In the offices where I worked, I also discovered a large old camera, complete with a tripod, that I was permitted to borrow. I looked quite official with all this gear, and it opened doors almost as effectively as a military uniform would have. Armed with my photo equipment, I gained access to places like the grounds and cellars of Schloss Johannisberg and Kloster Eberbach, two of the most famous wine labels on the banks of the Rhine River. We always made sure to sample the wine, of course.

———

My first CIA secretarial post was relatively routine, but it did afford me insight into some of the agency's inner workings, including its around-the-world support flight. Mirroring the worldwide flight patterns of Pan Am, one of the most respected airlines at the time, our planes flew on a reliable, scheduled itinerary, but of course, no one could purchase a ticket. The flights would drop off needed supplies and pick up others. It was almost like a classified FedEx service before FedEx existed.

The CIA logistics office where I originally worked dictated what would be transported where, when, and for whom. Part of my job was preparing the manifest and ensuring it was in order. Given that these flights, and their contents, were covert, there were guidelines around what was allowed on the plane. It was an unspoken rule that personal items were not permitted, a practice that was enforced by the honor system.

The protocol banning personal items was dutifully followed, except for one time when Jim, a friend of John and one of our logistics officers, was reassigned to the Far East. When he arrived on station, he was instructed not to drink the local water or even soft drinks, all of which could cause dysentery. After sending a request for beer—specifically, the local Henninger beer—his friends in logistics loaded twenty-four cases onto the next flight. This breach in protocol caused such an uproar that an entire new set of rules was put in place. Not long afterward, Jim was medically evacuated from his Far Eastern assignment with ulcers. What's that saying about karma? Within the CIA protocol reigned, and ignoring it exacted a price, one way or another.

———

As John's overseas assignment ended, he was given his next tour abroad, which would take us to the Far East. In between, we would do an exceptionally short, six-week leave tour in Washington, DC. While he continued to travel for work, I tried to get us ready to depart Europe, but was informed that I needed permission from my "sponsor"—a man, who in this case was John—to turn off the gas and close accounts, including those under my name.

We traveled home on the SS *United States*, the largest and most luxurious ship ever built in America and the world's fastest ocean liner. Our admin officer had used an obscure regulation to book us a first-class ticket. We soon discovered we were the youngest and least well-heeled couple in that part of the ship. Clearly in need of a cover story that would explain how we were affording such opulence, John posed as a rock 'n' roll DJ from Hollywood, figuring the many older passengers wouldn't challenge him on that. To hold up my end of the deal, I donned my form-fitting green velvet high school prom dress, which I'd already had shortened, and proceeded to win the dance contest partnered with the ship's handsome dance instructor.

Our five-day November crossing was rough from the outset. The ropes that lined each stairway and walkway kept us upright, but barely. With one step you were featherlight, and the next, downright leaden.

About a quarter of the two thousand passengers remained confined to their cabins throughout the trip. John was so concerned that I would get seasick that he, who had made this crossing multiple times with his parents, fell ill himself for the duration of the voyage. I felt fine.

As the great ship pulled into New York's harbor, passengers swarmed on the decks and for the first time, first-class passengers mingled with the others. We passed Lady Liberty in a fog so thick that we could make out only her feet. Bands played well-known show tunes on deck, and I stood at the railing, suddenly and unexpectedly fighting back tears. It was the first of many memorable returns to America's shores. Each one would deepen my gratitude for the country I called home.

Once back on US soil, we stayed with our friends and colleagues, Art and Nancy, in their Silver Springs, Maryland, home, always looking over the horizon. Still a mere "contract wife," a low-priority CIA employee, I didn't yet have a new assignment. I would have to search for a local CIA job once we arrived in-country. I was discovering that I hadn't married just John Goeser; I had married the CIA as well.

CHAPTER 4

The Far East

Walking through the airport of our new home city for the first time, I felt like we'd landed in a country that doubled as a convection oven permanently set to broil. I had grown up in the dry, searing heat of Kansas, but these high temperatures combined with humidity in a way that physically weighed you down. After a few years of cool climates in Europe, it took us months to adjust to this 24-7 sauna.

We spent our first several weeks living at a large hotel close to the US embassy. Mere months later, that hotel would burn down, killing many, including a foreign military man and his family that the CIA had placed there temporarily after he'd completed work for the agency. Once I began commuting to my job at the local CIA station, I would drive by the building's charred remains each morning, always noticing the soot-stained curtains blowing in the wind, reminding me of that heartbreaking ending to an operation. It took months for the local authorities to board up those windows.

During those first weeks in our new location, before I'd landed a new job, I hunted for housing while John reported to his new assignment. There were plenty of great options available, but I was intent on finding us the perfect place. When I discovered a modern building complete with a pool that was situated at the edge of one of the city's canals, I was transfixed. Traditional sampan boats roamed the waterways, some selling mangos and other fruit. Across the water were a Chinese school and outdoor theater. The whole scene was enchanting. Over the moon about our new home, I signed the lease one day while John was at work.

The whole city felt exciting, offering all kinds of new aromas, bright colors, and wonderfully welcoming people. Having moved away from the military environment in Germany, I no longer needed John's permission to sign papers or open and access our accounts. I felt enormously relieved to be able to function without an authoritative bureaucracy hovering in the background.

The second-floor balcony of our new apartment hung over the water, giving us a regular "seat" at the frequent nighttime Chinese opera performances. The music was dissonant to our Western ears, and so loud it could make you flinch. The boats, too, ran their engines at full throttle, roaring past our new home at all hours. There was a rumor that they were powered by used engines from American Chevrolets. Not long after moving in, John took to shooting me a look at dinnertime that expressed clearly, if silently, how he really felt about our new abode. He never did forgive me for picking that place.

Still an entry-level, field-hire contract wife, I began working inside the cipher-locked entry on the top floor of the local CIA station building. I was hired as the receptionist to replace a beautiful young woman named Faith who had been promoted and would soon become a friend. I was responsible for manning our field telephones to up-country sites, as well as greeting visitors. That job didn't last long; I was quickly promoted, receiving a simultaneous bump in GS grade, to become the secretary for Mr. Flowers, Executive Officer (EXO).

On my first day as the EXO's secretary, he sat me down in his office, took a puff of his cigar, and asked me if I took shorthand. Without hesitation, I nodded. He then put his feet on his desk, reclined in his chair, and began dictating. I scribbled furiously, clueless about how to take true shorthand, which I had taken in high school but had never used and had evidently forgotten. Determined, I made it up as I went along and was glad that I could make some sense of it later. That morning was when I began to invent my own personal version of shorthand, which I would continue to use throughout my career. It was so secure and so covert that even I couldn't make out its meaning sometimes. It was during that first meeting with the EXO, too, that I discovered a trait that would serve me far better than my "shorthand" in the years to come—my ability to perform at my best when working under pressure. The full importance of that characteristic, however, wouldn't be evident for quite some time.

Part of my role working for the EXO was to help slow down our operations officers, only administratively of course, just long enough for them to complete their yearly program reports and account for their activities—all duties they abhorred and were eager to avoid. The reports were arguably the most boring part of their job, but tracking agents' activity is critical for intelligence and counterintelligence gathering. For me it was a somewhat delicate dance, since making unpopular demands of them meant that I needed them to like me personally but also do what I asked. My mother had always told me to avoid confrontation at all costs; there was always a way forward without it, she'd advised. I kept her advice in mind as my people skills were put to the test—and honed—inside that station's fast-paced, high-pressure environment.

The EXO's job was to maintain administrative order, and his office was no place for laughs. Receiving a call to summon a case officer to the EXO's desk was rarely good news. Fortunately, I had Laura and Deb, all three of us seated at the front of the office. Our desks were arranged in a line known as Mahogany Row, and together, we were the links between case officers, intelligence analysts, technical operations officers, and the higher-ups. It was a pretty heady view, and one that came with a thrumming intensity and significant expectations. As a secretary, I wasn't privy to important information or aware of any direct correlation between our work and the Vietnam War, but we all felt the urgency of working in the same geographical region as our soldiers. We often worked long days and were expected to put in seven-day work weeks. On our occasional days off, we would sometimes head to the local salons for head-to-toe treatments—nails, hair, massage, the works.

The quick, easy friendship Laura, Deb, and I formed loosened the otherwise pin-straight mood in the office, which was especially fortunate given that we worked under the dark cloud of Bettina, the secretary for the Chief of Station (COS). She had a slim figure and wore sheath dresses so short you weren't sure what you'd see next. She also made no secret of her disdain for the occupants of Mahogany Row. When Laura went to the dermatologist about a rash on her arms, he asked if she was under any stress, she later told us. *Bettina*, Deb and I mouthed immediately when Laura recounted the scene.

One day, I was sitting in for Bettina at her desk just outside the Chief of Station's office smoking a Winston when an American military general, wearing perfectly creased pants and with a chest full of medals, walked in. Feeling called to attention, I promptly snuffed out my cigarette and dumped the ashtray in the trash can behind me. Unfamiliar with the workings of Bettina's desk, I was stumped when the secure, green phone began ringing. It was a special encrypted line that I wasn't sure I was cleared to answer. While I was quickly able to locate the jack that was connected to the flashing, buzzing ringer on her desk, the actual phone instrument was nowhere in sight. (For security reasons, all CIA phones were unplugged when they were not in use.)

As I frantically searched desk drawers, file cabinets, and nearby shelves, the general's voice suddenly rang out. "Your trash can is on fire, young lady!" Glancing toward the desk, I saw the flames spiking above the can's rim like a mini–dumpster fire belching smoke into the air. The general stood, but I waved him back into his seat. Even with his high-level clearances, he wasn't permitted to move freely through the CIA station, and certainly not with a fire-spewing trash can in hand.

Dashing into the empty Deputy's office nearby, I grabbed a half-full cup of cold coffee, ran to my desk, and poured it onto the fire. The can burped out a black cloud of stinking ash, but the fire was out. Smiling apologetically at the general, I sat down calmly as the secure, green phone continued to ring. When the COS finally emerged from his office, he greeted the general and ushered him inside. Just before closing his office door, he turned his head and glowered at me, eyes narrowed. The room was filled with smoke and the secure, green phone continued ringing, endlessly. Once the door closed behind him, I sat stunned, wide-eyed. *Bettina is going to kill me.*

In addition to overseeing the administrative affairs of the station, my boss, the EXO, was a key player in coordinating the CIA's work on interdicting the infamous drug trafficking in the Golden Triangle, composed of Laos, Burma (now Myanmar), and Thailand. The Kuomintang (KMT), remnants of Chiang Kai-shek's defeated nationalist Chinese party, was heavily involved in the robust local drug trade. Most of the KMT opium was packed south into this country via mule trains and then shipped to the US. Our goal was to help the local government stop that flow of drugs into America. It was a challenging undertaking that was further complicated by language barriers. Despite the relatively large number of near-native or native Chinese-speaking case officers within our reach, I was shocked to realize that we had no one who could communicate in the local dialect.

As fascinated as I was with our new city, it had a distinct criminal underbelly marred by drug addiction, prostitution, and rampant corruption. At night foreign tourists as well as American GIs on R & R from the Vietnam War sought out a hallucinogenic atmosphere, adding fuel to an already dangerous blaze. A number of our officers and their teenage children found themselves back in America earlier than planned after close encounters with the grislier side of the drug culture. My goal was to thread my way, carefully, between the CIA's stricter code of conduct and the city's exotic but sometimes dangerous street life, always staying within the guardrails laid down by the office.

There were so many American airmen in the streets, you might have thought the Vietnam War was taking place just outside city limits. The war's proximity generated a thrumming intensity that routinely permeated our office walls. Most weeks we worked seven full days, but on our rare days off we would head to the nearest beach, lie on the sand in our bikinis, greased up with Coppertone, watching the Boeing B-52 bombers take off. The planes flew low, weighed down by their payloads on departure, and then returned hours later lighter and quicker after their bombing runs. We would sip our local beers as the last of the daytime flights landed, feeling guilty and lucky at the same time. On Saturday night we would head for the latest hot club to hear a German band, headed by Gert Steffens, play popular American tunes as loud as they could. The club was full of American Air Force pilots on R & R from Vietnam. Jubilation and dread hung in the air, creating an electricity that felt palpable and surreal in equal measure.

Faith, the station's previous receptionist, rented a seaside beach house that stood on stilts over the water, right in the middle of town. It quickly became our favorite local hotspot. Upon waking each morning, you could watch the waves sloshing through the wooden floor slats below your bed. It was a fabulous place to decompress after an evening reveling in the town's notorious night life. The neighbors, of course, never imagined there was a CIA party going on every weekend right in their midst.

On the Fourth of July, Faith asked me to bring sparklers so we could all light them on her waterfront balcony that overlooked the sunset. It would be a small, festive reminder of home. I accidentally bought several boxes of local incense instead—they looked a lot like sparklers—so we spent our native country's birthday coughing, enveloped in a dense cloud of perfumed smoke.

———

One of the advantages of being abroad was the easy camaraderie among the local CIA community. We were all safe contacts for each other, which made socializing outside of work easy. In foreign offices, the different departments mingled more often, partly because altogether we made up a much smaller group than any single department at headquarters. With ample domestic help, entertaining was fun and easy. I enjoyed cooking and happily played my part, acting as hostess whenever John's and my schedule allowed. It was a part of our life that would flourish almost every time we were assigned abroad.

When we were away from the office, we also enjoyed the newly booming city around us. It had recently become a tourist destination, so there was a proliferation of high-end hotels and restaurants beginning to emerge in the city center. Amidst the local population of dark-skinned, dark-eyed, dark-haired citizens, my friend Deb stood out. She had a head of red hair so brilliant it looked like the sun was perpetually setting behind her. The locals were fascinated, always eager to touch hair of such a magical hue. As a woman, however, there were limits to what she, and all of us, could do in this part of the world. One day she took her basket to the market, intent on purchasing produce, only to discover that none of the local merchants would wait on an unescorted female. She promptly hired a houseboy to do her shopping for her. That need for domestic help would become a consistent theme during all of our faraway postings. Whether due to language or cultural barriers or both, we discovered that having help at home was essential for getting even the most basic supplies and services.

At one point Deb began dating Kurt, the food and beverage manager at the best hotel in town, a property that was eventually named best in the world. An Austrian by birth, Kurt introduced us to the elaborate outdoor buffet that even today takes place every evening at the hotel, sited alongside the slow-moving river that is the heart of the city. He also introduced us to the world-famous hotel's world-famous bar, which was already a popular hangout for our case officer colleagues. It was one of several likely places where they might meet the well-positioned, well-connected citizens that could make for good recruits.

One day John and I, accompanied by Deb and Laura, decided to take a small boat out onto the river to see how close we could get to a US submarine we'd read about in the local newspaper. It was on an R & R mission from Vietnam. As we approached the sub, Deb, Laura, and I stood up. "Permission to board, Sir!" Deb sang out, laughing, her long red hair billowing in the wind. To our utter astonishment we were allowed to climb up a short ladder onto the ship. Once inside the galley, the three of us began serving lunch to a group of sailors who had been at sea for god knows how long. They hadn't yet gone ashore, where their Captain was, which explained why we'd been permitted aboard at all. It was an unforgettable afternoon, partly due to the claustrophobia of the sub, which drew me back outside after about ten minutes. I needed fresh air, open space, and natural light. Pronto.

During that Far East tour, I once again enrolled at a local campus to study the language and history. This pattern followed me around the globe, as assignments took us to new parts of the world. On some level perhaps I was trying to make up for leaving WSU short of graduation, but only in theory, since I never did accumulate credits for my international studies. I was curious and eager to communicate with the local population and appreciate each place I was in. It made life overseas far more interesting. It would have been all too easy to go limit my life to working with Americans and then socializing with Americans. I wanted more out of a life abroad than that.

The longer we were stationed in the Far East, the more captivated I felt by the culture. The brilliant silks, the saffron robes, the unique, soaring rooflines of the temples, and the lemongrass, ginger, and chilies that made the food taste sour, salty, spicy, and sweet—all of it was seductive. A simple stroll down a back street became an adventure in sensory delight. Watching the people, you could tell they believed in fun, not as a frivolity but as an intrinsically valuable activity. Life was clearly not being wasted on the locals.

The busy, bustling street life often drew me outside, camera in hand. Unlike in Germany, where I'd had access to the local station's photography equipment, I couldn't borrow high-end cameras, but I did have the 35mm camera I'd purchased in Frankfurt. Most often I would venture out solo, heading toward Chinatown and to the Indian markets. The flower market, too, was dazzling, filled with striking blossoms and bold colors. When you'd had your fill there, you could roam around the temples, where gilded monk statues awaited, lined up in perfect rows of gleaming brilliance.

It was here, in this visual cornucopia, that I began to pursue my interest in photography in a more professional way. A new side of me was being born, but I didn't yet have a clue how far it would take me. At the same time, working for the EXO was giving me a better understanding of how the CIA functioned and how work flowed through the different branches and hierarchies. Increasingly, I was intrigued by the skills of our technical officers. While the case officers spotted, assessed, developed, and recruited foreign assets to provide intelligence, the technical operations guys (and, yes, they were all guys) provided the materials and equipment that were pivotal to operational success. If you needed to drill a pinhole-size hole in a hotel room wall and then install an audio bug, the techs would provide the equipment. An entry job into a foreign compound to emplace or remove something? Done.

False documents and/or a disguise that would allow you to clandestinely cross a foreign border? No problem.

When the time came to be reassigned, we bade farewell to our first Far East posting with mixed feelings. As always, I was eager for our next adventure, yet also reluctant to leave. A new part of me had come alive during our time in the Far East, a deep-seated affinity for foreign cultures and places blossoming inside me. I was fascinated by every aspect of these faraway destinations, the eternal student with an insatiable appetite for more. While the secretarial work I was doing could feel somewhat monotonous, in my ongoing letter exchanges with Jennifer, I couldn't help but notice an occasional twinge of jealousy in her tone. Only a handful of years had passed since I'd first landed in Germany, yet here I was, thriving in a life that was both thrilling and fascinating.

CHAPTER 5

Wichita

O nce John was informed that his Far East tour would be followed by one on US turf, we prepared to depart, opting to make a few stops in Europe on our way home. With Deb in tow, we stopped in Austria before heading straight for Grindelwald in Switzerland, where John and I couldn't wait to show her the awesome power of the Eiger Mountain's Wall of Death. Our enthusiasm was quickly overshadowed by dense cloud cover that masked the mountain entirely. We waited two days before resorting to buying her a postcard displaying the vista that we'd hoped to show her in person. Nonetheless, John and I delighted in the nostalgia of being once again in this place where we had skied and honeymooned.

Once stateside, we embarked on an altogether different kind of adventure—visiting Wichita, where he would meet my family for the first time. For John, whose early years had taken place almost entirely in Europe, Kansas must have seemed as otherworldly as Europe and the Far East had once been to me. Yet he adjusted almost instantaneously, charming my parents. After years of watching his daughters date one boyfriend then another, my father was thrilled that there was finally a male in the family who would stick around. He'd never been a man prone to emotional displays, and seeing how excited he was to welcome John into our family, I realized that this was as close to having a son as Dad was going to get. He had a lot of stories to pass on.

My mom, too, went out of her way to make John feel at home. After hearing about his love of peach melba, as well as his parents' jokes about how expensive their son's favorite dessert was in Europe, she had canned fresh peaches the summer before, expressly for this purpose. Just when we were scheduled to arrive, she found a recipe and made a dessert that she herself had never tasted. John was gracious and appreciative, savoring every bite.

PEACH MELBA

Blend:
½ pint fresh raspberries
1 tablespoon sugar
1 teaspoon lemon juice

Spoon:
poached peach halves into four dessert dishes

Add:
vanilla ice cream

Drizzle:

raspberry sauce

For the first few days, my younger sisters, who were now middle school and high school ages, walked wide circles around John, unsure what to make of this sophisticated presence in their midst. That was no small feat in the small house my parents had moved into since my departure for Germany. The second floor, where we stayed, had low slanted ceilings that made standing up straight impossible, particularly for John. We were also sharing a bathroom with my sisters. Perhaps due to our proximity to one another, before long, my sisters seemed to relax. Curious about their interests and plans, John peppered them with questions. *How do you like to spend your time? Where would you like to travel?* Sensing his sincere interest, they began to open up. The rapport between them never waned. They adored John, and their love for him only grew deeper over the years of our marriage.

Unsure when I'd return to Kansas, I checked in briefly with old friends, who were initially full of questions. *How was Europe? How was the Far East? Did I speak German? What was the food like?* But about five minutes in, they'd heard enough and promptly directed our conversation back to Wichita—who was engaged or married to whom, who had children or was pregnant, as well as who'd divorced already. I nodded and tried to think of questions, but we all felt the slack in the bonds we had once shared. I wasn't the same woman they'd once known. I had left to discover a wider world and in the process was encountering all kinds of people and pursuing possibilities that I'd once been unable to even imagine. There was no turning back now; home didn't feel like home anymore.

One friend, Skaye, stood out in a different way. I'd known her for years, and her life, too, had become an adventure. Married to a successful attorney, she had several kids and they were living an interesting life. She was as curious about my new life as I was about hers, and over the years she would remain a true friend, even during my more mysterious years when dropping out of many people's lives was a career prerequisite.

I also touched base with Don, my once true love at WSU. He, too, was married with kids and living a full life as an English professor. I would remain sporadically in touch with him for the rest of my life. But our paths had diverged for good.

During this time, John and I also traveled to Aspen to visit Jennifer. The town was great fun back then, a place where successful professionals went to take breaks from the intensity of their jobs. Many would spend their days skiing and their evenings working as waiters or bartenders, so when you ordered your cocktail, your server might be a cardiovascular surgeon or successful lawyer on extended leave. As always, we basked in the glow of Jennifer's popularity; everyone there seemed to know and adore her. She was single and dating and working in retail as a buyer for a premier fashion boutique, among other side jobs. While our lives had diverged in any number of ways, we remained close, and returning to the US always felt sweeter because I could once again see her and all my family.

When it was time to appear in Washington, DC, I felt grateful for the time with my family, but relieved, too, that our "real" life could resume. Our Far East assignment had felt like a palate teaser, an amuse-bouche to whet my appetite for additional overseas adventures and a more directed career, or so I hoped, in the office that was then called Technical Services Division (TSD) and would later be known as the Office of Technical Service (OTS). I set my sights on belonging to a sort of real-life Q, the infamous technical wizardry shop behind James Bond.

CHAPTER 6

2430 E Street

My first job as a CIA staff employee, rather than a "contract wife" abroad, was in the agency's Technical Services Division. I worked alongside Vera and Anne, the other secretaries. This was the storied beginning of most CIA women, including the renowned Eloise Page, who would eventually become my icon and symbolic mentor. After years of working as a secretary for General Bill Donovan, the first Director of the CIA, Eloise ended up helping to chase down Nazis during WWII and then rose through the CIA hierarchy. She eventually became the first female Chief of Station, the first female supergrade, and the first woman to head a major intelligence community committee. A tiny, dainty woman whose office was known for its elegant décor, all of which she brought in from her own personal collection of Oriental rugs and fine furniture, she was notorious and formidable. Upon hearing her name, male colleagues would raise their eyebrows and chime in with, "Oh, that old battle-axe?" After retiring from the CIA she became a counterintelligence instructor for the Department of Defense Intelligence Agency (DIA), where she taught until her death in 2002. I met her briefly once, while attending Dick Helms's birthday party. She wore white gloves that she draped neatly on top of her purse. I was so awed by her presence, I had to swallow hard to hold back my tears.

Many women who attempted to follow in her footsteps and pursue field work were deprived of the opportunity. Even as the world around us welcomed more women into higher levels of business, finance, commerce, and other demanding fields, decades after WWII, being a woman continued to seem like a liability inside the CIA. Women weren't cut out for espionage work, they said. Our foreign assets would be unwilling to work with women, they said. Besides, women excelled at clerical work. Who would fill those support positions if they were allowed to move into the field? The excuses for keeping women chained to secretarial desks were numerous, and to the men in charge, entirely legitimate.

Years before I arrived at the beautiful, red-roofed original headquarters of the Office of Strategic Services (OSS), the predecessor to the CIA, Eloise had recognized the agency's bias against women and banded together with others to spur change. During Allen Dulles's swearing-in ceremony as the Director of the CIA in 1953, Eloise and three other women confronted him about the persistent discrimination against female employees. After asking several pointed questions in front of his audience, Eloise and a larger group of women were appointed to the Committee on Professional Women, which men in the agency soon derisively nicknamed the "Petticoat Panel." The committee made a point of using that nickname in their report to highlight the agency's pervasive and flagrant discriminatory attitudes.

The committee's primary goal—pay equity for women—was bold, partly because it was unprecedented in the government offices of Washington, DC. (After all, this was still twenty years before the Equal Credit Opportunity Act.) The women met in a room inside a dilapidated CIA building the Director, Dulles, had referred to as "a damned pigsty." There the women spent the sweltering summer months without air conditioning poring over data and anecdotes about the treatment of women throughout the agency. After months of hard work—all while enduring demeaning comments from their male colleagues, one of whom characterized their work as "a bunch of old washerwomen gossiping over their laundry"—the committee uncovered startling trends. Over a period of years when agency salaries had risen 55 percent, women held 21 percent of CIA professional jobs but zero at the executive level, and were routinely given pay grades that were, on average, three levels beneath those of their male colleagues. Moreover, only 7 percent of field agents were women, and since the CIA was founded in 1947, the agency was steadily hiring fewer women each year rather than more.[*]

It was clear to Eloise Page and the other "Petticoat Panel" members that women deserved fair and equal treatment. However, the closed circle of high-ranking men who evaluated their report decided otherwise. At one point, Lyman Kirkpatrick, CIA Inspector General, went on record saying, "No supervisor in this Agency in his right mind is going to take a good stenographer or a darned good competent clerk and say, well, just because you got your BA . . . we are going to make a

---

[*] Nathalia Holt, *Wise Gals* (New York: Putnam, 2022).

Case Officer or Researcher out of you."* The message of the leadership was clear—regardless of their potential and efficacy, women were at the CIA to support the men. The panel's findings were hidden away for years, allowing the agency to ignore and justify its clear and persistent preference for male employees, especially in the field, where, it was widely asserted internally, "the real work" took place.

During my early years in the CIA OTS buildings, when I was first setting my sights on technical services, a critical aspect of field work, I didn't yet know about the Petticoat Panel report. Most of us didn't. It's possible that my muted awareness of the challenges I would encounter helped me in my pursuit of a technical career that, at least on paper, would have appeared hopeless. On the other hand, I could have wasted years chasing what could easily have been an impossible goal. Whatever the case, the agency's failure to address the glaring injustice revealed in the Petticoat Panel's findings undermined the potential of the vast majority of women at the CIA. It was unfair to us, but it was catastrophically shortsighted of the agency as well.

However critical, those issues didn't fit easily into the intense landscape of our workload. Even when your daily duties are tedious, as secretarial work often is, there's an imbued sense of purpose and duty that drives those of us who work under cover in the intelligence community. It's understood that a significant amount of personal sacrifice is required, including letting go of old friends, colleagues, and communities—and yes, individual needs, too. The work is unpredictable and intense, and it quickly becomes an exhilarating and all-consuming way of life. Inevitably, the balance between personal goals and organizational demands is weighted heavily toward the latter.

---

* "Challenging the Status Quo: Elizabeth Sudmeier's Historic Legacy," Central Intelligence Agency, June 26, 2015, www.cia.gov/stories/story/elizabeth-sudmeier.

It was hardly a time or place to complain, so I did what most of us did, for better or worse—put my head down and tended to the tasks at hand.

In my new day-to-day, I was mesmerizingly close to the technical guys and their work, including Art, the Deputy of our branch, who was our very own Q, our internal James Bond–style weapons-lab genius. His fiendishly creative brain produced mind-bogglingly innovative weapons intended to terrorize the Soviets. Some of his clever inventions would eventually be featured in the movie *Charlie Wilson's War*. He became a friend of mine and John's and someone we invited over for dinner, along with our neighbor, whom Art was dating. Art's work fascinated me, and while he couldn't discuss it, knowing him personally felt akin to befriending a celebrity.

As the new junior secretary in the office, I asked a lot of questions and suggested simple ways to organize supplies and help the office run more efficiently. I also began helping with the trip reports and project reports for the engineers, who were technologically brilliant but not the best writers. Being able to dictate their reports directly to me while I typed was a relief for them, and a process that resulted in better reports that were submitted faster. That part of the work wasn't challenging, but it was gratifying knowing that I was contributing to the branch's effort. I was also learning the business of hiring and managing contractors as well as handling classified projects. That was fascinating, like going to school all over again. I loved it, and quickly realized that I wanted a future in clandestine intelligence work.

Little by little, I felt myself inching closer to the world I aspired to be a part of, including at home, in the apartment John and I rented. Just three blocks from the White House, it sat at the corner of 20th and F Streets, diagonally across from the F Street Club, which played a quiet but important role in domestic politics and international relations since the Depression and Prohibition, when it was turned into a Washington, DC, members-only social club. Since then, diplomats have used it to discuss matters like the founding of NATO and any number of other high-priority international relations issues. Eleanor Roosevelt, Jackie Kennedy, Jimmy Carter, Ronald Reagan, George H. W. Bush, and Bill Clinton, as well as several famous journalists, are all on its roster of historic guests.

On weekends John and I would pour ourselves a glass of wine and watch out our corner window as political, congressional, and ambassadorial invitees paraded up the steps of the club. Small crowds of students would gather hoping to see Henry Kissinger, who was a frequent guest. Some students would linger, awaiting the tray of canapés that the club staff, dressed in white tie, would invariably serve them at the end of the evening. John and I would just sip from our glasses, quietly satisfied in the knowledge that we, too, were doing our part to serve our country.

Wondering if OTS could be a place for me to begin building a longer-term professional future, I scheduled a meeting with David Chime, Chief of Personnel for OTS. I was still a branch secretary, but it seemed like a logical next step, even though the few secretaries who did move up typically did so through negotiations between the divisions and branches. David was a friendly guy who promptly broke the news to me that the only way of moving up in that office was by getting an advanced degree in engineering, physics, chemistry, optics, or some other esoteric technical specialty. Leaving his office, I felt deflated yet determined. Somehow, someway, I would have to find a way out of secretarial work.

During this time, the dynamics at home had shifted, too. We'd been married for over twelve years, and John was now a full-time student at George Washington University, where he was completing a degree in international affairs. Once he graduated, we'd agreed, it would be my turn to take leave and complete my university degree. What's that old Yiddish joke about making plans? Life, I'd eventually discover, had something else in mind for me.

The best perk of my job was the commute, a five-minute, three-block walk from our apartment. Running was enjoying its heyday as the new and preferred way to stay healthy, and more Americans were regularly strapping on their Nikes to log more miles. At lunchtime, I happily joined them, changing into my running shoes to jog up and down the long, grassy strip that extends from the Lincoln Memorial to the US Capitol. On other days, I'd veer onto the sand paths beside the massive reflecting pool or join the group that ran across the Theodore Roosevelt Bridge that spans the Potomac River. When tourists would stop to ask if there was a race going on, I'd smile, shake my head, and explain that this was typical lunchtime behavior in the nation's capital. Perhaps running gave us all some relief from the intensity that had rocked the capital in recent years. Watergate had occurred while we were in the Far East, but the scandal remained relatively fresh in the American psyche. The Vietnam War was still raging, dividing people into two opposing ideologies. Despite it all, we could still match our strides. Running, I would continue to discover, was a powerful unifier, bringing all kinds of people together here at home and around the world.

I was delighted to discover that, even as entry-level clerical staff, I qualified for a temporary duty trip (TDY), which was any assignment that took an officer abroad for several days to several weeks. My first one took me to the Panama Canal Zone, where I would help enter data from index cards into a new digital system. The work was deadly boring, but the trip wasn't entirely without excitement. Upon reporting to the local station on my first day, I sat down for an interview with the Chief of Station. I didn't know it at the time, but this Chief was somewhat of a legend within the agency. A tall, elegant man, he was friendly but authoritative, and years later would be the subject of several books.

"I have one request before you tend to your assignment," he began, peering at me intensely.

"How can I help?" I replied, eager to make a good impression.

"The officer you'll be working with, Rob, has lost track of a unique piece of equipment. He had it yesterday, but it seems to be missing. I need you to go to the Chief of Support and find out where this unit has been placed. It's called a skyhook."

Feeling gratified by this opportunity to support the Chief, I found my way to the Chief of Support's office and inquired about the skyhook.

"I saw it yesterday," the Chief of Support replied, gazing at me intensely. He squinted his eyes slightly, as if remembering the last time he saw the equipment in question. "Check with the Finance officer. He'll know where it is."

Nodding, I thanked him for his time and found my way to the Finance officer's office, which soon became the next step in an afternoon-long pursuit of the mysterious skyhook. Finally, I met Rob, the officer I'd be working with for the remainder of my trip, without the equipment in question and out of ideas of where to look next.

"There is no such thing as a skyhook," he confessed, laughing. "It's a joke we play on all first-time TDYers."

I would never be that naive again, but I had passed their hazing with honor.

During the second weekend of that trip, I booked a day trip to the San Blas Islands, a flight that took only an hour. After being picked up in the Canal Zone promptly at eight a.m., we arrived at the airfield, where I climbed aboard a tiny, twin-engine airplane. I was the only passenger, and I told the two pilots that I didn't have a ticket yet, that there had been no time or place to pay. "Not a problem, we'll handle it when we get back to Panama City," they assured me. Once we landed on the island, I visited several villages on foot and talked to some of the local Kuna people.

After eating lunch with the pilots, I went on my own down to the beach. It was my first time swimming alone in the ocean, and I was totally unfamiliar with the geography of the coastline. The entire San Blas Archipelago consists of over 350 islands, and the one I visited had a sand beach inside of a naturally protected harbor. The clear water and breathtaking fish lured me around the bend, until I was suddenly outside of the calm area and felt myself being powerfully pulled away from the shore. I wasn't a particularly strong swimmer, and even when I neared the shore, I struggled to get back on land. The slippery, sloping volcanic rocks I needed to grab on to were covered with live crabs. Afraid to get out of the water and afraid to stay in, I remember thinking that if anything happened to me, there would be no record of where I was, or even who I was with. That was my first time realizing just how invisible I was becoming in my new life at the CIA.

Adrenaline kicked in and I found the strength to get around the bend and back on land. I changed clothes, found the pilots in the open-air bar, and we left as scheduled. When we landed, I asked again about payment. The office was closed, they said. I would have to take care of it another time.

Following protocol, I reported the trip to the office the next day. "Nobody comes out to the residential area of the Canal Zone to pick up passengers," I was immediately told. As a woman traveling alone, I was already cautious about being targeted. The office wanted to know if I had given the pilots any personal information. I had not. When I called the next day to try to pay for the tickets once again, I was informed that the flight records were closed.

That mystery remains unsolved.

———

It took me two years to climb up to the front office of the one-thousand-person OTS. After working as the Deputy's secretary, I moved up to a new boss, David Brandwein, who was the Director. From my perch at the very top of the secretarial pyramid there was a lot less work to do. Brandwein conducted his transactions verbally. When he did write, it was short and sweet. He would periodically ask me to write short papers for his signature, but otherwise my job consisted primarily of keeping his calendar and inking in the *New York Times* crossword puzzle, with his occasional assistance, to pass the time.

Despite my persistent boredom, I felt a sense of belonging in OTS. We were cut from a different cloth than our Ivy League cohorts in Operations at Langley. Their job was to recruit foreign assets, which I always thought sounded incredibly challenging. How do you convince a foreign national to betray their own country? Invariably, a successful career in Operations might consist of a few productive recruits over a multidecade career. Techs, on the other hand, were brought in only after a foreign asset had been deemed worthwhile, which meant we participated only in high-stakes operations. That was a distinction our contacts at Langley could not claim. While there was mutual respect between OTS and Langley and a shared recognition that we needed each other to do our jobs, there were subtler divisions that played out beneath the surface. The Operations guys were recruited almost solely from prestigious universities and social-register families. They were the so-called intellectuals, well-heeled by their exclusive educations, pedigreed in ways we were not. Our technical officers were budding chemists, physicists, and engineers who had graduated from state universities and colleges. Proud to claim our status as "techs," we had a global responsibility that mandated a worldwide presence. Travel was a major part of our duties, so each morning when you walked through the doors, you never knew where you might be sleeping that night. Cairo? Havana? Tokyo?

To keep track of an office that could easily have devolved into chaos, Brandwein conducted a weekly "around the world" exercise on Fridays. In his conference room, on a map behind an enormous wall of drapes, the Chiefs of our operational divisions would gather to brief the Director on where his people were on that day and what they were doing. One by one, they would detail the various operations and targets, what equipment was being used, and which officers were on the scene. Those meetings were the only time that all senior management would know which operations were underway where, with whom, and why.

As the Chiefs described each op, someone would place pins on the twenty-foot map to demonstrate what was happening where. Red pins indicated audio, blue were clandestine photo ops, and other colors represented covert communications, paramilitary ops, and disguise/false documents. During my early days, one of my responsibilities was gathering information for the weekly around-the-world meeting. Then I began posting it on the map myself. To do that, I first had to collect status updates from each of the department Chiefs.

The first time I entered the office of Fred, Chief of Audio, to get his report on the microphones and bugs that his techs were installing worldwide, I immediately noticed an incredible display on the wall. Fred was a formidable man, and in his office, which had once been occupied by

Allen Dulles, hung a collection of ropes, pitons, and other gear, all of which would be needed to summit Mount Everest. However, Fred had never scaled a mountain. He had used those tools in a European capital while hunting down a target twelve stories above street level, where he was to place a "bug." It was a famous operation within the agency, but also a secret one. Inside our walls, the story had been retold countless times. He'd become a hero among us, although nobody outside of CIA buildings would ever know it had even happened.

The buildings where we worked held countless secrets like this one, of course, as well as some important history. Once the headquarters of the OSS, the institutional predecessor to the CIA, the square footage we used every day was described in one government brochure as one of the most beautiful "secret" squares in the city. The address was 2430 E Street, the famous birthplace of modern American espionage. Hollywood director John Ford, who had been one of the first staff photographers at OSS, once described the agency's founder, General Bill Donovan, as "the sort of guy who thought nothing about parachuting into France, blowing up a bridge, pissing into Luftwaffe gas tanks, then dancing with a German spy on the roof of the St. Regis Hotel in Paris." Long before Ian Fleming introduced us all to the iconic James Bond, Donovan had been our spiritual leader. We all wanted to be like him: debonair, clever, fearless.

As the OTS Director's secretary, I was keenly aware that I had earned a certain status. The conduit to the branch's most senior boss, I could have wielded a quiet power, but my memories of working under Bettina's constant scrutiny in the Far East still loomed large in my mind. Instead of emulating her example, I went out of my way to be helpful and create a more inclusive atmosphere. I wasn't planning ahead so much as I was trying to avoid recreating a past I hadn't enjoyed.

Nonetheless, the goodwill I sowed with colleagues and administrative staff alike would pay me back repeatedly over the years.

———

My sparse workload and resulting boredom weren't the only downsides of being the Director's secretary. I soon learned that the joke was on me; I'd reached the pinnacle of my secretarial career. I was now a GS-09 and there was no next level. No next rung of the ladder. My only chance of being promoted was if the Director rose in the ranks, was reassigned, and chose to bring me along with him. I was at a dead end. I needed a plan.

Feeling smothered by yet another secretarial job, I knew that there was a more meaningful job for me elsewhere. Sensing that Brandwein had my best interests at heart, during a conversation in the outer office one day, I pointed to the Smithsonian Castle building on the National Mall, a majestic, red-brick Victorian building I looked out on each day. I told him I thought there might be a better job for me there, perhaps one with more substance to it. I needed a challenge, ideally one that would get me out from behind a desk. He challenged me back, suggesting that I, an enthusiastic amateur photographer, take some of the office's photo courses, typically reserved for our clandestine operations officers. Energized by the opportunity to spread my wings, I jumped at the opportunity.

One week later I dashed across an airfield in southern Virginia to board a small twin-engine plane. The motor was running, and a man stood on a ladder nearby painting out the tail number. The plane's doors had been removed, and I could see a harness hanging inside the doorway. The flight and harness were for the only passenger—me. Once I was lashed into the rig, with the microphone secured around my head and earphones clamped over my ears, a flight tech handed me a 35mm SLR camera with a huge, extended 1000mm lens. Moments later, the pilot and I took off, flying first over a small river that wound its way to the Chesapeake Bay.

While strapped into that harness flying high above the landscape, wearing a mic to communicate with the pilot and bulky earphones to buffer the engine's loud roar, I pinpointed this day as my entry point into a real career at the CIA. The course was called Airborne Platforms, and its purpose was to assess how well you could resolve small details with a handheld long lens. The "platform" was, of course, the airplane itself, which vibrated constantly. The goal was to develop a technique that allowed you to steady the lens enough to capture, say, the license number of that pickup truck down below going 60 mph while kicking up a cloud of dust as it traveled down a dirt road.

We flew through a clear, cloudless sky, soaring over the water and heading to several lightly populated areas. The tail number on the plane was obscured so the flight remained anonymous, even to other pilots, as we navigated the skies in a somewhat unorthodox manner. As we flew over a small city, I asked the pilot if we could fly lower so I could focus my long lens on a nearby radio tower. When we flew over railroad tracks, I focused my lens on the train signals. Swooping down over a winding river, the plane slipstreamed behind a flock of geese that, at the same altitude and same speed, were easy targets for my camera. And when I asked the pilot how low we could go, he glanced back at me, smiling devilishly as his eyes lit up. Then the plane swooped down. My stomach dropped, but I laughed as he took us below treetop level and we skimmed along the surface of the water. Hours later, we landed, and my knees were shaking. It was one of the best days of my life.

After dinner I retired to the huge darkrooms at the Farm, a training facility available to only some CIA employees. There I spent the evening alone in the glow of amber safelights, developing my film as I swayed to big band music. The jazz that Don and I had listened to at WSU—Stan Kenton, Ella Fitzgerald, Frank Sinatra, and others—played on the radio. I wondered what he would make of my new life and the future that I could now practically taste. Immersing the exposed photo paper into three separate trays—developer first, then fixative, followed by a cool water bath—my new goal took shape as I clipped the prints to a wire drying line. I would become a technical operations officer, specializing in photography of all kinds, from the micro to the macro. The idea was thrilling. I couldn't wait for my new career to begin.

Fortunately, Brandwein continued to support my new aspiration. After spending that day in a harness flying high and low, I was granted permission to take numerous other photo courses. This, I understood, indicated that I'd done well enough to warrant additional opportunities. That was as much praise as I could reasonably hope for, a reality embedded in the necessarily clandestine culture of the CIA. As John's wife, I'd perhaps been able to learn this more easily than most. He continued to share insights into the organizational culture and support my desire to do work that mattered.

Since graduating from university, John had returned to the CIA to work as a polygrapher. It was a specialty the agency took seriously and valued enormously, putting each polygrapher through its proprietary internal polygraph school. The job required a certain confrontational intensity since passing the polygraph was required for all assets. It was a strict pass/fail system that offered no second chances. If there was any indication an asset was untrustworthy, all ties to the agency were cut promptly and completely. I didn't yet realize it, but John's "no nonsense" approach would become an important counterbalance in my career, helping me to learn how to assert myself in situations that required it.

As my training advanced, my existing skills with a 35mm SLR camera, a single-lens reflex camera, expanded. I learned new ways to use it. I was also exposed to subminiature cameras. Among them were the Minox, of James Bond movie fame, and the Tessina, which could be hidden inside objects of various sizes—books, bags, cigarette packs, and the like. You could hide a subminiature inside a jacket button or a logo on a purse, or within the barely visible slit of a briefcase. I also learned how to shoot pictures with an infrared filter (IR) over the flash, allowing us to take high-quality photos in complete darkness, a feat that was possible only because the IR flash is silent and invisible to the naked eye.

I also learned how to use photographic settings in covert circumstances. For example, you could preset the hyperfocal distance of a hidden camera in advance. That determined parameters for the depth of field, which indicates what's in focus. A shallow depth of field might be useful if you wanted to blur the background. Alternately, you could preset the hyperfocal distance so that everything from eight feet to infinity would be in sharp focus. That was especially useful for field work, when you might need to capture people, places, and things as you walked down the street or into a crowded bazaar or hotel lobby. The photography courses were engaging and the espionage capabilities nearly limitless. Invigorated by my new professional prospects, I dove headfirst into this new world of technology that I couldn't seem to get enough of.

As I became increasingly invested in cultivating a technical career inside the agency, John, too, remained devoted to his work. He'd begun to travel more frequently, occasionally returning home with interesting tales. One guy he polygraphed began an interview by placing his gun on the table. During another, John struggled to concentrate, distracted by the enormous snake that was coiled around the curtain rod at the opposite end of the room. He, too, seemed to enjoy the thrill of doing meaningful work that offered ample adventure.

When we were both at home, our professional lives remained separate. He worked at Langley, several miles outside of DC, down the George Washington Parkway, and I in the heart of the city. Our offices served different functions, and our work virtually never overlapped. Unlike overseas, where CIA employees from different offices mingled regularly and easily, at home each section—he was part of the Office of Security, I was in OTS—was large enough to comprise its own subculture. Fortunately, one couple we'd known abroad, Tim and Josie, were now at home too. In our free time we had a great time attending Josie's grand parties. She was a fabulous cook and a skilled entertainer. Now that we were back at headquarters, John and I rarely had dinner parties. On US shores John seemed to prefer watching football to mingling and exploring. His ideal vacations were Caribbean cruises that docked in ports that featured an endless array of duty-free shops, but no culture or history at all. This new side of John provided a stark contrast to the adventuresome man I'd met in Europe, but I didn't worry. We had long careers and several more overseas assignments ahead of us.

My training soon segued into an assignment to the office of our Chief of Operations in Technical Service, where, for the first time since joining the CIA, I was no longer a secretary. My title was Administrative Assistant, which meant I was responsible for writing a good bit of the operational correspondence that crossed the desk of my new boss, Ed. He was gruff with a crew cut and the bearing of a military officer, but he, too, turned out to be a supportive boss, encouraging me to pursue my dream of becoming a technical operations officer. I had been, and would continue to be, blessed by great bosses. Most of the time, that was.

CHAPTER 7

Cultural Tremors

During a Hawaiian vacation one year John and I visited Kilauea, one of the world's most active volcanoes. I was fascinated by what I learned, for example that volcanologists listen for harmonic tremor, which indicates that a volcano is building pressure it may not be able to contain. When detected in conjunction with earthquake swarms, these tremors are seen as warning signals that a volcano is nearing eruption. The tremors, volcanologists claim, sound a lot like a scream.

In the late 1970s the CIA "suits" that occupied the seventh floor of the agency's headquarters at Langley heard a different but equally disquieting kind of tremor. In 1977 a female Directorate of Operations officer, Harritte Thompson, filed her historic lawsuit against the agency. Hers was the first complaint to turn into a discrimination lawsuit, which began in 1979 and concluded in 1980. Her case asserted that the agency was "oriented primarily toward male operations officers." The women of the CIA had been screaming for years, and they were only getting louder.

The ensuing investigation found that the Directorate of Operations believed women could not run agents. Many male operations officers believed that in Latin America, Africa, the Near East, and Asia, women were second-class citizens, and as such, unqualified to perform the agency's "real" work in the field. Harritte Thompson won her case and was retroactively promoted two grades, from GS-14 to GS-16. She went on to cultivate a long and successful career in clandestine operations in the CIA, but the story of her lawsuit remained largely unknown, even inside the agency, for many years.

On paper the CIA was on notice that sex discrimination would not stand. The case should have marked a new day when women within the CIA began to exert public pressure on the agency, demanding that it take action to address the sex discrimination that had pervaded the agency's culture since day one. However, the CIA promptly exercised its right to keep the case secret, which largely voided the potential impact of the lawsuit and the likely public blowback.

At around the same time, the CIA began to feel other kinds of pain resulting from its long-standing policies that worked against women. Increasingly, female spouses were pushing back against their husbands' overseas assignments. *No, I won't uproot our life, give up my job at home, which has a much bigger paycheck, and accept whichever low-level secretarial post the agency "asks" me to take.* And *No, I won't sacrifice my professional future and return and find that I can't get my old job back, or any equivalent position.* As more CIA wives asserted their right to pursue their own careers, both inside and outside of the agency, more CIA officers (and husbands) were forced to choose between family and their latest, greatest assignment abroad.

The agency had always counted on the accompanying spouse, almost always the wife, to fill low-level positions overseas on a contract basis. Similar to how the US military operated in Germany, the women, as a group, were taken for granted and expected to provide operational support, typically without compensation. As Bina Kiyonaga wrote in *My Spy: Memoir of a CIA Wife*: "We lied about our husbands' jobs, stalled inquisitive policemen, befriended ministers' wives, kept our ears open at parties, deflected the children's questions, and worried in silence alone. We were the CIA wives. You never knew us."

The CIA was not alone in its expectation of wives; State Department also considered the wives of diplomats, even the nonworking wives, to be part of the "team." For this reason, there was widespread internal approval of professional married couples like me and John, who both worked inside the CIA. The coupling of clandestine, undercover officers was convenient and good for the agency. Only by marrying another CIA employee, after all, could two officers share common experiences in the office. Only by being married could two officers track each other during overseas trips and understand the unique stress and pressures that came with the job.

Usually that's the point of being married—being able to share your day, your work, your fears and successes. If that option is unavailable, as it was when an officer married outside the agency, the inability to communicate typically takes a huge toll on a marriage. With a considerable—and growing—percentage of wives unwilling to leave behind promising and more lucrative careers, staffing worldwide case officer posts, as well as the (often unpaid) overseas support positions, was becoming increasingly difficult. While there was always the possibility of separated tours, agreeing to live thousands of miles apart for at least two years often indicated that an officer's marriage was, or would soon be, in trouble. That distraction was no more beneficial for the agency than it was for the officers being sent abroad.

Times were changing, and the CIA wasn't bothering to keep up—until its overseas staffing problem became so undeniable that suddenly, it had to try. To address the agency's worldwide staffing problems, the Task Force on Working Married Couples was formed. I was thrilled to be asked to join the task force as a representative of the Directorate of Science and Technology.

Like many other CIA wives, as Mrs. John Goeser, I understood the career jolt of leaving a position at Langley to accompany my husband overseas. Each posting abroad had resulted in me being hired overseas as a contract employee at a much lower grade and pay rate. Upon returning to CIA Headquarters after each tour abroad, any promotions I'd received on foreign soil were rendered null and void. At headquarters I was rehired at an entry-level grade, forced to start over yet again. The fact that each assignment had allowed me to deepen and broaden my understanding of how the agency worked made no difference.

In addition to accepting this obviously biased and unfair system, CIA wives overseas, myself included, were expected to spend evenings and weekends organizing social gatherings, chatting up a foreign ambassador at an embassy function, or pre-positioning an operational car. I'd enjoyed hosting parties abroad, but that didn't make me immune to this injustice. It is one thing to offer to entertain, and quite another to be expected to do so merely because you're a woman. Far too many women within and married to the CIA were on full-time duty even as underpaid contractors. We were expected to organize our entire lives—professional, personal, and everything in between—around what was convenient for an agency that at best we didn't choose and at worst actively exploited us. At long last the wives' low-level groaning was turning into something much harder to ignore: refusal to participate at all.

I had watched a similarly biased system play out with my mom, one of the few working mothers I knew as a young girl. For most of her career, she had worked in the computer section of Boeing, shoulder to shoulder with men, many of whom did the same job as she. Each time the aircraft giant was forced into a round of layoffs, she was always among the first to be furloughed. While she sat at home, waiting for a recall, the young men she had mentored would move into her position. When at last she was called back to work, she would end up working for them. This was the rhythm of her "career" during my formative years. I'd long assumed this was how the world worked. All these years later, however, I, like many other women, was getting restless, increasingly frustrated with a career that looked like a shaky stock market graph. No more, I told John. While the work I wanted to do was in the field, which meant overseas, I wasn't interested in any assignment abroad that would require me to sabotage my GS grade or future career prospects.

As the task force took shape, I was hopeful we could come up with solutions. The men, however, seemed content to maintain the status quo, repeatedly offering the same misogynistic retort—*this is how the system works*, as though the system happened to them rather than reflected their own design. In fact, the solution to the agency's growing overseas staffing problem was obvious and simple. The CIA needed to guarantee the accompanying staff spouse, who was typically the wife, their same grade and job, or an equivalent one, upon returning to the

United States. When our recommendation was accepted and turned into official policy, I felt an overwhelming sense of accomplishment and satisfaction. We had had an impact that would reverberate through the agency for decades to come.

Feeling liberated to pursue the technical services career I desired, I eagerly sought out our next overseas posting; the trick would be finding assignments for John and me in the same location at the same time. To gain internal support, I approached Ed, my current boss, hoping he could help arrange a tour that would meet our needs. I had made things better for women at the agency. Now it was time to make things better for myself.

CHAPTER 8

A Return to Europe

I was on a TDY, a temporary duty trip in Europe, visiting a case officer when his wife came running into his study. There were police at each end of their street, she announced, gasping for breath. Their street had been cordoned off. The case officer gave me a sharp look before exiting his residence to reconnoiter the situation. A lone briefcase was sitting on the sidewalk, he discovered, and police were worried it might be a bomb. Terrorist activity was becoming more common in this country, so we were relieved when the briefcase's owner was located and its contents were confirmed to be innocuous. Crisis averted.

I had arrived in Europe on Pan Am One, and as the plane descended, the Middle Eastern women on the flight, who had boarded in Beirut or Istanbul, lined up for the restrooms, entering in dark burkas, exiting in high heels, form-fitting Western attire, and full makeup. To everyone's surprise, we arrived in the midst of a rare and massive snowstorm, which had caught even the Queen off guard.

I was met at the airport by an office car whose driver reported that the Queen and her driver were stuck in a snowbank and had found shelter at a small country hotel. When I arrived in the capital city and entered the Hilton hotel lobby to meet my foreign agent and his case officer, I noticed a group of the Muslim women from my flight. They looked shell-shocked, carting their mountains of luggage as they teetered forward in stilettos. Their male escorts were busy registering them for rooms since the women were not allowed to do that for themselves. None seemed to have heavy coats or boots. Some were given shawls, but those wouldn't keep them warm during this frigid blizzard.

I had been sent there to handle my second operational case, a significant recruitment from an Asian country considered unfriendly to the United States. We had issued this gentleman a subminiature camera system for copying documents in his office, but he was not using it. We figured he was scared. My job was to resolve the problem.

I met him at the Hilton. He brought his Tropel subminiature camera, which we had concealed in an expensive Montblanc fountain pen. He was sure he could not use it in his dimly lit office, he explained. To demonstrate the extreme sensitivity of the camera and its film, I flooded the room with light and had him take several photos from the daily newspaper. Then I began removing light sources, turning off lamps, lowering and then closing blinds, and so on, taking photos as the light dimmed. The next task was the hard part; I had to develop the film, then and there, to prove to him that the camera could capture images in low lighting.

Setting up a temporary darkroom in a hotel suite is usually no big deal. The work with a Tropel had to be done in total darkness, wearing infrared goggles and illuminated by an infrared light source, all of which I had sent ahead. However, doing all of that in the most expensive hotel in the city proved to be challenging. The elegant bathroom was sheathed in marble, and there was no place to clamp the IR light source; the bathroom's modern, rounded edges provided no point of attachment. Returning to the sitting room, I dragged the six-foot ebony coffee table into the bathroom, carefully standing it on its end, and hung the Do Not Disturb sign on the suite's outer door. The elevated legs were perfect for the clamp, and the tall glass tubes were ready to receive the chemicals.

Thirty minutes later I emerged with the developed film. I promptly unpacked a proprietary viewing device and sat down to review our results. At all levels of light except complete darkness, the camera had captured the text of a black-and-white document. The asset was embarrassed. He was prepared to take risks for us, he said, but saw no point if his success was not assured. With him now convinced that his efforts would be worth the risk, I was relieved and chalked his concerns up to inadequate training by our original photo operations officer. He returned to his home country and provided the CIA with invaluable intelligence over a long career using our small, subminiature cameras. And I experienced the satisfaction of a job well done.

Tony Mendez, who was now Chief of the Clandestine Imaging Division, the photo shop back home, sent a cable of congratulations when I returned to my home office. It was my first contact with him, but not my last.

After an extended period at home, John and I embarked on our third assignment overseas. This was our second assignment in Europe, but in many other ways this tour felt like my first real posting abroad. I was once again working on another continent, but now as something other than a secretary. Instead of taking shorthand, I'm going on trips where I might encounter a bomb threat or train a foreign asset. Ed, Chief of Operations for OTS, had been instrumental in finding me this new job as a photo lab technician. I also now had a guarantee of an equivalent GS grade upon my eventual return to DC. It felt like a fresh start, and the prospect of a tech career finally seemed within reach. I was determined to put this opportunity to good use, negotiating my way out of the lab and onto the street.

The first roll of film my new (all male) colleagues handed me on my first day was meant to be an initiation that was undoubtedly intended to inform me of my place in their ranks. Assuming a serious demeanor, one of the photo officers handed me a roll of Kodak's 1414 high-definition aerial reconnaissance film. I'd never seen it before, much less worked with it. It was a specialized type of film that had an ultrathin backing that made it a lighter load for satellites. Handling it was like working with Saran Wrap, and my task was to thread it into a Nikor reel. While I struggled to load the film in the darkroom, the guys waited in the outside office, giddily anticipating my failure. When I emerged with the developed film, they grew quiet, the air suddenly sucked out of the room. To their surprise, and perhaps chagrin, I did it. I often perform best under pressure. Once they'd recovered from the shock and disappointment of my success, they broke into brief, half-hearted applause. My darkroom skills were never questioned again.

This "joke" soon became a turning point for me. Most of my new male colleagues were Rochester Institute of Technology graduates who quickly realized that I was willing to take pains that they no longer felt they needed to bother with. Rather than immediately trying to develop a roll of unknown film, for instance, I would cut off a tail piece and develop that. East Germany's ORWO film, for example, had sloppy production values, and their ASA, or film speed, labels could not be trusted. This sometimes resulted in losing an entire roll of film. By cutting off a small piece to develop first, I could discern whether I had the correct chemical bath for that film, adjusting it accordingly before developing the whole roll. Confident that precious intelligence, which was often provided at great risk to our assets, was safe in my hands, my colleagues soon trusted me with increasingly important, sensitive materials.

One of our most experienced photo ops officers, a true old-timer, was especially generous with me, taking time to pass on his darkroom skills and considerable knowledge. He was a retired staff officer who had chosen to remain here with his wife and kids. It was a striking contrast to the younger photo officers, who were happy to hand me their work but never went out of their way to mentor me. Perhaps the idea of passing on their knowledge and skills never occurred to them, or perhaps they didn't yet perceive me as a threat. As men, they exuded an unfailing confidence that they would inherit the "real work." Even after proving myself repeatedly, in the darkroom and with assets, they seemed oblivious to the possibility that I, a woman, would or even could surpass them in responsibility or rank.

When the old-timer photo officer fell ill after a series of trips to Africa, we watched from afar, aghast as the medical staff at the huge US Army hospital tried, but ultimately failed, to cope with a set of symptoms they'd never encountered before. That was possibly my first look at the AIDS epidemic that would soon take so many lives.

In the photo labs we stayed busy, concealing cameras in laundry baskets or in the bellies of fake pregnant women, hiding them in a man's tie or the buttonhole of an overcoat. We could place a camera almost anywhere on you or in your belongings and have you ready to photograph a person, a building, a street scene—anything and anyone.

Various types of cameras were doled out according to role and purpose; the Tropel cameras, our most sophisticated, were often nested inside the fancy ink pens or key fobs we gave to our most valuable agents. The Tropel lens was made of eight tiny, precisely ground glass elements stacked one on top of another, resulting in crisp photographs of documents.* We, as lab techs, would never employ it ourselves. We would never get close enough to the subject, or to a head of government, or to a Prime Minister's desk, to take the pictures we wanted, for instance, but our foreign agents could.

On the streets of the city, my colleagues often used cameras in active concealments in support of those operations. One of our staffers might have a concealed camera inside a bag. Another case officer would wear one in a tie, while another, possibly a technical officer, would carry an attaché case, taking pictures through a razor-thin slit on the side. There were a million ways to hide a camera, and the pictures each one took were indeed worth a thousand words. During the Cold War we amassed reams upon reams of film at an unfathomable rate.

While I had continued to earn the respect of my fellow photo lab techs, there was one aspect of the darkroom that still made me feel out of place. Since day one, the walls had been plastered with pinup

---

* "Tropel Fountain Pen Camera," International Spy Museum, www.spymuseum.org/exhibition-experiences /about-the-collection/collection-highlights/tropel-fountain-pen-camera.

nudes, some of which were life-size. I hated them, but also knew I had to be careful how much attention I invited as the sole female in the darkroom. I was working in a man's world, and if I wanted a tech career, I would need to blend in. One afternoon an officer from a different building wandered in with his five-year-old son. When the boy asked about the photo of the lady with the big nose, the men all smiled, knowing the boy was too young to initiate into their club quite yet; Hilda, as she was captioned, was a statuesque, life-size black-and-white nude with luscious blonde hair spilling over her shoulders. I didn't like seeing the poster every time I walked into the darkroom, but I also knew I couldn't "be a girl" and complain about it. That would only validate their assumptions about me, which had everything to do with their misogyny and nothing to do with me, my qualifications, or my potential.

Our large, third-floor apartment in our new European home city had lots of windows and lots of light, an important feature in an often gray, dreary city. One urban legend claimed the local government had offered huge tax incentives to building owners who painted their exteriors any color other than gray. As far as I could see, it wasn't making a difference. Our apartment unit also had unique curtains and a good washer/dryer. The other wives in the building noticed every one of these details and didn't hesitate to inquire about us and complain about the disparities in our living quarters. The wives, we soon realized, likely posed a bigger threat to our cover stories than foreign nationals. The Soviets weren't looking for us, but the American wives, with their discerning eyes and finely honed sense of hierarchy, absolutely were.

The wives' questions sometimes caught me off guard, and each time I had to do some fancy verbal tap dancing, always ensuring our cover story was plausible. Consistency was also critical, and often the more challenging part; if the wives swapped conflicting stories, we might attract unwanted attention, and worse, more questions. Much of this casual redirection fell to me of course; none of the wives would have dreamt of asking John about the mundane details of our housing or décor.

John, an excellent tennis player, enjoyed playing on the red clay courts at the local club, where the tennis pro was Pakistani and the club members came from all around the world. While I didn't play tennis, I was fascinated by the multicultural social interactions. It was there that I met Liz, a Brit who was somewhat addicted to tennis. John and I both loved spending time with her. She was a foreign-currency dealer for Chase Manhattan, my old stomping grounds. As two women carefully building their careers inside a maze of men, we soon discovered we had quite a bit in common.

Liz was funny and loud, characteristics that would turn out to be typical of my female friends. She was fearless, aggressive when she needed to be, as well as gregarious and charming. She would have made a pretty good CIA operations officer.

Instead of learning tennis, I focused more of my attention on skiing, which Liz also excelled at. We took weekend trips, often with the International Ski Club. While I never did match Liz's expertise on the slopes, we shared an inordinate affection for the sport.

John had learned to ski in high school in the Swiss Alps, and his skill level was on par with Liz's, but I didn't mind for a minute. We'd take a bus that would depart from our housing area promptly at 6 p.m. on Friday evening for a weekend away. Each traveler would be provisioned with a box dinner and a personal bottle of wine. By the time we arrived in France, Austria, or perhaps Switzerland, it would be midnight, or close to it, and some of us would be asleep while others might be passed out in the aisle.

As my love of skiing deepened, I also continued running, preferably in the beautiful park located between the office and our housing complex. There was a leafy trail, a circuit that was about a mile long that I would run as many times as my schedule permitted. The only downside was the view in warm weather, which Europeans seemed to define as any temperature above fifty degrees. One after another, on every "warm" day, they would strip down to sunbathe nude, entirely unfazed by their audience.

As this tour unfolded, John and I each became increasingly devoted to our work, although we didn't discuss the details of our assignments with each other. Occasionally, if something especially upsetting occurred, we might touch on how we were feeling, but we always avoided getting into specifics. We were also both traveling more frequently, often with minimal advance notice, so we kept a "guest" notebook in our foyer that we used to communicate our whereabouts. For instance, I might come home from work one day to find a note from him inside saying he would return on Friday evening and would be sure to bring home a wheel of Parmesan cheese. That would let me know that he was in Italy. During weekends when we were both at home, we spent many of our Saturday afternoons sampling vintages in a wine cellar owned by new friends whose family owned a local vineyard. We all had a great time sipping their wines, often talking for hours that sometimes extended through dinner. The wine was spectacular and the friendship welcoming and lively. Whenever I had a dinner party featuring Indian or Thai food, I would end up in their kitchen choosing the wine, usually a Gewürztraminer to complement the spicy food. They told us amazing stories of WWII, when they buried their wine in the fields, worried that foreign soldiers would steal it. The wife often sent me home with a huge bouquet from their flower garden as well. To them, we were employees of the American government, and to me, they were a welcome window into a world of new knowledge, a reminder of how much more I had to learn.

Still, nowhere was my education more vital than at work, where one challenge rarely looked like the next. One day I was asked to assist with a uniquely delicate situation. Some of the agency's military colleagues asked for help with developing classified film that was needed for a court case, which meant the CIA couldn't touch it. It had been secured by a military intelligence officer, but they'd encountered issues in the darkroom and couldn't complete the process. The one military soldier who had the technical prowess and necessary secret/top secret clearance was unavailable due to a personal security matter.

When I sat down with their replacement technician, I showed him how to load a piece of dummy film onto the Nikor reel I'd brought with me. Then the film reel would need to be placed carefully inside a light-tight stainless-steel container. Loading the film was the only part of the process that required a specific skill, especially since those first steps would need to be completed in total darkness to avoid damaging the film. Once the film reel was secured inside the container, the lights could be turned back on and the remainder of film development followed like a recipe for baking a cake.

With my guidance the technician practiced loading the film repeatedly. He was noticeably clumsy but still able to perform these critical steps, so we ventured inside the darkroom, where under no circumstances was I authorized to touch the film. He promptly positioned himself at the counter and I on a nearby stool. Before beginning, we made sure he knew where everything was, since he would need to locate each item in absolute darkness. A can opener to pop open the film cassette was on his right, scissors to cut the film were in the middle, and the Nikor spool and steel can were on his left. He would need to pick up those items in that order.

Once he seemed ready, we turned off the lights. I heard him fumble for the opener, then heard the film cassette pop open. I heard him pick up the scissors, then drop them on the floor. When I heard him struggling with the film, trying to load it onto the reel, my body instinctively shifted forward, now perched on the edge of the stool.

When someone was loading film correctly onto a reel, it was nearly silent. There was a silky, smooth sound that confirmed the film had been handled successfully. When the film wasn't loaded correctly, there was a crackling sound that indicated there would be huge "purple hearts" on the developed film, obliterating the image underneath. As soon as I heard the crackling sound, I told the technician to relax, put the film down, and take a moment to catch his breath. When I heard him set it on the counter, in the pitch-black darkness I moved to the counter, quietly picked up the reel, and manually checked his work, entirely by feel. To complete a thorough check, I had to unwind the film back to the beginning and then rewind it in absolute silence back onto the reel. The entire process took less than a minute. Once I was confident that he could proceed, I gently laid the reel back on the counter and told him we should move on to the next step. He picked up the reel and placed it inside the steel can before turning on the lights. I stayed with him while he developed the film, making sure I never touched it. The developed film was perfect.

———

John and I lived in a group of buildings that were embellished with some exceptional add-on features, like maid's quarters for each apartment.

Unfortunately, none of us had live-in maids, but the extra space was great for storage. We lived in a lovely housing area where State Department staff typically lived, but we weren't State Department employees either. We were neither fish nor fowl.

Eager to take advantage of our new European home base, John and I took personal trips whenever our schedules permitted. Through these trips, as well as the TDYs I was being sent on, I was meeting new CIA colleagues in various field offices, including Mick, one of our tech ops officers. An outgoing guy who usually traveled with his guitar, he could be found after hours in a local pub, drinking Czech Pilsner Urquell beer, an exquisite European brew, while he entertained local Germans by strumming American tunes. He was fun to be with and sitting at his table almost felt like being back home.

Along with Joe, a new, young colleague, Mick and I were on a TDY conducting a mail cover operation at the local airport, a cavernous facility built by the Nazis between 1936 and 1941. Joe struck up a conversation with an older woman who was directing the work. When she mentioned the bombing of Berlin during the war, Joe asked how long it lasted. The woman just looked at him. Days? Joe prompted. Silence. Weeks? Shaking her head, she spoke quietly. "Years." Almost half of the population of the city, 1.7 million people, had fled during that time. Joe was quiet for the rest of the afternoon. We all were. While the German people did suffer during the war, the suffering inflicted upon millions of Jews by the Nazi regime they had tolerated, or even supported, was far too great to ignore. Rather than initiating a conversation likely to incite anger and pain, we resorted to silence, all too aware that no words could undo the brutal slaughter of Jews that had occurred in and around Germany.

During our trips to Berlin, we frequently met up with Allen, another new and engaging CIA colleague. The trip there was an easy train ride from Frankfurt, and we treated each one as a festive getaway. Each time we made sure to arrive early enough to gather supplies for the journey: chilled Riesling wine, Hungarian sausages, cheese, fresh baguettes still warm from the ovens, and chocolates. We always bought a little extra, hoping to exchange cigarettes or chocolates with the junior guards standing on the platforms at each stop. They carried long guns and wore heavy, ankle-length coats and huge hats. We were amazed to realize they were merely kids, some looked to be only fourteen or fifteen, and they were as interested in us as we were in them. Opening our windows quietly, we'd gently toss out packages of Western cigarettes, breaking all the rules nearly every time the train stopped.

One memorable moment from those trips occurred on a VIP helicopter tour of the wall. It was an exceptional invitation from a high-level CIA officer who was about to become Chief of Operations for the agency. While I had followed the headlines daily and understood the politics at work in this divided city, I was emotionally unprepared for the view as our helicopter traveled above the death strip that was nestled in the no-man's-land on the Eastern side. The wall was an open, festering wound running through the heart of Berlin, complete with gun emplacements, barbed wire, and snarling German shepherd dogs. As we flew above, armed guards eyeballed our helicopter from the guard towers in a way that I found unnerving. I had heard the stories of escapees who'd been shot down as they tried to race across this open ground. Directly below us was further proof—beds of nails that were sunk below each bridge where the wall crossed water, intended to impale any East Berliner who tried to leap toward freedom.

I was glad to be in a helicopter with a stranger who would not notice the tears welling up in my eyes as we landed. When Allen met us on the tarmac, he nodded but didn't say a word.

I was grateful to also be aware of the incredible covert work being done underneath the wall itself. Tunnels were being dug nightly by West German students, whose efforts allowed more than 300 of their compatriots to escape from the East. By comparison, 140 died trying to cross that almost suicidal strip of land aboveground that divided the city. None of these lifesaving tunnels were visible as we peered down from our helicopter, but I knew they were there.

OTS, where I worked, was the go-to unit for the American intelligence community if and when a tunnel was needed. We had been the driving force behind the famous Berlin Tunnel dug under the city in the 1950s to intercept Soviet communications, but that effort bore no resemblance to these current, homegrown efforts. To my knowledge we were never involved in these West German–led tunneling efforts, but we were as aware of them as we tried to be about just about everything going on in the city.

Aboveground on the Western face of the wall, a new style of art was flourishing. West Germans painted ladders up to the top on their side of the wall to symbolically encourage their fellow countrymen to escape and climb down. That side of the wall became one of the largest art canvases in the world. Artists from around the globe eventually flocked to it. Today, segments of those murals are exhibited in various countries.

———

I first met Sergeant Bob after enrolling in an evening photography class that he was teaching. A retired Black US military Sergeant with an exquisite level of skill handling color film in the darkroom, he had an equally deep knowledge of the backstreet jazz joints, underground art galleries, and offbeat new restaurants in our staid and dreary city.

Before long, Bob became a real friend whom John and I would meet to attend a Friday night art gallery opening and then end up with at an impromptu balalaika performance in a Russian-themed bar. Combined with his sophisticated taste and knowledge of the city, his courses breathed new life into my photography.

In the darkroom at work, I was growing increasingly familiar with the caustic chemicals used during hand processing, many of which could cause chronic skin problems. When I suggested that we purchase a Royal Print professional color-printing machine, the guys in the office were dubious. Almost everything that we processed was in black and white, they countered. If we didn't offer color prints, they seemed to think, there would be no demand for them. If we *could* handle color film, I argued, it *would* become the standard tool. Color photography showed more detail and provided more accurate and thorough intelligence.

My thinking proved sound. Not long after we purchased the machine, our CIA colleagues began using more color film than black-and-white. I was put in charge of the care and feeding of the machine, changing the color chemistry weekly as the demand for color prints rapidly increased. I was glad to take on that additional task, even though we all knew it was the guys' way of making me pay for getting them to agree to color printing. I'd been instrumental in elevating our intelligence, and we all knew it, even if none of them would admit it.

As my skill and confidence in the photo labs increased, I began trying to convince my boss, Ted, to give me more opportunities to train foreign assets. A gray-haired, bespectacled chemist whose white lab coat pocket sported a full row of pens, he was atypically religious and optimistic compared to the younger, more cynical tech types that dominated our office. While hands-on operational training was not in my current job description, one day when an emergency came up, he sent me, confident that I could handle the work.

The assignment was to meet with and train a wealthy Middle Eastern businessman who lived and worked locally on how to use secret writing. That seemed simple enough, but there was a twist. The man I was training would be a "bridge agent." It was the first time I had heard that term. Essentially, my trainee was not the asset, not the one in the country of concern who had access to the intelligence we needed. That person was his relative. The man I was supposed to meet could travel back and forth to the country of concern with an ease that we could not. As the "bridge agent," he would be responsible for training his relative, who would then collect and transmit valuable intelligence back to the CIA. I was not simply training our bridge agent in how to use secret writing techniques; I was also training him in how to train.

Even locally, in a relatively benign working environment, we had to be discreet when meeting foreign assets. We were constantly reminded that there were no friendly intelligence services. We'd been trained to assume that the local intelligence services, whether domestic or foreign, would have their eyes on us. As a result, surveillance detection runs, or SDRs, were mandatory before meeting any agent, regardless of nationality.

Once a thorough SDR had been completed to ensure I was not being observed, I met my bridge agent in a room at the most refined hotel in the city. He was dressed in a three-piece suit, his gray hair immaculately coiffed, the very picture of the accomplished businessman he was known to be. He and I would not be alone for long; his case officer would join us after an hour. In the meantime, I was to teach him the intricacies of preparing a secret-writing message that could pass smoothly through international mail censorship.

Before our meeting got underway, we followed the protocols, preparing for unanticipated intrusions, including the possibility that security might begin pounding on the door. How much time did he have? Had he encountered problems in attending the meeting? What were we doing there, together in a hotel room? What was our cover story? Often, a man and woman in the same room might pretend to be engaged in a sexual tryst. Oftentimes all that would be required to prop up that story was hopping into bed and pulling the covers up to my chin. In most cases that's all it would take, so that's what we agreed to.

At this time there were still very few meetings between members of the opposite sex. The foreign agents were always men, much like the technical operations officers. I was the outlier.

During our one and only meeting, I introduced myself as "Jane from Washington." He was focused and seemed perfectly comfortable working with a woman. We talked about him and his relative at some length, and at the end of a three-hour session, I felt confident that he could successfully provide him with the necessary training.

The illustrious hotel where we met was distinguished by a huge circular outdoor courtyard in front of the lobby entrance that was covered by a tent-size, orange umbrella. It was a great spot to reconnoiter after a meeting, especially in the city's typically gloomy, wet weather. When the case officer, who had seemed bored during the training session, paused with me at that spot on my way out, I was surprised to learn that he was especially pleased with how the meeting had gone. After he'd complimented me on establishing a rapport with the subject, we stopped for a quick cup of coffee. As we sat down, he explained that this training was one of many in a huge operation they had just put together. I was proud to be involved in this program and was beginning to feel the satisfaction of being part of the CIA's operational machinery.

Weeks later we received the first message from the operation; it had been completed perfectly. The foreign asset also sent a hello to "Jane from Washington." For the next several years I received hand-drawn holiday cards from this agent, whom I never met, written in secret ink, annotated with his version of an American Christmas tree. By sending these cards, he was violating several of the security rules I had taught the bridge agent, but that made it a bit exciting, like a secret holiday flirtation. Merry Christmas!

During these early meetings with foreign agents, I consistently confirmed something I'd suspected all along—that my gender was more helpful than harmful in this line of work. While many of the OTS guys were still convinced that foreign assets, all of whom were male, wouldn't listen to a woman, all the assets I met with consistently paid close attention when I told them how I could help them keep safe, avoid getting arrested, and protect their families. Often, these men, who were understandably frightened at the prospect of getting caught, seemed to feel comforted being trained by a compassionate woman with high-level skills and some cultural understanding. The so-called soft skills so often attributed to women were an asset, not a liability, especially in a technical field where this ability to build rapport and earn people's trust is so critical, yet so undervalued.

While I would make the most of my "soft" skills throughout my career, my technical skills continued to be paramount. Fortunately, the technical aspects of my job were my favorite part. Having earned the trust of my boss and colleagues inside and outside of the darkroom, I was now being given foreign assignments, initially to various countries within Europe. During one of those early trips, I opted to take the train rather than fly the short distance. Pleased to be seated in a plush, first-class compartment, I settled in, quickly discovering that my neighbor was George David Woods, a former President of the World Bank. Since I would be working in the CIA offices on arrival at my destination—not meeting operational assets or doing anything clandestine, at least not in a public setting—I simply told him I was meeting a friend. On trips like this, there was no need to devise a complicated cover story.

Mr. Woods was on his way to a conference in Geneva where he would give a speech on economics, but what he wanted to talk about was a play he was writing. He'd had a long-standing love affair with the New York theater community, he explained, and had backed several Broadway productions. A spectacular conversationalist who seemed to enjoy meeting someone outside of his sphere, he read portions of his play to me while we sped through Bavaria and then over the French Alps. He had a deep, booming voice and a knack for reading the lines with the appropriate emotion, as if onstage. I sincerely enjoyed his performance and our ride together. When he invited me to attend his talk, however, I declined, confident I would be busy with "my friend."

Indeed, I was busy, processing a secret message that required me to boil alcohol to reveal the writing. Unbeknownst to me, all alcohol commercially available in this country was laced with camphor, which is best known as an ingredient in Vicks VapoRub but is also used in plastic, paints, and mothballs. Adding camphor to alcohol was the local government's way of preventing its citizens from setting up illegal stills under their kitchen cabinets and turning it into the ever-popular schnapps, or eau-de-vie, flavored with pears, apples, plums, or cherries. These alcoholic beverages, like Poire Williams, or pear brandy, were wildly popular and heavily taxed in-country. As a result, purchasing pure denatured alcohol required a prescription from a medical doctor.

The secret, it turned out, was to cross the border and buy your alcohol in the adjacent country, where they would never restrict the use of alcohol in such a heavy-handed way.

The odor that boiling camphor-laced alcohol makes is not only overpowering and repulsive, it's also potentially toxic to breathe. Not yet aware that the locally available alcohol contained camphor, I set about my lab work as usual, boiling away. Before I knew it, the entire building had to be emptied for several hours, as the fumes had entered the air-circulation system and put everyone at risk.

Feeling humiliated by the entire fiasco, I consoled myself in a café. Hoping my reputation hadn't been permanently tarnished, especially with the tech guys whose respect I'd had to work so hard to earn, the next day I returned to my home office sheepishly; the dramatic story of my mistake had beat me home, but the guys were nonplussed. We were too busy to dwell on the past, and this was the CIA, where anything could, and often did, happen.

As usual, however, there was little time to focus on myself or my error. The next day Alex, a friend and coworker, landed in Beirut on a TDY. Arriving at the American embassy there, he had made a brief detour to the men's room after checking in with the case officer for the operation. Moments later, as he stood at the bathroom sink washing his hands, a bomb detonated at the center of the seven-story building. The building promptly collapsed, each floor falling onto the one beneath like a gigantic, deadly pancake stack. Eight members of the CIA's station, including Kenneth Haas, Chief of Station, were killed, and a photo of the destruction soon appeared on the cover of *Newsweek* magazine. There was a body still visible in the photo, hanging from the wreckage. Alex, who had been encased inside the reinforced cement-block construction of the plumbing and electrical core of the building, survived. He was pulled from the rubble in a harrowing rescue as large tractor-like vehicles removed the tons of material under which he was buried.

We were all devastated by this horrific event. I soon learned that John had recently done a routine polygraph on one of the working wives at the station. She, too, had been killed in the blast. At moments like these, our daily duties took on a darker hue, reminding each of us in vivid, terrifying technicolor of the immense risks we were surrounded by at every moment of every day. The tragedies, the deaths, left us with a haunting feeling that made an indelible mark. Decades later, on June 24, 2021, when news reports featured the fallen condominium on the beach in Surfside, Florida, I shuddered as I stared at the tattered remnants of the building hanging off the side of the still-standing structure. Praying that some would be found, still alive, as Alex had been, I turned away, unable to watch anymore.

———

As my trips became more frequent and spanned longer distances, I would occasionally marvel that I was sitting at an outdoor café in Paris, or London or Madrid, expected to provide mission-critical results. Amazed that the life I was living was real—not some daring, enchanting fantasy—I reveled in the path that was unfurling in front of me. *What would Don, my first true love, think of my new life?* I wondered on occasion. In college we'd listened to the big band music he loved—Stan Kenton, Tommy Dorsey, Woody Herman, and others. That had led to me expanding my reading repertoire to include authors like F. Scott Fitzgerald, another favorite of Don's. Through this immersion into his world, a new side of me had come to life. Suddenly, I'd been able to access the keen sense of wonder inside me, which acted like a kind of inner fire, propelling me outward and forward, eager to discover all that I didn't yet know, hadn't yet seen, couldn't yet experience. At one point, my mother had remarked to Don, "You helped raise Jonna." He didn't understand her meaning at the time, but if he could see me now, perhaps he would. Still, though, neither I nor Don had ever imagined me in *this* life—not back then, at least.

Yet here I was, and with each new challenge it was becoming clearer that I was my best self when doing the work. In a hotel room working with a foreign asset, showing him—and yes, they were still strictly male—how to collect information more safely, and how to protect himself and his family from discovery. The work I was doing came with significant risk, yes, but it was also protecting critical information and the very important individuals who dared to collect it on our behalf. What I was doing every day mattered. A lot. Although I became aware of the CIA's imperfections over time, I always believed in its broader mission, and felt a strong sense of purpose around my work. That never got old.

Up until this point, most of my operational work had been done on my own, as a solo. My next TDY would be as part of a two-person team. My partner for this assignment was Mick, whom I'd first met while visiting Berlin. He was going to do the "outside" part of the job, while I would be the "inside" person, taking the film he returned daily and developing and printing the "take." It was a new experience for me, and I was intrigued.

I knew Mick as a technically accomplished officer and a gregarious guy who naturally drew people in; his was a personality the CIA recruited for when looking for case officer candidates. He had a positive, infectious approach to life and operational scenarios. I was glad to be working with him. I checked into our hotel, the fabulous Plaza, almost next door to the train station and, more importantly, directly across the street from the city's landmark entertainment center and lavish gardens. We were here because a long-term operation in the city was about to bear important fruit. Our job was to assist in the matter.

We registered at the desk and happened upon the hotel bar, one of the city's best-kept secrets. Designed to emulate a posh men's club, it had all the necessary accoutrements—soft leather chairs, walls of leather-bound books, a vaulted stained-glass ceiling, and miles of oil portraits and ornate murals. We ordered drinks and sat down to plan our operation, anticipating that this might be the only moment we had to relax for a while. Without realizing it at the time, this bar became the benchmark by which I would measure all other bars and clubs from that point forward. The closest match would be the Metropolitan Club in Manhattan, although that was more ornate and larger than the bar at the Plaza. Both made my heart swell—I have a soft spot for a well-appointed bar to this day.

Over the next three days we developed a comfortable rhythm, meeting for breakfast before Mick would leave to make the next meeting, leaving me free to explore the city and its world-class gardens. Then at lunch he would drop the first batch of intelligence, and we would reconvene at six o'clock each evening to review what I had developed. It was one of my first closely coordinated team efforts, and our work proceeded seamlessly.

To top it off, the Chief of Station was an old friend of Jack Goeser, my father-in-law. This friend of John's family was the quintessential man-about-town in the city, far better known than most COSs, who worked hard at preserving their low profiles. Fortunately for us, he also stepped forward to ensure that Mick and I had everything we needed. Mick was amazed that I knew him as a family friend.

It had been an incredibly smooth and rewarding trip, until the last night. Once Mick and I had finished our evening meeting and stashed the last of the material, he suggested we grab a quick bite and check out a movie. That sounded like the perfect close to a successful assignment. The theaters in town showed first-run American movies in English, so I told Mick to choose whichever one he wanted to see.

About ten minutes into the film, I started to realize that this was not just any movie. Billed as a historical, erotic drama on the poster in the theater lobby, *Caligula*, to my surprise and horror, was a violent, pornographic movie in which the Roman emperor Caligula turns his palace into a brothel and makes his horse a priest, at which point the "fun" begins. Sitting in my movie theater seat, I realized that the first darkroom "joke" the tech guys had put me through had only been a tryout. This was my first real test as a woman in this man's world I had elbowed my way into.

More than anything, I wanted to walk out of that theater without hesitating or looking back. I was a married woman with a newly blossoming espionage career that required levels of courage and daring many people struggle to fathom, yet I sat there, furious and humiliated, feeling oddly pinned to my seat. I remember thinking that I couldn't let myself walk out. That story would circulate at our home office in a matter of hours. Jonna had, what, stormed out? *Ha, such a typical woman! She couldn't take it!* Unwilling to feed that fire, I sat and stared at one revolting scene after another, a temporary prisoner of the decidedly masculine world I'd worked so hard to join.

I have made plenty of mistakes in my life, and a good number of them in my career, but staying in my seat and sitting through that movie, against every instinct in my body, remains in my personal hall of shame. Too unsure of myself as Mick's equal to take a stand, I shrunk, closing my eyes when the scene playing out on the big screen grew darker and more demeaning. If I could have done so clandestinely, I would have plugged my ears too. Afterward, Mick and I endured a long, largely silent walk back to the hotel. He wasn't a bad guy, and perhaps he hadn't known the details of the movie, but he had crossed a line and we both knew it.

A movie, of all things, had torpedoed my professional confidence, leaving me to question whether I could soldier on as an equal among my male colleagues. Was the entrenched misogyny within OTS and the CIA overall too dense for me to penetrate? Mick could have stood up and said, "This is awful," and we could have both left, but he didn't. How would I ever be taken seriously as a professional when this kind of disrespect was dished out so thoughtlessly? Where I had once seen affable coworkers, I now saw red lights and alarm bells. I didn't feel physically threatened, per se, but I did briefly wonder if my professional dreams were dissolving before my eyes. I'd always known that pursuing this career would require me to develop a backbone, abandon my mother's cautions against direct confrontation, and stand up to the blatant sexism that had plagued her work life. How I would accomplish all of that, I didn't yet know. But I needed a new playbook, and I would have to write it for myself.

When Mick and I returned, I waited for the weekend and then headed into work. I opened our office, marched into the darkroom, and pulled the nudes down from the walls, one by one, before crushing them into the trash can.

Hilda was never seen again.

CHAPTER 9

The Middle East

My boss, Ted, made a beeline toward me as soon as I arrived in the photo lab early one Friday morning. He'd been notified of an urgent hand-carry assignment, he explained, and it would necessitate a quick flight, stat. Forever eager to indulge my love of field work, and excited to travel to the city in question, I said yes before Ted could complete his request. Being childless and married to a man who was traveling around the globe for the agency on a perpetual, almost nomadic circuit made split-second decisions like this one a good bit easier.

Moments later, the administrative machine began ticking forward. One person would walk my travel request through the office for signature, another would book the travel and pick up the tickets. The entire process, which could have taken up to a week back at headquarters, was accomplished in a single morning. It was one of the perks of a high-priority field assignment; the impossible became possible in the blink of an urgent TDY. At this point in the process, my job was the easiest of all: to make the five-minute walk home, toss some things into a suitcase, and return to the office ready for takeoff within an hour or less. I would be a courier, hand carrying something so important and so classified that I never even learned what it was.

Upon returning to the office with a small suitcase, I stopped briefly to pick up my tickets, cash advance, travel orders, and passport. Nearby, a small cluster of secretaries had gathered. I smiled as I approached them, knowing what they wanted: cartouches, which were solid-gold pendants with their names carved in hieroglyphics. Each of these necklaces was handmade, personal and popular at the time. Once reserved for the deceased, who were buried with a cartouche to identify them and allow them access to the afterlife, they'd since become custom-made trinkets for tourists that were also readily available in the city I was traveling to. The CIA was a perfect source for them if you knew somebody. Now that I was suddenly that somebody, I accepted six or seven requests, as well as several envelopes of cash, and was then driven to the airport to board my Lufthansa flight.

The plane was shockingly empty; it was just me and perhaps a dozen other passengers. With so much room, little chance of bathroom lines, and an abundant supply of snacks and drinks, the trip was comfortable and the flight attendants exceptionally attentive. As we settled in, a fellow passenger named Mr. Gentleman—I kid you not, that was his actual name—began talking to me. A Texan in manner and stature—he was a physically large man with thick silver hair, a full mustache, and an equally loquacious, jovial manner—he worked for a huge American construction company. He had been injured on the job, left with a few broken bones, and flown home to the States to get serious medical care. Now healed, he was "rarin'" to get back to work, he told me excitedly. Within a few minutes of talking—he did most of it—I became "little lady." Each time he saw the flight attendant, he would say, "Hey, miss, would you bring me and the little lady another drink?"

I sat back and let him entertain me with his stories, which were soon followed by an unveiling of the very special wooden box he had stashed in the overhead bin. It was, he explained, his "fixin's box," and it contained all the ingredients a Texan needed. Inside was an assortment of the herbs, spices, and sauces needed to make a proper chili or a sumptuous barbecue. One by one, he removed the lids of a few of the small bottles, describing each precious ingredient as he wafted the pungent aromas toward me with one hand.

About an hour out from landing he stopped talking long enough to inquire about my trip—where was I going and staying and what would I be doing while there. I seized the moment to test the light cover story I had devised while hurriedly packing my suitcase a few hours earlier. I was visiting an old friend, I told Mr. Gentleman. She worked at a private bank and had an extra room where I would be staying. Simple, short, and sweet, specific enough to satisfy but general enough to offer no details to double-check or follow up on. *Nothing to see here*, a good cover story would convey. *I'm just going about my average life.*

As the pilot executed a smooth and feather-soft landing, Mr. Gentleman generously offered to take me under his wing. After briefing me on the inner workings of the airport and the potential problems one might encounter at immigration, he offered tips for navigating the arrival process. I listened intently; Mr. Gentleman couldn't have known that I'd studied CIA maps of the entire airport at the office.

Before even boarding the plane, I'd already known the precise location of every choke point, where to find immigration and customs, and more. Upon returning to my home office, I would also annotate any discrepancies I'd noticed in the airport layout, security or otherwise.

"You just stick with me, little lady," he said as we stood up to deplane. "Stay close and we'll slip right through the formalities. I know my way around this airport."

When we walked toward the exit, I was about ten feet ahead of Mr. Gentleman. Before proceeding down the stairs to the tarmac, he paused to hug each flight attendant while I advanced toward a small cluster of uniformed military intelligence officers. They were each wearing freshly starched khakis studded with brass. Behind them a black limousine waited, its rear passenger door open. One of the liaison officers stepped forward and addressed me by name, with the correct parole. I then handed him the hand-carry package. Without ever stating his name, he guided me to the car and slipped in beside me as his colleague closed the door. Pulling away from the plane, I looked back just as Mr. Gentleman, who was now halfway down the stairs, his fixin's box clutched to his breast, watched us drive off. I always have wondered what he was thinking in that moment, as the "little lady" left with a military escort.

After my hand carry was in the right hands, my assignment was complete, but instead of returning immediately to Europe, I planned to spend the weekend here as a tourist. My only concern was all the cash I was carrying—the secretaries' money for cartouches plus my cash advance and per diem; I was eager to turn all that green cash into money orders. When I paid my courtesy call to the Chief of Station, he informed me there was an American Express office nearby. It was a ten-minute walk, so I set out on foot, happy to get my first look at the city. Street life has always fascinated me, and this city was dominated by a cacophony of honking horns, which I recall vividly even now. As I walked down the streets, I wondered if traffic might lessen, or even stop altogether, if there were no horns.

After entering the lobby of the bank, I walked up to the cashier, reached into my purse, and began fishing around. Bewildered and then suddenly panicked, I realized that my wallet was gone. I had been pickpocketed. I looked up at the cashier, speechless.

Stepping aside to let the next customer take my place, I mentally retraced my steps, recalling a gentleman wearing a long, flowing white robe. The streets were crowded, but he had caught my attention, partly because he'd come a little too close to me. Thankfully I always carried my identity documents separately from my money. I would still be able to get through immigration and return to my home office, but it was hard to believe all that money was gone.

Without the secretaries' funds in hand, I opted not to visit the souk where the cartouches were made and sold. The local office advanced me extra pocket money, which I spent on a taxi to visit the architectural wonders in the area. My taxi driver was a young man who seemed to enjoy practicing his English. I told him what had happened, apologizing for not having enough cash for a real tip. He seemed almost embarrassed that I had been robbed in his country. When we arrived at the site, which is one of the most visited tourist sites in the world, the scene was flooded with camel-riding "guides"—aggressive young men eager to give tourists a tour of the site, for a price. As I exited the taxi, the driver climbed up on the hood, where he was at eye level with the guides on their camels. "This American woman," he began, pointing at me, "has no money. None." He then explained that I'd been robbed and that they should treat me with respect as a result. He said it all in

English, and several of the camel riders nodded in agreement. I was then able to spend the entire afternoon wandering through the massive structures with my cameras, undisturbed.

I had lost money but been given a window of time to enjoy the area, once again becoming a flaneur, an urban explorer. Meandering through the vast site, I made eye contact with a shy little boy who looked about seven years old, standing by himself, away from the groups being led by tour guides. I smiled at him, and he nodded in reply, turning and walking around the corner. I followed him as he proceeded toward the remnants of some ancient temples. After stepping down a route that led into a square opening, the boy turned to me, beckoning me to enter the shaft behind him. I followed him down the stairs. Ahead of me was a long, dark tunnel with doors on either side. Roughly carved hieroglyphics covered the walls, resembling the entrance to a massive subterranean world.

I noticed a flickering light down the tunnel and continued walking. As we got closer, I saw an older, gray-haired man with a beard. He was holding a torch. When the little boy spoke to him, I froze, suddenly regaining my senses. "What are you doing?" I whispered to myself as I pivoted abruptly and hustled toward the entrance, threading my way through the shafts and chambers and then back into the blazing sunlight.

Moments like these would continue to pop up throughout my career, highlighting one of the tricky parts about field work and foreign travel. You must be willing to take risks, but also know when you're about to go too far. Not for the first time or the last, no one knew where I was. If I disappeared, no one would even know where to look. *This is how people vanish into thin air*, I reminded myself. Of course, I might have been perfectly safe deep inside that dark tunnel with that boy and that bearded elderly man—or not. Neither instinct nor the thinking mind makes for an infallible guide. Figuring out when to trust which was never simple, a struggle every woman on earth has faced in one way or another, though perhaps not with as much frequency as I would.

Most of my photos from that weekend came out overexposed, probably because I was distracted by my inner turmoil over being pickpocketed. *How had I let that happen? Why had I ignored my instincts silently warning me that the man in the white robe was getting too close?* I could have compensated for the picture quality in the darkroom, but the photos themselves weren't as interesting as they should have been. Instead of taking the time to fix them, I focused on the man who had probably pocketed my cash now being able to support his extended family. The money he had so surreptitiously plucked from my purse, the COS told me, would last them for years. That gave me some comfort.

Years later, wearing a solid-gold cartouche with your name spelled out in hieroglyphics was akin to flaunting your CIA badge outside Langley's security gates. That one trinket announced your CIA connection loudly and clearly. Just like that, we all stuffed them into the back of our jewelry cases until we retired, but by then, of course, they were no longer fashionable.

———

When my good friend Liz left the country to begin her new job at Chase Manhattan in New York City, friends asked me to arrange her farewell party at the International Tennis Club. Happy to do the honors, I reached out to her colleagues at the bank as well as other mutual friends. Nearly everyone was eager to attend; it would be a special night for all of us, toasting someone who had brought so much fun into our lives.

At that time, we had a great local tradition of home beer delivery. Like old-fashioned milk delivery here in the US, once you'd signed up, a truck would pull up to your address every week or two with big plastic crates full of beer bottles. After offloading your crate and wheeling it up to your apartment, they'd pick up the previous crate of empties and take it down to the truck. You never had to lift a finger, except to pop the ceramic cap off the next beer you drank.

On the day of Liz's farewell party, the beer truck pulled up to the tennis club with the many cases I'd ordered. Pleased that the party planning was going according to schedule, I directed them to the club's gigantic walk-in refrigeration. Hours later, shortly before the party was about to begin, we heard a series of muffled explosions sounding off at the back of the club. Alarmed, I set off to investigate the source. Several cases of beer, all in glass bottles, had detonated like miniature bombs, coating the room in a dirty slush that dripped from the ceiling, creating beer stalactites as it froze. Evidently, I had directed the beer delivery men to the walk-in freezer. Fortunately, the white wine, which had made it to refrigeration, was drinkable. Years would pass before Liz would let me live that gaffe down, and to this day, it still makes us both laugh.

Although I hated to bid Liz farewell, I knew our friendship was only beginning. Living in so many places around the globe made the world seem smaller. I was a good letter writer, often swapping news with Jennifer from wherever I was. Liz and I would stay in touch, too. Our bond didn't seem like one that would wither because we were a few time zones apart.

I had always thought that if you were going to spend a major part of your life working, you should tackle something that made a difference. We used to refer to this as "touching the wire," CIA shorthand for delicately, in some small way, helping to nudge history in the right direction. Of course, everything we did required a team effort, and success resulted from countless little moments training a foreign asset, adjusting a tool, disguising a colleague, performing a surveillance detection run, or putting up a signal, to name just a few. All of it, every piece of it, mattered. I loved being part of the team.

At the same time, I was discovering how difficult it was not to be able to discuss my work. It didn't feel natural to be so discreet when you felt overcome by relief, elation, and pride after a successful operation. The discretion was a central job requirement, but it was also new to me and, I would discover, disqualifying to many CIA applicants. Each success and failure had a distinct impact on your psyche. Having to keep your cards so close to the vest could take a toll, and loneliness inevitably set in at moments.

Yet John and I had grown comfortable with the unpredictable nature of our life. We understood that waking up together at home offered no guarantee that we would see each other that night; at any given moment, one or both of us might need to jump on a flight and disappear for a period of days. Upon returning, we couldn't divulge where we'd been or what we'd done, although I might drop in some mention of, say, the delicious croissant I'd had if I'd been in France. While some level of disconnection is inherent within any marriage, the covert, confidential nature of my career meant that even close friends, including those inside the CIA, couldn't act as confidants either. The ups and downs of a given day or week were strictly need-to-know. Still, though, I didn't envy my friends who were living a more conventional life, many juggling work and child-rearing. Repeatedly, they told me I didn't know what I was missing by not having children, but I had no desire to be a mother. My work fulfilled me in so many important ways that I couldn't imagine giving it up for any reason.

CHAPTER 10

CID and Southern Europe

The letter on my workbench looked innocuous, like any other piece of airmail. It bore German postage with cancellation stamps, and it hadn't yet been opened when it was couriered by hand to Washington, until finally it was placed here, in the Clandestine Imaging Division (CID) laboratories for examination. The highly classified, compartmented operation that generated this piece of correspondence was on shaky ground. Some within the agency wondered if one of the principals had been compromised. This letter I was holding in my hands was, in fact, a test, sent to find out if it would be opened by censors or a hostile intelligence service. It was, as we referred to it in CIA vernacular, "trapped" in several ways, designed to detect unauthorized opening.

After positioning the envelope on the laboratory microscope, I examined the sealed flap for tears, searching slowly and methodically for fiber disturbances in the paper substrate. Nothing. That was a start, but there are many other ways to enter an envelope. Next, I inspected the bottom and side folds of the envelope, which could be carefully, expertly slit, allowing the contents to be examined, and then resealed with a minimal amount of glue and fiber tears. That technique was called a French opening. Once I'd confirmed that all three closed sides of the envelope were intact, I looked at the envelope under UV and IR light. Finding no suspicious markings, I felt my shoulders lowering and my body relaxing slightly as I began to arrange the next set of tests.

A wax trap had been applied to the outside of the envelope to guard against the steam pot, a common and difficult-to-detect method of opening a piece of mail. When performed carefully, a steamed envelope displays none of the fiber disturbances I'd searched for initially. The steam melts the glue, allowing the flap to lift easily. However, in this case the steam would also liquefy our invisible wax grid. The only way to detect this kind of tampering was by applying GCR, a proprietary solution developed for this purpose. Holding a small paintbrush, I dipped its fine fibers into liquid GCR and then softly spread a thin ribbon of the chemical across the top half of the envelope. Holding my breath, I watched as the envelope turned a deep magenta where the GCR penetrated, revealing a blown wax trap and other signs of steaming. As quickly as the bloom appeared, it faded away and my envelope looked normal again. The flash could be triggered only once.

I called Ted, my boss, to report the results. He then promptly called our Chief of Operations, who soon arrived at my lab. He asked me to describe again what I had seen and stood silent for a moment, deep in thought. Several weeks later, I would learn the consequences of my finding. Three of our officers had been promptly moved out of a European capital city, and one foreigner, a permanent resident of that city, was relocated to another country, all based on that brief but undeniable flash of evidence of tampering in my lab. The GCR had confirmed that this communication channel was in fact compromised, the details of which were, of course, need-to-know. What mattered was that the operation was at risk, vulnerable to sabotage, and along with it, several officers' safety.

———

Since our last overseas tour had ended, John and I had returned to Washington. He had continued to work as a polygraph officer, and I'd secured a position in CID, the photo division where I had longed to work. My new job meant that I was no longer a darkroom jockey. At long last I was a professionally validated woman working in the original CIA offices across the street from the State Department.

John Ford, the Academy Award–winning director, had organized the agency's first Field Photographic Branch in 1940, sending for some of Hollywood's top cameramen to help him get it started. Together they set up quarters, including a mess, in the South Building at this Navy Hill complex. Their laboratories and studio were in the basement, where I was now working. I didn't know any of these details of the branch's history until years later; we were so focused on today and tomorrow that there was little time to consider yesterday.

Since Ford's days, CID had expanded beyond pure photography to include technologies around secret writing, microdots, low-light-level video, and a variety of other chemistry-based techniques used in clandestine communications. Soon after starting my new position, I found myself working half-time in a chemistry lab and half-time in a photo environment. The work was varied and gratifying, offering instant feedback: success or failure.

Immersed in the intricacies of our unique capabilities, I found the work energizing and engaging. Eager to learn and willing to come in early and stay late, I soon mastered the equipment and began to travel more frequently on short and long TDYs. Being married to John, who was equally invested in his career, paved the way for me to do what I most wanted to—dive full mind and body into my work. In her book *Fair Game*, Valerie Plame Wilson discusses her first CIA training course. After taking the Myers-Briggs psychological profile test, she learned that she, and all her fellow trainees, were ENTJ, or extroverted, intuitive, thinking, judgmental. "ENTJ personality types tend to be strong leaders and feel the need to take command of a situation," she explains. According to the Myers-Briggs description, an ENTJ is often "tireless in the devotion to their jobs and can easily block out other areas of life for the sake of work." Valerie adds, "ENTJs appear in approximately 5 percent of the population; apparently, that's what the CIA was looking for in its future operations officers. We were drawn to one another, not just because we would be doing the same training and ultimately the same job, but because we had similar personalities." This personality type dominated in the agency's technical offices where I worked, and although I tend toward introversion, burying my head in books whenever I can, I, too, felt right at home, never hesitating to give the agency everything I had. That often meant working holidays and hopping on a flight with only a couple of hours' notice. My bosses and colleagues noticed all of this, and they liked it. I did, too.

There were several other women working in CID, primarily on the research and development side of the office. Linda made the biggest impression. Her extensive background in chemistry made her imminently qualified to work shoulder to shoulder with the guys in R & D. Her unique and secret chemical recipes meant that the films our agents used, if confiscated overseas, would reveal nothing when developed using standard chemistry. While she knew the value of her contribution, she perhaps also sensed that simply being qualified wouldn't suffice for a woman working at the CIA. Determined to flex rather than curtsy, she leaned hard on her dazzling capability for using profanity. Never missing an opportunity to show off her extensive off-color vocabulary, her strategy worked shockingly well. In her presence the men were always slightly off-balance, and the more senior her audience, the more nervous they would become.

Most officers would have been penalized for that level of profanity, but her obvious intelligence and clearly demonstrated competence seemed to act as a kind of hall pass in her case. She had found a way to make the double standards that we, as women, inevitably faced within the agency work in her favor; who was I to judge?

—

My next foreign assignment was in Latin America, and the trip was intended to be a routine training trip. I would be working with several foreign groups using a package of high-priority materials that I had to bring with me and keep a close eye on. That meant ensuring the package was loaded into the belly of the plane and watching the doors close. It also meant deplaning in time to see the hold door open before the baggage handlers even approached the package. Last one to board, first one off, ensuring the security of the material. When we stopped in Miami, more passengers and their luggage were loaded. Before the hold doors opened, I deplaned to stand on the tarmac while the luggage compartment was opened and the new bags stowed away.

Taking an extra measure of precaution, I decided to check on my package. The baggage handlers motioned me inside the cargo hold, a privilege afforded to me by the government's arrangements with the airlines. I removed my heels and stepped onto the slow-moving conveyer belt, shoes in hand. Suddenly aware of the passengers on the plane peering out their windows, their mouths agape as they watched me inch into the belly of the plane, I looked ahead, pretending not to notice. Once inside the small compartment where my package had been safely stowed in one corner, I gasped. Packed inside the same small space they'd also stowed a coffin and a German shepherd traveling in a kennel. The coffin had a brass plaque on it that read: *Maria*. Meanwhile, the dog was barking in utter terror as my little but important package cowered in the corner. As I headed back down the belt, the door to the compartment began closing behind me and the dog started yelping and whining. He was going to have a long flight with Maria, in the dark, at 35,000 feet.

My work in CID, which was eventually renamed the Clandestine Communications Division, continued to be intellectually challenging and operationally interesting. No day was like the previous one, making boredom an impossibility. Every day felt like climbing a new mountain, and the sense of accomplishment I felt never failed to exhilarate.

One day during a European tour he was taking, the Deputy Director of OTS in Washington requested an interview with me. When he asked what assignment I was anticipating when I got home, my mind went momentarily blank. Lacking an answer, I thought of one of my favorite lines often attributed to Ralph Waldo Emerson, which had acted as a kind of personal mantra since leaving Kansas:

Do not go where the path may lead,
go instead where there is no path
and leave a trail.

Without much forethought, I replied that I wanted to be considered for our office's Career Development Program (CDP). I knew of only one other woman who had taken the course. I also knew it was a big ask and that my candidacy would be out of the norm. It was unlikely that I would be chosen, but why not try?

CDP was an elite, yearlong course that provided in-depth cross-training in all the technical disciplines OTS used to support CIA espionage operations around the world. Out of the approximately one thousand technical officers in our office, only eight middle-grade officers were selected each year.

Looking back, it's amusing how many of the bigger moments in my life felt like virtually nothing at all. My request to be considered for CDP seemed spontaneous at the time, but perhaps on some deeper level, it was the product of a slower, more significant evolution. I had long since outgrown Jennifer's shadow, but it had taken years longer for me to take myself seriously as an espionage professional with viable potential. At long last I was ready to let my deeper desires be known. I wasn't concerned with how few women had ever occupied the kinds of jobs I aspired to. I'd already done the "impossible" by getting myself out of the CIA's typing pool. I knew what I wanted next—a career inside OTS that offered ample field work around the globe—and I had every intention of going for it.

Months passed, and even as we finished our overseas tour, I'd heard no feedback or updates about CDP, including whether I was even being considered for it. When I found out that I would be one of the eight to attend that year, I was equal parts stunned and thrilled. I later learned that Tony Mendez was on the selection committee. He confirmed that the Deputy Director had nominated me after I'd expressed my interest in CDP. Tony, along with others, had supported my candidacy for the program. I would be one of two women to qualify that year. Two! I already knew the other woman, and looked forward to working with her.

As the shock wore off and the reality began to sink in, I realized that I, a photo operations officer, would be cross-training in electronics, audio devices, document counterfeiting, and disguise. We would learn short-wave radio techniques and how to decipher Morse code. We would learn how to drill in a wall a pinhole so small the naked eye couldn't see it, install bugs, and then plaster over the hole. Plaster! A dying art, even then. I would also learn how to color match paint by eye years before the items at Home Depot would enable you to do it perfectly. We would be instructed in the fabrication of concealment devices, including everything from a leather purse to a piece of wooden furniture. To be able to do all of this I would be taught woodworking and leather tooling. We would also take classes on defensive driving, physical protection, and shooting. To top it all off, we would take the Operations Course at the Farm, a requirement for all case officers and necessary for OTS officers who would be working overseas.

The course took place over one year, a total immersion away from the office, mastering new skills the agency needed us to know very, very well. The curriculum was varied and, to me, exhilarating, like nectar for the eternal student inside me. Being there was a privilege, and we were expected to perform at the top of our abilities. I dove in headfirst, determined as ever to make the most of this unique opportunity.

All our trainers were men, and as one of only two women in the course, I couldn't help but note the sexist attitudes of some of the men in our class. To them I seemed to be nothing more than the Director's former secretary, a token allowed into the course by special treatment rather than merit. It was the attitude most military men carried when women dared to venture beyond a secretarial desk. I noticed the bias, of course, but was too engrossed in the contents of the course to give it much thought.

At one point during the course, our office Director, Peter, announced that I'd been selected for promotion; opportunities to move up were evaluated annually by grade, so for instance, all eligible GS-09s were reviewed by the promotion panel at the same time. The evening after my promotion, the Director, who was visiting the Point, a location on the water south of DC, asked me to sit at his table. Henry, a classmate, made a point of voicing his disdain for the "special treatment" I was being given. I made note of his slight, figuring he was jealous I'd been promoted ahead of him, and promptly placed my attention elsewhere.

Given the increased international terrorist bombings of American facilities, our course included a weeklong training on all manner of explosives. By learning to create explosive devices from everyday materials, we would become better able to recognize and search for them in the aftermath of terrorist incidents. Locating the seat of the explosion, we would learn, is the first step in discerning what triggered a blast and sometimes how it was constructed and who made it.

That explosives training, the "bang and burn" component, took place at the Point. The air was hot and humid and the swamp that surrounded that base let off a terrible stench, like being smothered by a wet Army blanket. I had a pounding headache the whole time, feeling almost like I might suffocate.

Before explosives training could begin, however, a fifty-five-gallon drum of some unknown chemical had been sent by the chemistry branch and now needed to be disposed of. I accompanied Mark, a colleague and friend from Washington, to the warehouse to check on the project. When we arrived, Mark noticed that the metal drum containing the liquid was beginning to bulge, indicating that the chemicals were reacting to something. *It must be that putrid swamp smell,* I thought to myself. Whatever was causing the reaction, it wasn't a good sign. After putting on a face mask and safety gloves, Mark gently removed the cap, but accidentally dropped a small wrench into the barrel in the process. Almost immediately, the chemical soup inside began belching out a roiling cloud of black smoke. Without hesitation, Mark grabbed me by the arm, probably aware of what was in the barrel, and jerked me away from the fumes. He quickly notified the base commander, and afterward the base ordered an immediate quarantine of all personnel: *Everybody inside!*

Over many years, the small town near the base had grown accustomed, however begrudgingly, to the rumbles that came from this site, periodically shaking storefronts and causing hanging light fixtures in homes to swing. It was difficult to conduct the explosives training without making some noise. However, the cloud of fumes that was now coming from the drum was toxic and potentially poisonous. If it drifted off base, the health of local civilians and livestock would be in danger. We couldn't risk additional blowback from a dangerous chemical cloud drifting over an inhabited area. Within a matter of hours, OSHA employees in hazard suits flew in and discreetly took care of the chemical "eruption." The wind had remained quiet, and the cloud had dissipated. Another disaster had been averted.

When the training did begin, it was grueling. At the end of another long day we wandered toward the student bar, as we'd done the night before, staying out late drinking into the wee hours. By the time I walked in, the mood was already getting rowdy. A group of Navy SEALs visiting the Point for their own unique training was huddled at the bar, playing a drinking game. As I passed by, Henry glanced up briefly. Immediately afterward, his group laughed loudly as a few of the SEALs stole glances at me. Were they laughing at me?

We were on what Henry thought of as his turf; as he glanced at me from across the room, I decided to extend an olive branch. I picked up my beer and walked over to him. As I approached, he commented to his military colleagues loudly that having a female on the firing range was unlucky—dangerous, in fact. Then he turned toward me, daring me to react. Without a thought or moment of hesitation, I raised my glass and poured my beer over him.

The room fell suddenly silent as Henry stood, glowering at me, beer dripping down his chest. One by one, the SEALs began to laugh. Henry's face remained ice cold, his darkening eyes zeroing in on mine. Wondering if he was preparing to take a swing at me, I walked back across the room and left the bar.

"Boy, are you in trouble," somebody said as I headed for our barracks-style quarters. "He's going to come after you. He'll want to get even. Look out!" I suddenly realized what I'd done: embarrassed him in front of military colleagues, tarnished his reputation by making him look weak. There was no greater sin to a man like Henry. I'd put up with him for months without reacting, but there was a limit. That night I closed my eyes with a clear conscience and slept like a baby.

The next morning, we arose early, due back on the firing range to continue testing bombs we'd made from everyday materials you could pick up at a hardware store, materials readily available to a terrorist. After retreating to a dedicated bunker, we proceeded to detonate our handiwork, marveling at the destructive power of our "homemade" devices. We destroyed yellow school buses, blew up vehicles purchased at used-car auctions, and exploded deuce-and-a-half trucks as well as metal file cabinets, noting the exponential increase in damage when the drawers were closed. Afterward, we would examine the blast site, learning how to find the seat of the explosion, how to investigate a bomb incident, noting everything from the color of the smoke to the triggering mechanism. It was only the third day of our training, and already the base office was receiving the usual litany of irate complaints from neighboring residents. Their ceilings were cracking . . . again.

Henry was the instructor for this training, along with Jake, who was equally large and muscled but had a heart of gold. Both had come to the CIA from military backgrounds. While we were all students in the CDP course, they were taking the lead in this explosives section because of their extensive munitions experience. Since the beginning, they had repeatedly drilled us on firing-range protocol. While both men were prone to joking around, neither would ever kid around on the range. Cigarettes, matches, and lighters, too, were forbidden. We were working next to wooden sheds full of munitions, armaments, and explosives; causing a catastrophic accident wouldn't take much. There was a protocol to doing this work that demanded respect, they insisted. At all times, under all conditions, we were expected to obey the rules. Ignoring the rules was akin to smoking in a fireworks factory, they insisted repeatedly.

One particular moment during that training stands out in my mind. It's a memory of mine that has not changed over the many years that have since passed. We were working outside, as usual, when I heard a male voice yell, "Hey, Jonna!" I didn't have to look over my shoulder; the voice belonged to Henry. I walked away from the group and turned toward him. He was standing about one hundred feet away, holding a grenade in his hand. When he pulled the fuse on the grenade and rolled it across the bare earth toward me, time slowed to a strange and sudden crawl. Figuring he was trying to scare me, I assumed the grenade wasn't live and tried to stay calm, hoping to deprive him of the reaction he was hoping for. Instead of running, I stood my ground, staring at the grenade as it rolled toward me in an almost dreamlike state. Somebody yelled, "Run!" but I barely heard, as if the voice had come from a great distance.

The grenade rolled to about ten feet from me before stopping. Then it went off, the bang roared, and my body began to vibrate like a jackhammer. Jake immediately ran toward me, taking me by the arm and leading me to a bench outside of one of the sheds. He sat down beside me, with his arm around me, scowling at Henry, who had just broken nearly every rule in the book, *their* book.

Some of the class gathered around me. Somebody brought me a cup of coffee, but I was shaking so hard, I couldn't hold it, much less drink it. I only knew that I couldn't cry. I couldn't act "like a girl"; that was what Henry was looking for. Instead, I sat in one spot, my body quaking endlessly. Class was promptly adjourned for the day. As it turned out, Henry had defused the grenade, so while the explosion had made a tremendous noise, it was incapable of causing physical harm.

Nobody in the hierarchy at the training base was aware of the incident, and I decided that I wouldn't be the one to rat Henry out. Privately, though, I was so shocked by what he had done that my mind struggled to digest it. His behavior belied his training, his military rigor, and his standing as an expert instructor. I, too, had reacted unprofessionally in the bar, but nothing justified what he'd done in response. He had become so unglued by an upended beer glass that he had let his ego overtake his senses. It was, in fact, a firing offense, and we both knew it.

Two days later Henry asked me to take a drive with him. He apologized for his actions, acknowledged that he had overreacted, and asked me to forgive him. I told him I would, but I lied. I was still furious. He never would have pulled that stunt on one of his male colleagues, no matter how badly they offended him. I was a female, which to him meant that I was inherently inferior. Yet I had been promoted, and then I had had the gall to embarrass him. One slight to his ego was all it had taken to pull his fuse and render him too emotional to make responsible decisions. With one misogynistic move, he could have blown up his entire career.

When the CDP course concluded months later, I was told that I was at the top of the class and feeling reenergized and better prepared than ever to resume my work at CID. Our new abilities would enable us to handle a wide array of assignments, including worldwide TDY travel as "singletons," in which we would participate in operations on our own around the globe. The idea was exhilarating, and I felt restless, eager to see what lay ahead. Once a somewhat quiet and shy young woman, I was finding my voice, often leading workplace discussions. The future looked promising, and I felt ready.

———

Keenly aware of the investments the agency was making in my career, I knew my office was watching me closely when they sent me on my first TDY to southern Europe after CDP. As my skills and opportunities grew, so did my dedication to the work at hand, as well as to the agency behind it all. I also knew that I wouldn't keep getting those chances if I didn't put my head down and do the best possible job I could. The work was all-consuming, all the time—focusing on the task at hand was essential.

On this six-week trip I would be filling in for a Technical Operations (TOPS) officer, who could handle almost any technical requirement that the station needed, but who had been called away. I was responsible for handling any requirements that arose and having the good sense to know when to send for help, if needed. It would be a real test of my newly sharpened problem-solving capabilities.

The station booked me into a cheap hotel, anticipating that I would do as my male colleagues did and stay in an out-of-the-way hotel so I could pocket the excess per diem. But that was not how I traveled. I booked myself into a once grand, historic hotel located in the heart of the old city, a property that was walking distance from most tourist sites and had been known as a preferred destination for toreadors. From France to Portugal, the southern tier of Europe was still sprinkled with small bullfighting rings. Jet-lagged and exhausted by the late social hours of southern Europe, which began its evening at 9 p.m. and didn't shutter until well after midnight, I fell asleep with my shoes on.

My room turned out to be the suite where the local toreadors used to stay. When the first loud bang sounded, I was sure it was a gunshot. Startled awake, I leapt out of bed, suddenly on high alert. Slowly, I moved toward the windows, thinking the sound had come from the roof. When a hesitant reconnoiter revealed nothing, I walked down the suite's long hall, which was lined with large, black-and-white photos of toreadors at work—but still, nothing. For the next two nights these same sudden banging noises woke me repeatedly. Arriving at the reception desk early on the third morning, I requested a new room. Smiling, the concierge asked what the problem was. I told her I was uncomfortable in my current room and needed a new one. She nodded, calling a porter to carry my bag to a much more drab and ordinary room. He spoke minimal English, but as we navigated the hallways to my new room, he muttered, "The phantom," just loudly enough for me to hear. Seems that this had happened before.

However bleary-eyed I felt from those first nights of poor sleep, my work absolutely could not suffer. My first challenge appeared in the form of a malfunctioning telephone cut-out device on an apartment rooftop where we maintained a safe house. The safe house was occupied by a single American woman, a professional psychic who lived in the apartment under a unique arrangement. She paid us no rent but allowed us to use it for meetings. When a foreign asset called the station's unlisted number, the call was supposed to go through this communication device, which had been buried in a large cement planter. Each caller was, in fact, dialing in to a flowerpot. The cut-out device would then reroute the asset's call, disguising its actual origin in the process. That small and well-hidden technical device was providing necessary security and protection to CIA's operational assets when they called their handlers.

The device had stopped working once before, a malfunction then attributed to the city's enormous traffic; the heavy vibrations from the street could throw the device out of proper line-of-sight alignment with the receiver on the station's roof. Assuming this would be a situation where I would have to call the audio techs in to fix it, I nevertheless went up to the roof to inspect the planter. I saw nothing obvious that might explain the malfunction. Knowing the planter was too heavy to move, on a whim I kicked it just hard enough to cause a brief but noticeable flash of ankle pain. When I returned to the station that afternoon, to my great surprise, the cut-out device was working perfectly. The Chief of Station was so pleased with my work that he sent a cable to my home office praising my efforts. The men in my office were amazed that I had "repaired" this sophisticated piece of equipment. I took their praise in stride, never revealing how I'd managed this remarkable feat.

Skill and luck, I eventually realized, were critical to any successful career, and this moment was no exception, earning me my stripes in a decidedly male-centric organization. My regional base Chief was so pleased by my success, in fact, that he flew over to bask in the glow and accompany me back home to our offices.

Before leaving that city, however, I allowed myself a glimpse into the local culture. Curious about southern Europe's passion for bull-fighting, I accepted an invitation from Davina, whom I had known in Washington and who now lived here, to attend a fight. Feeling ready to witness the magic of the sport, we entered the packed local arena and settled into our seats.

Having read Hemingway's *Death in the Afternoon*, I figured I had some grasp of the romanticism attached to the bullfighting display. As I watched the toreador in his suit of lights seducing the bull and the crowd, I soon realized how unprepared I was. Watching the proud bull being poked and prodded then superficially stabbed by the pic-adors before the final coup de grâce was delivered by the matador, I felt almost physically sick. The performance is not merely ritual or dis-play; the bull is always killed. As the crowd roared its approval, my eyes teared with horror and sadness. *This is not a sport*, I remember think-ing, *this is a sadistic ritual*. I shot two rolls of film that day but threw the bright yellow Kodak cannisters in the trash on the way out of the ring. I had no desire to develop those images or relive those moments.

Women were historically forbidden from entering a bullfighter's hotel room the night before a fight. Females were viewed as bad luck because they might "sap" the toreador's energy, I was told, and increase his chances of being gored by the bull. After hearing this, I told the Chief of Station the story of "the phantom" and the mysterious banging noises in my original hotel suite. He promptly asked for the room number. His mother-in-law was planning to visit in the spring, he explained with a sly grin and a gleam in his eye. He wanted to see if he couldn't get her assigned to that same room.

CHAPTER 11

On TDY in the Subcontinent

Turning to steady one of the several dozen oversized pages I'd been sent here to photograph, I backed up slightly. When the skin on my arm touched one of the enormous lights I'd set up in a small upstairs room in our safe house, I heard a brief but unmistakable hissing sound. Leaping forward, I gasped, barely able to breathe as a bolt of searing pain overwhelmed me. Glancing at the bulb, I could see the thin layer of my skin that was now emitting the stench of burning flesh. Staring in disbelief at the red scorch mark on my arm, I held my breath as the pain persisted. Under no circumstances could I make another sound; the asset did not know, and could not know, that I was in the safe house too.

Wincing, I took off my headband and wrapped it gently around the wound. Surrounded by the hot lights I needed to photograph several dozen pages of foreign intelligence, I could feel sweat pouring down my face and trickling down my back. Knowing that I'd be working through the night inside an unventilated closet, I'd arrived wearing my running clothes—a headband, T-shirt, and running shorts. The work I needed to complete before the morning was meticulous and time-consuming; I'd made sure to dress accordingly.

Time was everything—the asset, who was meeting with his CIA case officer downstairs, could be out of pocket for only a few hours. He had to have the document returned to him by early morning. Our safe house was in a residential compound, and the asset had brought a new Soviet military equipment manual. It was the espionage equivalent of a gold mine, and my job was to photograph it while the two men drank ice-cold beers and reviewed details of their operation one floor below me. The manual I was handling in this walk-in closet contained large foldout diagrams and schematics that were challenging to capture on film with the necessary precision.

The manual would be returned to the foreign asset only after I developed the film, working overnight in my darkroom to ensure that every frame was legible. It was going to be a long night.

After photographing every page of the manual, I put it back inside its case and began to remove the film from the elaborate Recordak document copy camera. Next, I would develop the photos, producing more than eighty feet of printed photographs, a span so long that I had to hang it from a series of wire lines that had been set up specifically for this purpose. The film would then need to be inspected, frame by frame, to ensure that every detail of every page had been fully and accurately captured. Only then, as the sun rose in the east over the subcontinent, would the original document be handed back to the case officer. All in a night's work.

Once the assignment had been completed, I applied aloe to the burn and prepared for bed. I had signed up for an unpredictable career that promised a sense of purpose; the CIA was delivering on that promise. To this day, I bear the scar from that night. I wear it proudly.

It was an exciting time to be working against the Soviet target. During the Cold War, India and the Soviet Union had a strong strategic, military, economic, and diplomatic relationship. Traditionally, the Indo-Russian strategic partnership was built on five major components: politics, defense, civil nuclear energy, anti-terrorism cooperation, and space.

Put simply, the Indian government was in bed with the Soviets.

That Moscow-Delhi relationship forged a sturdy link between the world's leading communist/authoritarian superpowers during the Cold War, even as India's idealistic leader, Jawaharlal Nehru, worked to secure the country's fledgling but enthusiastic democracy. That alliance meant that India was a happy hunting ground for Soviet intelligence. The manual that I had just finished photographing showed design plans for a new piece of military equipment. Soon afterward, a second informant would offer us the exact same documents. It was a huge get.

Not long after my first TDY after the CDP program and my too-close encounter with the toreadors, I was sent on this extended TDY to the subcontinent. I was filling in for Helga, a CIA officer who was returning to the States, going on "home leave" for the summer. Helga was an old friend from OTS in Washington, and she and her husband, Dave, acted as my informal hosts, showing me the ropes during the first weeks of my trip. A career chemist, Helga was working as a CIA contract wife while she "accompanied" her husband on this assignment. She handled multiple requirements at this CIA outpost, from basic disguise and document copy photography to secret writing and more. She was granted access to a huge lab with an attached, well-equipped darkroom, all of which would be at my disposal during her absence.

The site was situated in the desert on the edge of a stretch of large, rolling sand dunes that was like a dry sea, an ocean-like expanse of blazing sand. Yearning to explore this incredible, unknown landscape, I soon began planning trips in the region. Several colleagues offered to show me the local sights in and around the city, but to my surprise, nobody was willing to join me on the trip into the desert that I had been imagining. It involved an overnight train ride west that I soon booked for myself. Feeling brave and apprehensive at the same time, I departed with basic supplies and my cameras. The second leg of the trip included a train-issued sleeping bag, which I declined, worried about fleas.

I had arranged to be met by a driver who would be joined by a translator. From there we drove their Jeep off-road, quite literally, driving through a seemingly boundless stretch of desert that looked and felt like the edge of the Earth. Each of us had to carry at least one gallon of water per day. I think we drifted back and forth across an international border several times, but I could never locate the villages we visited on a map. Throughout the area, village huts were constructed from dried camel dung, which was in abundant supply and required no water.

Most of the villagers had clearly never encountered a Westerner, and certainly not a Western woman. They were as interested in me as I was in them. In one village, I was invited inside the school. The children were sure that rainfall, which they'd never witnessed because of the region's yearslong drought, was a fairy tale. The town's "lake," which had long since dried up, was also the stuff of legend. Imagining a vast expanse filled with water was outside of their life's experience, and water too rare and precious to visualize in such volume. To wash dirty dishes, villagers used dry sand, which seemed to work rather well.

On visits farther west I was delighted to discover seashells among the sand dunes. Some of the natives showed me the whale and shark teeth they had found. In prehistoric times, forty-seven million years earlier, this area had in fact been a sea. We were traversing the floor of a long-ago ocean. Today, the state it's located in is known for its magnificent architecture, vibrant culture, and beautiful arts and crafts. The lake that locals believe was formed from the tears of Lord Shiva now hosts the area's annual camel festival.

It didn't take long for the region to cast its spell on me. Like a flame to a moth, the desert and the culture of the area drew me in. I was captivated.

My photographs from these trips to the desert often featured the richly saturated textiles worn by its inhabitants. Even at a distance you could tell what part of the country a person was from. The men had unique ways of wrapping their turbans, typically using fabrics specific to their village. The women followed similar practices, attending local festivities dressed in saris cut from the same bolt of cloth and wearing ornate jewelry from the same goldsmith. They would usually travel in groups, resembling one large family. The colors they chose were electric: fuchsia, chartreuse, and what I called "mustard on a Coney Island hot dog" yellow. All were bold colors that could be seen at a distance, across acres of blazing sand. The women, who seemed to do most of the manual labor, would walk single file along the top of the dunes, balancing on their heads copper pots full of water from the few deep tube wells. Perched behind my lens, this photographer was in heaven.

Hundreds of miles away was a strikingly different view: the campus of the American embassy in New Delhi. The outer wall of the chancery, its main building, was covered in filigree, beckoning you inside toward the large indoor tropical pool. Nearby, birds flew over the lagoon, where water lilies bloomed with abandon. A bit farther into the grounds, you stepped onto the meticulously groomed, lush, green landscape, and suddenly, the stark beauty of the sand-soaked oasis seemed a whole world away.

The embassy offices were arranged around the perimeter of the building on two levels, the upper floor a mezzanine overlooking the water. From the outside it bore a distinct resemblance to the Kennedy Center in Washington, DC, which was logical since both were designed by architect Edward Stone.

Nestled inside the walled residential compound you could easily pretend you were in America, perhaps at a resort or golf club, and many did just that. The familiar comforts of home were there: an American commissary that stocked our favorite brands, a club where you could order hamburgers and hot dogs, and a pool that was anecdotally the largest swimming pool in an official American compound anywhere in the world. Evidently it had been proposed in one-foot metrics and mistakenly built to one-meter specs. It was three times too big, but to us the size was just right. There was even a regulation-size baseball field.

Beyond the fence, however, lay a cityscape that triggered all my senses. As the musky, sweet scent of sandalwood floated from storefronts, I found myself transfixed by the striking beauty of the country's people. Endless crowds flooded by as camels pulled carts and the odd elephant or two meandered down the street. Large oxen, too, moved through the city at night, pulling immense loads of steel beams and other construction material.

This was no place for black-and-white film; only Kodachrome would do.

During my sixty-day stay, I joined an international running club called the Hash House Harriers. Originally founded by the Brits and Aussies, the organization has local chapters around the globe. Each run begins with a bugle being played and ends with drinking beer, a kind of Monty Python running club open to anyone and everyone who wants to lace up and have fun. While case officers sometimes joined local clubs to meet potential foreign assets, that wasn't among my job responsibilities. I joined for strictly social reasons, and because I continued to love my routine of running five miles per day no matter where in the world I was calling home. In my running shoes I had sailed through Victoria Park in Hong Kong, dashed through Retiro Park in Madrid, leapt over open sewers in Kathmandu, and dodged nude sunbathers in Europe. I wasn't about to miss what this region had to offer.

The locals who didn't run—we foreign nationals were often a minority—did not always appreciate our club's rowdy antics. One day while running in a Hash-emblazoned T-shirt and shorts, I noticed an elderly bearded man in a turban wobbling down the road on a bicycle that appeared on the verge of collapse. Sweating and huffing in ninety-five-degree heat, he took one look at me, swerved over, reached out, and slapped me hard. Stunned, I stopped abruptly. Without saying a word, he rode on at about two miles an hour, as though nothing had happened. Figuring this was his country, I decided to ignore it and resumed my run. Women weren't supposed to dress so immodestly in this part of the world. I had no desire to offend anyone with my outfit, but I was equally unwilling to compromise my lifestyle to meet his expectations of me as a woman. It was often over one hundred degrees outside. Modesty be damned.

Some days we ran through squalid streets and into beautiful land-scapes, dodging sacred cows with rhesus macaque monkeys howling behind us as small packs of wild dogs ran alongside. Other days we ran through open-air bazaars and across empty fields that were, I eventually learned, "shiggy" fields, or outdoor toilets. As we noisily thundered through the local outdoor bathroom, people squatting down in the brush would suddenly bolt up to stare at us like we were crazy, which of course we were. Several times we were overtaken by blinding sand-storms that barreled in from the desert as we ran through parts of the city we had no map for. With so much sand swirling that you couldn't see your hand in front of your face, you would have to stop and stand perfectly still, pulling your shirt up to cover your face to protect your eyes. For women that meant standing on the street in your bra, but the sand was so thick that nobody could see.

At the end of each run we would barrel through the gates of yet another embassy (they were expecting us), and most of us would run straight into the swimming pool, fully clothed, shoes and all; it was that hot. Afterward the pool would have to be drained. As the old saying goes, only "mad dogs and Englishmen go out in the midday sun." It was great fun, an easy way to meet people, and for CIA, a good way to meet contacts in foreign embassies.

Once my two months were up, I knew I needed to find a way to come back. Upon returning home to DC, I set to work on my new career goal: finding an assignment that would bring me back, prefera-bly for much longer.

CHAPTER 12

Disguise Training

Once back in DC, I made an exploratory visit to Tony Mendez, our office's former Career Management officer. He was now back as Deputy of the Graphics and Identity Transformation Group in the Central Building. He was respected and well-liked, someone with connections within the agency. He had been supportive of my performance at CDP, a program he helped to oversee, and he seemed like the right person to help me take charge of my next move. It wasn't just a matter of securing me a position in the subcontinent; John was open to working overseas again, provided we could both be assigned to the same location. His career, too, was advancing nicely and he was eager to continue that progress.

When Tony told me that there would be no open photo operations position in the subcontinent within my desired timeframe, my heart sank. There would be a Disguise position available in about eighteen months, he added, although that would require a sudden, hard career pivot. After spending years establishing myself as a photo operations officer, I would have to learn an entirely new trade. Intrigued, I fixed my eye on a new goal—becoming a dual expert, in clandestine photography and disguise.

With this project Tony and I were putting the CIA's commitment to working married couples to the test by seeing if the agency would assign both me and John to the subcontinent at the same time. It was a big ask. How committed was the agency, really, to helping me, once a "contract wife," build a substantial career in the agency? Only time would tell.

Tony quickly created a single-student training program specifically for me, and just like that, the Disguise labs became my new hub. I began by creating ear impressions, a process that's like making dental impressions. Using silicone and translucent paints, we could construct custom-fitted earflaps. The first earflap acted as a pliable, flesh-toned covering for a Phonak receiver, a tiny radio earpiece that fit inside an officer's ear canal. The second earflap served as a filter for ambient street noise in the other ear.

Creating these earflaps was meticulous work. Once completed, there was no telltale wire emanating from the ear canal. Instead, we devised an antenna that could be worn as a free-hanging, invisible necklace that lay underneath your shirt and attached to a small receiver that was worn on the body. When this work was done well, the Phonak was invisible, even on close inspection. This was important technology for our Moscow-bound officers, who would be listening to KGB surveillance frequencies while on the streets.

The next disguise project involved the making of what can be described only as stunt-double masks like those used in Hollywood. The stuntman, or stuntwoman—present-day Hollywood's Zoë Bell, for instance—takes all the risks on set while wearing a rubber likeness of a studio actor. CIA field officers often needed to conceal their identities, too, with much higher stakes.

The technology for making these masks came to us straight out of Hollywood, compliments of Tony and his deep connections in the Los Angeles film industry. After seeing *Planet of the Apes* years earlier, Tony had convinced Oscar Award–winning prosthetic and makeup artist John Chambers to become a confidential CIA contractor. John had developed several sizes of masks, all based on the facial impressions of well-known movie stars.

Fabricated from latex rubber that was poured onto aluminum molds and heated to high temperatures, the masks were then finished by hand. Little by little, I mastered the technique for working with liquid latex, and after that, the meticulous artistry required to turn the blank masks into convincingly lifelike people. Using Dremel airbrushes, we painted them with multiple translucent layers of pigment. Finally, we would attach hair goods—wigs, and sometimes mustaches and beards too. The completed devices could conceal the presence of mixed ethnicities in apartheid South Africa, for instance, or obscure the presence of a Western visage in North Korea.

Earflaps and masks were just the tip of the iceberg. To perform the job I was hoping to step into, I needed to gain mastery over a vast range of additional materials and techniques. Wigs, prescription glasses, and colored contacts, all kinds of facial hair, skin colorants, dental appliances, and various clothing modifications were all skills that I needed to acquire, and quickly.

The work required a lot of manual dexterity, and initially my hand skills were only adequate. That meant I would have to work even harder, especially since I was surrounded by professionals at the top of their game.

Kristina, a statuesque Black woman, was one of those professionals I looked to, and a force of nature. When a problem arose, we were all grateful to have her on our side. Not everyone agreed with her, but she always commanded attention, often swaying managers to her advantage.

Andi was a tall, sleek blonde whose excellent hand skills were matched by her interpersonal and admin abilities. At her workstation you would often find her humming Sade while doing a discreet samba in her stilettos. To my enthusiastic applause from the sidelines, she eventually went on to more senior administrative positions within the agency.

Williamson was the most artistic of the group, but I worried about him because of his barely concealed homosexuality, which could easily have cost him his job. John, who as a polygraph officer tested job applicants regularly, had to comply with CIA regulations that banned gay applicants from becoming employees. The rationale was that homosexuality could be used for blackmail, putting the agency at risk. John and I used to have heated discussions about that regulation. While John was generally against rocking the boat, I countered that if a person was openly gay, his or her sexual preference could not be used as leverage against them or the agency. Years later the CIA would come to its senses and allow declared homosexuals to be employees.

Among these new coworkers, I was the newbie, working hard to race through training they had completed methodically over a period of years. Intent on taking my comparatively unproven skills abroad, I buckled down, not yet aware of just how long it would take me to earn the respect of my new colleagues.

One day I arrived at work to discover that I was being temporarily diverted back to photography. A young man, a mujahid from Afghanistan, needed training in tracking and photographing aircraft with an impossibly long lens. He was in the DC area for a limited time, and it was imperative that he learn the necessary skills before departing. The effort was part of the active support the US government was providing to the mujahideen who were trying to oust Soviet troops from their country.

My trainee would need to be able to use the hyperextended lens while the target aircraft was flying. That meant he had to learn to pan with the camera, using one arm as a steadying unipod while smoothly following the flight path with the lens. It's not as easy as it sounds. This young man had an uncle, a more senior mujahid, who was also fighting the Soviets. The uncle was a doctor who was being paid by our government with medication that he couldn't acquire in Kabul or Peshawar. He and his nephew were risking their lives daily for a few more crates of penicillin.

This small, slender, handsome young man was generally on horseback in his country, often traveling long distances through desert and mountainous terrain. That provided an unusual opportunity to observe the movements of Soviet troops, encampments, and equipment. There was continuous Soviet aircraft movement throughout the area he worked in, he noted, yet another opportunity for them to see him.

Lying side by side on the ground at Gravelly Point Park, perfectly situated next to National Airport with unobstructed views of plane landings, he and I discussed the ins and outs of his logistics and the Pentax 35mm SLR camera he was holding. It had a long telephoto lens that stuck out atop the grassy knoll as we awaited the next plane, which would make its approach to the airport from straight down the Potomac River, following it like a highway into the heart of Washington, DC. Arlington National Cemetery was on our left, and down the long riverside path on the right was George Washington's Mount Vernon home. We were sandwiched between two parcels of hallowed ground, but here we were in a US government–sponsored outdoor classroom where I was the professor. Listening to him talk, I fully expected to learn someday that he had been one of the fighters to shoulder one of the Stinger missiles that the US had recently sent to his country. That weapon would eventually drive the Soviets out of Afghanistan.

Initially the session seemed like a straightforward photo training, but I soon discovered a few unique problems. My student's English was halting, and since I spoke no Dari or Pashto, the language barrier slowed our progress. This was also his first time being outside of Afghanistan, which meant he was unaccustomed to being escorted and taught by a woman. Both proved to be time-consuming hurdles. How could my husband "allow" me to do such work? he inquired. Confused about who I was and what I was "permitted" to do, he expressed his utter amazement that a woman would conduct the training. Or even could. Several times, always hesitantly, he asked what my husband thought of this arrangement. While this line of questioning was delaying the urgent task at hand, I quietly enjoyed explaining that in America women performed the same work as men. Work was conducted in a professional manner, eliminating any need for a third-party chaperone, burka, or veil. Slowly but surely, as I continually returned to the training at hand, he acclimated to the idea, which allowed us to shoot a dozen rolls of film.

As we eased into the photo training, we got some looks from nearby cemetery visitors, who no doubt thought we made an unusual pair. There I was in my expensive designer pantsuit, standing or lying adjacent to him in his sand-colored shalwar kameez and small woven Chitrali cap. We were strikingly mismatched, but we each carried a knapsack full of photo equipment—film, tripods, lenses, and backup cameras.

As he grew more comfortable, he mentioned that he would often stumble across pieces of equipment that the Soviets had stored or discarded. I asked him to photograph anything that might be of interest to the US military. I showed him how to add common items—a coin or bill, a soft drink bottle or can, or a package of cigarettes—to provide a sense of scale for the object he was photographing.

Hearing him talk, I began to worry about how visually exposed he would be on his horse, riding alone through what might quickly become hostile territory. At the time there were approximately 130,000 Soviets in Afghanistan, and the slightest anomaly could cause them to zero in on him from above. The metallic shine of the equipment he carried, including some of the items we were issuing to him, might attract unwanted attention. The camera and its accessories would be painted a matte black prior to his departure for Afghanistan, I assured him, and anything else he acquired could be modified with black duct tape.

After only a week working together, I felt fully invested in his safety and success. He, too, had begun to relax, which made his English easier to understand. As we reviewed the different places where he would be carrying and using this equipment, he described the bazaar in Kabul, where you could find anything, he boasted proudly. Legal or illegal, Russian, Afghan, or from anywhere else in the world, all of it was available there. He made it sound like the most fabulous place to shop in the entire Middle East, except that the price of goods could be unacceptably high—not excluding your life.

It was clear to me that he was immensely proud of his country and committed to pushing out the Soviets by any means necessary. Over the years I worried about him, wondering what happened to him. Did he survive, and if so, did he go along with the mujahideen when they turned against the United States? Did he eventually join the Taliban and plot against the US government? As I watch the Taliban clamping down on women, revoking even more of their rights, I wonder if he remembers our conversations.

There was a good reason that we, as CIA officers, didn't get too close to foreign assets. It was a distraction that we could not afford. Still, I do think about him on occasion, always hoping he made it.

———

After returning to the Disguise labs, I got to work helping to prepare a new group of pipeliners, Soviet and East European Division case officers being trained for their Moscow assignments. It was a special category of disguise work that pushed the boundaries of our normal process; we not only issued them materials, we insisted that they practice on the streets of DC. We were working directly with officers from the operations directorate, and my overseas experience allowed us to speak the same language on the streets. One of our goals was to be able to create new disguises remotely from Langley while they were in Moscow. Then we would either send out the disguise materials or travel to the Moscow station for final fittings with the officers in question. Using the information we'd collected—photos of each officer from multiple angles, face impressions, hair samples, clothing measurements, skin-tone palette, even eyeglass prescriptions when needed—we could practically build a twin of any of these officers without seeing them in the flesh. The process was exhaustive and meticulous, but we now knew we could do it.

For me, learning how to create semi-animated masks, which we called SAMs, proved the most challenging. Without any formal artist training and little experience in the area, I was stretching well beyond my natural abilities. The most difficult part of the process, however, was fitting the mask around the eyes. The result had to be seamless so the viewer couldn't see where the mask material ended and the delicate skin around the eyes began. When done well, the result bordered on magical, but achieving that required multiple attempts.

My advanced SAM skills were put to the test during a TDY in Africa with Bill, our senior Disguise officer. We'd been sent there to complete two mask fittings but were soon tasked with an additional requirement as well. The local station believed that they might have an Asian man preparing to defect; his race was important information. Studying the physical features of the local population was critical in disguise work. We spent a great deal of time researching and matching the precise hues of skin and hair color in each region, as well as the size and shape of other facial features. Disguising someone as a local in, say, Taiwan would be effective only if the skin color of the mask blended in seamlessly with the local population's. When we used SAMs, which covered only part of the face, we had to be sure the mask perfectly matched the wearer's skin color and texture and facial contouring. Lives were at stake; every aspect of a person's appearance informed the disguise we created for them, and no detail was too small to consider.

Worried about how to get this potential defector out of the country, they asked for our input. Bill and I devised a scenario and proposed it to the Chief of Station. The man in question was about the same height as one of the uniformed guards, so we could disguise him in a guard uniform, adding an artificial facial wound that the station could claim had occurred when a grenade "accidentally exploded." The station would then call in an American medevac helicopter and transport the "guard" to the helicopter on a spinal board with a cervical collar. He could then be transported to wherever the station decided, details we had no need to know.

The two SAMs we created during that trip, along with a lifelike facial wound, prompted Bill to sign off on my advanced SAM skills certification. Months of training and practice had paid off. I was finally ready to be a Disguise officer.

CHAPTER 13

Hostile Interrogation and More at the Farm

Like many CIA operations officers, OTS traveling technical officers often spent over half of their time away from their home offices. Because that travel increased the risk of encountering hostile situations, whether aboard an aircraft or elsewhere, the Hostile Interrogation Course had been created to prepare us for those dangerous possibilities, including being taken hostage. The real value of the course, however, was observing yourself in extremely dire circumstances.

It was one of the most useful and disturbing courses I ever took.

After arriving at the Farm, south of Washington, DC, we were asked if there were any special cases among us—any physical or psychological constraints they should know about. I was the only woman in our group, and I volunteered almost immediately that I was claustrophobic. Even the idea of being put into the trunk of a car or any small enclosure sent my heartbeat racing, I explained. Nodding, the instructors noted my comment.

Lesson number one: *Never reveal your weaknesses to your captors.*

On that first morning, we listened as several ex-military POWs described how they survived years of interrogation and incarceration. Think of John McCain, a Navy pilot who in 1967 was taken captive after his plane crashed in North Vietnam. Five and a half years, several injuries, and countless interrogation and torture sessions later, he was released. He bore the scars, but he went on to live a long and productive life.

The instructors taught us the concept of "peeling an onion," how we could slowly and deliberately reveal information to the enemy if captured. It always had to be done in an intentional way to keep the heart of the onion, the truth, concealed. Give them a little something, then a little bit more, but never the core of the matter. Never the goods.

They described the monotony of a long incarceration and how to withstand the never-ending procession of hours that had to be filled every day. Some had done mental projects—built houses, solved intricate math problems, redesigned their favorite old cars, even played imaginary chess games with themselves (which they always won).

The last instructor discussed "special confinement"—times when he could not bear to be where he was because there were rats or snakes or when he was suffering from intensely painful wounds. He talked about mentally vacating his surroundings, transporting his mind to a place he would rather be, and then spending his day there. It took true focus to do, he explained, but if you wanted to leave badly enough, you could.

Listening to him speak, I wondered if I could focus like that if I ever needed to. I flashed back to years earlier, in college, when I worked for an anesthesiologist who used hypnosis for patients who couldn't tolerate anesthesia. He wrote a book about medical hypnosis that I typed and retyped. Fascinated, I asked him if he would hypnotize me. He declined, explaining that I was too interested in the technique itself. That distraction would prevent me from having the necessary focus.

At lunchtime we boarded a bus to the cafeteria. About five minutes in we heard the deafening roar of a nearby explosion. As clouds of smoke began to surround us, what looked like a platoon of black-masked military men bounded onto the bus, taking us captive. They swiftly put hoods over our heads before leading us off the vehicle. Just before my hood was on, however, I spotted an old friend galloping down the aisle: Shaughnessy, a huge chocolate Lab I knew as well as he knew me. John and I were in his house often; Tim and Josie, our good friends of many years, were his owners. Even with the hood secured over my head, Shaughnessy happily greeted me, covering me with so many slobbering kisses, they had to restrain him.

My momentary delight was soon disrupted. A minute after the hood was placed over my head, claustrophobia set in. "I'm having a little trouble breathing in here," I said. My captor said nothing, yanking me off the bus as he twisted my arm even tighter. After being hustled to a new location, we were told to change into the military uniforms they'd given us. Mine was so large, I had to run the tail of the shirt through the pants' belt loops to keep them on. When they took our clothes and personal effects, they told me to remove the gold studs in my ears.

"I just had them pierced two days ago," I said, putting my fingers in the classic T formation for time-out. "They're like raw hamburger right now."

My captors insisted that I remove them, so I did. I was beginning to realize that this course was like no other I had ever taken. Nonetheless, I made enough noise that an instructor came over to survey the situation. He agreed that I could keep the gold studs, but when my captors told me to put them back in, I shook my head from side to side. I would vomit or pass out if I had to do it myself, I explained, before insisting that they had to do it. They did, but roughly, shoving them in my raw earlobes backward, with the gold balls in the back and the sharp tips in the front. I didn't care. The recent piercing had required two martinis and moral support from two good friends. I had skin in this game, and I had no intention of letting the holes close and heal without a piercing in sight.

In theory, knowing this was a training regimen should have made the experience a lot less frightening. I was fortunate not to know what a comparable real-life scenario felt like, but still, this simulated version felt scarier than you might imagine. The experience got so real, so fast that it took the wind out of all of us.

When it was my turn for questioning, I was tossed in front of a very hostile interrogator, and he quickly began his probe: name, age, height, weight, eyes, color of hair?

"It's brown," I replied, pausing as he wrote "brown" on the blank line in pencil.

"Actually, there is some gray starting now, so I color it brown. It's really ash brown with some gray."

He looked at me blankly.

"Except that most of my friends would tell you that I am a blonde."

I was trying to stop talking; I really was, but my jittery nerves kept tripping me up.

The interrogator continued to stare at me as he erased his writing. He then scribbled more words than it seemed like he should. Watching him, I couldn't help but wonder why he suddenly had so much to add to my file. When the course was over, I saw what he'd written: "This bitch thinks this is a game. Let's show her what real pressure looks like!"

The unspoken animosity between the CIA trainees, who considered themselves to be the well-educated intellectuals, the "smart ones," and the interrogators, the brutes, was playing out in real time. This was going to be a competition, and this time, the interrogators were holding all the cards.

We were stripped of our shoes and taken to individual cells that were barely large enough to allow you to sit, but only with your legs bent close to your chest and your arms tightly folded on your torso. Once the cells were locked, we were told to remain standing and stay completely silent. For hours, we stood barefoot on the cold concrete floor without water or food. When I needed a bathroom break, I dared to break the deafening silence. A military man appeared, unlocking my cell just before putting a hood over my face. He then escorted me to the bathroom, where I'm pretty sure he stayed with me the entire time, glaring and staring as much as he wanted. It was humiliating.

Night and day, bald, bright white lightbulbs stayed on, and every hour or so, they patrolled the cells, flipping open a small window to peer into each enclosure and ensure we were still standing. Throughout my captivity, I did as I was told, usually standing with my arms crossed. Lee, from our false documents branch, was in the cell next to me, and every time they opened his window, he was sitting on the floor, resting, maybe even sleeping. "Get up!" they would yell at him each time, but the moment they left, he slowly slid back down the wall, landing with a muffled thump. I thought he was showing weakness but later realized he was conserving calories and energy, which I should have been doing too. My intent to show them how tough I was cost me a lot in fatigue and stress. As the only female in the course, I knew I needed to appear stalwart, sturdy, and brave—probably twice as much as the guys.

Eventually, a single cup of sticky cold rice and a glass of water were shoved through the small window in the door to my cell. Many hours later, another small cup of that same awful rice appeared, again with water. Those two sparse servings were the only food and drink we were given over the space of two days and two nights. As we endured the long hours of our captivity, static played on the radio, punctuated with Muslim chants and loud diatribes in other foreign languages.

We were each periodically hustled into a small, barren room for questioning, and as these interrogation sessions began piling up, I made sure to stay with my cover story. The interrogators were very rough, and several of my male colleagues "left early," a nice way of saying that they were escorted out of the course. We had been closely screened before they allowed us to enroll, but some medical issues arose, and probably a few psychological problems too. The experience was unsettling on a level that's challenging to describe. We were attending a training, yes, but the experience got so intense that at times you didn't feel like you'd make it. There was no end in sight and no reassurance or comfort to be had.

Several interrogation sessions in I realized my cover story was becoming more complicated than it should be. I'd been on a work trip with my "boss," I'd said, to attend a scientific conference being held in the (fictional) Republic of Virginia, i.e., the Farm. The interrogators wanted more. What was the specific part of the agenda that interested my boss—and me? Too quickly I felt myself getting sucked into a lengthy vortex of lies that my scientific knowledge could not support.

Just as I felt myself being chased down that rabbit hole, the lead interrogator stopped cold and stared at my ears, first one and then the other.

"What the fuck is going on with the earrings?" he asked. "Why are they on backward, with the points sticking out?"

Just as I was about to reply, his phone rang. Imagining our exchanges were being monitored by his command-and-control people, I assumed they were telling him to get back on track with the interrogation. As soon as he hung up, I quickly answered his question, telling him more than he ever wanted to know, including how I was about to throw up and on the verge of fainting when they put them back in. My strategy proved surprisingly effective; he soon lost his rhythm. I was promptly escorted back to my cell, my blood pounding through my veins. I had won.

When I heard keys jangling and others being released from their cells, I breathed a silent sigh of relief. I'd made it. *Phew.* Once my cell door was unlocked and opened, I was hooded once again. After a short walk inside the same building, the hood was ripped off just as I was shoved inside a box that measured maybe eight inches in depth. As soon as the box was closed, I was enveloped in darkness, unable to move a limb in any direction except perhaps a few millimeters to the right or left. Immediately, I felt my breathing grow jagged and my heart begin to race. I was trapped inside a claustrophobe's nightmare, except this was happening in real time and I had no way to "wake up." *I won't make it through this one*, I remember thinking. *Someone's going to have to get me out of here.*

As the minutes piled up, I remembered what the POWs had told us about mentally vacating your surroundings. Breathing deeply, I tried to envision places I'd loved. It took many tries, but eventually, I discovered that while standing in a mattress-size box so narrow that I couldn't rotate my shoulders, I could in fact mentally escape captivity. While literally boxed up, I could enter a glistening green world like using night-vision goggles in a darkroom. My newly imagined landscape shimmered: a sea of grass that I knew well—the Flint Hills of Kansas, a vast, tallgrass prairie that I loved. It was there, in that familiar landscape from my upbringing, the one I had worked so hard to leave behind, that I survived this nightmare enclosed in a box.

At one point, I heard footsteps and then several seconds of silence. "Are you okay in there?" a voice asked quietly. I hesitated, briefly wondering if the question was a trap or a trick, but then quietly replied. "I'm okay." When the box finally opened, I felt relieved, but not yet sure I'd "made it" through the training. After being hooded yet again, I was led straight ahead and then around a few bends. As soon as my hood came off, I was pushed into a container so small that most people would look at it and swear they'd never fit inside. My military escort promptly barked at me to kneel, so I entered on my knees, only to discover the "floor" was covered by a bed of gravel. The discomfort was undeniable, but after surviving the mattress box, I felt strangely resilient, sure I could endure this, too.

On the morning of what turned out to be the third day—I could no longer tell night from day—I heard footsteps. When my containment unit was opened, I slowly and painfully unfolded my limbs. My knees were numb, and possibly bloody, too, but I didn't have the energy to care. Mentally and emotionally, I felt vacant and bottomless, incapable of experiencing much emotion at all. When no hood was placed over my head and I walked out without a military escort, I knew it was finally over. We were being released. I was one of the first to walk over to the mess hall, which was not officially open yet. I asked for a cup of coffee and sat down in the cavernous, empty room, still wearing the military fatigues I had been issued, the pants still held up by the shirt tails. A heavyset man with unshaved stubble on his chin soon emerged from the kitchen carrying two cups of coffee.

"You from that course?" he asked as he sat down across from me, sliding one of the cups across the table.

I looked over at him and nodded. I still felt a bit shell-shocked, not yet ready for conversation.

"They wouldn't even let me put salt in the water when I cooked up that rice," he said. He stood, rubbed his hands on his greasy apron, and picked up his coffee to return to work. He could see there was no conversation to be had.

I had gone almost entirely without food and water for two and a half days. I had been simultaneously sleep deprived and mentally assaulted. I had learned more about myself than I ever would have imagined, including how I would react instinctively and then how I *should* react. Be meek. Go unnoticed. Don't make eye contact. Rest when you can. Give them something, but never too much. You just might survive.

Right after the course, Damon, our OTS Chief of Training and a psychologist by training, was admitted to the hospital. He had sustained nerve damage to his feet from standing barefoot on cold concrete for two days and nights. I would never know what had happened to the men who were removed from the course early, but I did later learn that my class had made a mark; they either abolished the course or paused it for an undisclosed period.

Hours later, revived by a shower, food, and a change of clothes, I got in my car and drove to the outlet mall nearby. The following day, I was scheduled to return to the Farm, this time as a trainer. I had packed an appropriate outfit but felt a sudden urge to buy something new. Mere hours after facing my claustrophobia in the scariest way possible, I felt a rush of energy coursing through my body, a visceral, almost electric buzzing. I wasn't the same woman I'd been a few days before, and I needed a new outfit to reflect that.

As I flipped through the racks, feeling bold and vaguely elated, I paused when I happened upon a yellow dress with big flowers and a circle skirt. I'd always worn tailored clothes and this dress was the opposite—unapologetically feminine and flowy. It was unlike any I'd ever bought, but as soon as I slipped it on, I knew it was the one. It fit me like a glove, and wearing it, I felt newly empowered, not despite being a woman but because I was one. Being female and claustrophobic, both of which are considered weaknesses in a military context, hadn't held me back. I'd lived through my personal nightmare, and emerged victorious, unlike several of the men in my group who hadn't made it. The next day, I slipped on that dress and sat on the lawn at the Farm, making notes for my presentation.

Something had changed inside me, and the rush I felt stayed with me as I entered Arena B, where I would train a hundred or so new ops officers in the operational use of disguise. I'd never had difficulty with public speaking, but this time felt different, like a switch had flipped. I don't remember what I said or how long it lasted, but I do recall how I felt afterward. I'd given the best talk I'd ever given, and I knew it, even before Tony Mendez, who'd been my boss since I began training in disguise, approached me to tell me he thought so too.

That day, I realized that whatever limitations I'd faced—as Jennifer's somewhat invisible little sister and then as a claustrophobic woman in a man's world—none of it could stop me now. Just like that, my potential seemed to unfold before me, a vista so full of possibility, I had no need to question it. The future I wanted was mine; all I had to do now was reach for it.

———

Having been a student at the Farm a few times already, I stepped into a second role there, as a guest lecturer. The drive down to southern Virginia from Washington, DC, is famously peppered with speed traps. Driving my secondhand Porsche 928, I took great pains to stay within the speed limit. I believed then, and maintain to this day, that I was periodically pulled over because my car *looked* too fast. At times when I was part of a group of cars that was speeding simultaneously, I would be the only one stopped. Behind the wheel of my sports car, safety in numbers didn't work to my advantage. Regardless, each time I shamelessly attempted to talk my way out of those tickets. It rarely worked, but I was a young, attractive woman, so I figured it was worth a shot.

My office conducted several training courses, and I felt honored to contribute to the careers of these new recruits. For many officers, that hadn't always been the case. For years, being assigned there permanently as a staff instructor had been viewed as punishment. It was where failed officers were sent after their covers were blown. It was also a convenient place to hide an officer with a drinking problem. That attitude has since changed. Today it's considered an important assignment; only the best and most innovative officers are asked to educate our new cadre.

The SRB was the student bar at the Farm—and far less tame than the faculty's separate facility. Its reputation as the rowdier drinking hole, however, explained why it was favored by students and instructors alike. Eventually the SRB's reputation turned into an official complaint. The OTS officers, the Farm's Chief alleged, had violated all sense of decorum by playing a drinking game fondly known as "aircraft land-ings." To begin the game, you set up a series of long tables end to end, forming a runway. Then pitchers of beer are poured along the length of the tables. Allegedly, OTS officers would then take a run at the tables, landing on the first one with a belly flop. Points were scored based on how far down the "runway" they slid. This, the Chief claimed in his complaint, was accompanied by loud cheering and whistling.

According to a witness present at the conversation, our office Director, Corley, paused after hearing the full complaint. He then proceeded to deny it all, asserting that his OTS officers, who were highly trained professional intelligence officers, would never waste good beer like that. We already loved him, but we loved him a little more after hearing this story.

He did not deny, however, that some of his officers might have helped move the beer machine out of the SRB and into the dormitory lobby, where it clearly belonged. "Who needs a beer machine in a bar?" he asked.

———

Defensive Driving was always a popular course, and when it was my turn to attend, I couldn't wait to get started. What spy hasn't had James Bond fantasies of being behind the wheel of an Aston Martin careening over the Alps?

This course was not that.

At the start of class, the instructors asked about the cars we drove in our personal lives. By this point I was driving a Volvo, which got the instructors excited. "Like a tank!" one exclaimed. To personalize the training, they wanted to match us to the type and weight of our personal vehicles.

The course was necessary for any spy but had become especially relevant given the history of violent kidnappings in Europe, many carried out by the Baader-Meinhof Gang, or Red Army Faction (RAF). They were an extremist left-wing Marxist-Leninist urban guerilla group founded in 1970. Classified as a terrorist group by the West German government, they'd also conducted bombings, assassinations, shoot-outs, and bank robberies. Some of the group's earliest members, including at least one founding member, were women, who might, for example, suddenly pull a gun from the baby carriage they were pushing to play their part in a kidnapping.

Europe was hardly the only place where danger lurked; agents had been abducted and subsequently killed by terrorists and insurgents in any number of places around the world. Wherever your next overseas assignment might be, knowing how to power your way through a potential roadblock situation was well worth the time it took to train in that skill.

Driving cars without windshields and while wearing football helmets and protective goggles, we learned how to run through two cars blocking the road ahead nose to nose. After we were finished wrecking the cars in our path, we would blow them to smithereens during demolition courses.

The key to running through the roadblocks was knowing the weight distribution of the two cars in your path as well as the one you were driving. If the blocking cars were both front engine, you would want to hit the rear end of the lighter car, at the axle. There was no braking involved, only a fast-paced powering through. We were given opportunities to do this multiple times. It felt like a life-size, fast-moving game of bumper cars, but with a lot more at stake.

Another maneuver involved avoiding the roadblock entirely by executing a reverse 180 turn just before hauling ass in the opposite direction. Right as you approached the two cars, you'd slow down, coming to a full stop about four car lengths away. At this point the bad guys would get out of their cars and approach you, probably with guns in hand. While they were on foot, you would throw your car into reverse and floor it. You wanted to be going backward at around 45 mph, eyes fixed on the rearview mirror, at which point you would pull on the emergency brake. This raises the front tires off the road, and you'd use the steering wheel to turn the car in the direction you want to go while shifting into drive. When the front tires set down, you apply more gas, hopefully leaving nothing but a cloud of exhaust in your opponents' faces.

Sound hard? It is! Now imagine executing this maneuver while looking down the barrel of a gun. This was not for the faint of heart, but it was just the kind of heart-racing, adrenaline-pumping challenge we tended to seek out. I always believed that I could and would ram a roadblock if necessary. More recently, former CIA officer Valerie Plame executed a brilliant reverse 180 in an ad she ran while running for a US Senate seat in New Mexico. She has my admiration!

Shooting instruction was another component of our training. The course focused primarily on teaching us how to fire handguns and AK-47s. Some people seem to have a natural ease with guns, but I was not one of them. My aim, especially with handguns, was subpar, which put me at risk of failing the shooting portion of the course. My team captain promptly brought in Buck, an American Indian OTS officer who taught only the most recalcitrant students the ways of his world: how to shoot, how to detect surveillance, and how to live in the woods and even thrive there. Acting as my private handgun tutor, he quickly assessed that I was anticipating the jump, or kick, of the gun. To solve this problem, he balanced a penny on the barrel each time I prepared to fire. By concentrating on keeping the penny in place, my aim improved enough for me to pass the tests. When Buck gleefully called the other instructors over to watch me during skeet training, I knew I'd finally arrived at a good place. My aim and timing when shooting skeet was uncanny; I almost couldn't miss.

Prior to the shooting course I'd been afraid of rifles, but as I gained skill in shooting, I came to understand that guns were another tool that I could master and use confidently. I eventually qualified as a marksman with a Smith and Wesson .38 revolver and a Colt .45 automatic and could hit the targets from one hundred paces. The only disappointment came from a series of exercises the instructors orchestrated to demonstrate how hard, even impossible, shooting at a target from a moving vehicle is. Reluctantly, with a heavy heart, I let go of that fantasy.

The final portion of that training series was on personal physical protection. Our instructor, Chuck, was a paramilitary officer, and he later went on to become the public face of the CIA in liaising with Hollywood projects. A highly skilled officer, he taught us how to leverage our weight, where the body's soft spots are, and how and where to deliver a particularly painful, even crippling, blow. It was good training, and he did an excellent job—with one exception. Talking amongst ourselves, my small group of women felt he'd been dismissive of our part in the class. We'd all learned a lot, but only because we'd made sure to; without a doubt, Chuck's attention had remained fixed on the men first and foremost. We, his inattention seemed to convey, were mere sidekicks.

When Friday morning rolled around and it was time to leave, Chuck placed his military-issue duffel bag in the trunk of his car just as he was about to depart. The women in our group quickly decided this was our chance to execute our farewell plan. As some of us made a point of saying goodbye, a few of us even giving him a brief farewell hug, *somebody* stashed an open bottle of Midnight in Paris, an infamous, cheap eau de toilette, in his bag. As he drove away, we smiled and waved, bemused by the thought of the slightly musky, sweet scent that was now seeping through his belongings.

CHAPTER 14

The Subcontinent, Again

The plan Tony Mendez and I had hatched succeeded: the Disguise assignment I'd been seeking in the subcontinent was mine. John would "accompany" me, which was US government lingo labeling him as my dependent. In fact, however, he was a career CIA staff officer with a full-time position in the Office of Security at our new station. Instead of working as a polygraph officer, he would now focus on physical security, managing safety protocols and systems in critical locations. We were both embarking on new phases of our careers and eager to expand our skill sets and experience. Throughout this assignment, he would travel as much as I did around the subcontinent; between the two of us, we'd clock some major miles.

Nonetheless, in the eyes of those around us, he was secondary, a spouse merely along for the ride. None of that was true, but a lot of men would have vehemently objected to this assignment and the apparent demotion—in personal and professional status—that it implied. However, John Goeser was paying me back for his years at George Washington University and paying it forward, should he get another overseas assignment where I would need to play the role of tagalong wife. He went along with the plan without complaint or regret. Ours was a CIA marriage, and it didn't follow the "typical" rules any more than our covert, work-centric lifestyle did.

By this point we'd had countless conversations about the challenges married couples were facing in the CIA. The staff permanently assigned at Langley were fine, able to be home for dinner and on weekends. Among field officers, however, the divorce rate was high. There was a lot of drinking, which probably didn't help but was a common side effect of the job. None of it was easy on a marriage, especially when extensive travel was involved.

John and I had both noticed that the married male field officers always seemed "fine." They'd get assigned to a new part of the world and before long be on yet another flight to a TDY, returning to their foreign "home" only for short periods of time in between. Meanwhile the wives were left to fend for themselves and their children in a part of the world where they knew no one and probably didn't speak the language or know the customs, school system, or neighbors. Plucking your wife and children from everything and everyone they knew at home and largely abandoning them to fend for themselves in a foreign land was a lot to ask. Still, John and I always remarked that the kiss of death for any marriage was separated tours, in which the wife and children stayed back home while the husband completed a two-year tour in a different part of the world. Above all, we were determined to avoid that. While we spent considerable time apart, each of us traveling to different places at different times, we both understood how much this career path demanded. Provided we were both assigned to the same "home" office at the same time, we knew we could make it work.

One of our strengths as a couple was our commitment to the agency. As my career blossomed my increasing focus on my work earned me a professional advantage. Tireless dedication was a characteristic the agency looked for, especially in field officers. This job requirement consistently worked against women, and it was a poorly kept secret that women who had kids were quietly put on a shelf when opportunities for promotion arose. Married women, too, were typically overlooked; it was just a matter of time before they would get pregnant, the thinking went. In that way I was a relative anomaly, married to John and the CIA in equal measure.

Due to the nature of our work, OTS officers were exclusively involved with live operations that were likely to produce valuable results. That was part of what made the work so exciting, and so rewarding. The more of this work I did, the more I loved it.

As someone who could do disguise and rudimentary false documents with a secondary set of in-depth photographic skills, I brought valuable flexibility to the unit. Our terrain was broad and the geography we covered varied, stretching from Kathmandu in the Himalayas to the tropical shores of Colombo, and from the Khyber Pass to the slums of Dhaka. The only shadow lurking in the background was our new Chief, Tom Smallwood. He hadn't yet arrived, but his reputation had. Before John and I left DC, Tony had cautioned me about Smallwood, reminding me, in his pithy way, to keep my head down. Smallwood could be trouble.

My lab was the largest room in the station, surpassing the Chief's own office, with lots of windows and odd, baby-blue carpeting. Every morning the cabinet surfaces would be covered with a layer of fine desert sand, even after I'd sealed the lab's windows with silicone caulk. During my long hours inside those walls, I would play cassette tapes sent to me by colleagues at headquarters containing contemporary music like Huey Lewis and the News and Phil Collins as well as PBS recordings of Garrison Keillor from Lake Wobegon. They also sent videotapes of Super Bowl games. When I traveled around my newly assigned region, I was briefly the most popular person at the local station, offering my tapes to anyone eager to view them. Football was not my thing, but I was happy to share these little slices of home.

———

Soon after arriving, I began searching for our housing. After touring several possibilities, I set my sights on a pink-and-white stucco house, a mansion done in the European rococo style. The marble floors on the ground floor extended up the open, three-story circular staircase that ended at a rooftop terrace. The house had an extensive garden that came with a full-time gardener, a man who was highly skilled but so old I worried he might expire at any moment. I was enchanted the moment I saw the house. Without thinking, I swooped it up. It was simply too good to pass up.

Once I'd hired our housekeeper, Maggie, our new life quickly fell into place. Her entire family worked for either the American or British embassies and was well-connected in the diplomatic communities. A fabulous cook, she had learned her skills from her father, who had worked for the British in Burma during the war. Having such a genuine, caring woman in our home would prove to be invaluable, both personally and professionally. She would become a lifelong friend.

In one of the second-floor rooms, there was a bay window where I placed my desk and caught up on correspondence whenever I could. I had a view of our lovely street in the southwest quadrant of the city and a stack of stationery in the middle drawer; it was my personal command center. For security reasons I wasn't sending international mail from the countries where I was working. The list of people I now wrote to had also shrunk to family and a few friends; by this point I had disappeared into the world of clandestine operations, fragile situations, and flimsy cover names. I also quickly lost track of new people, often unsure if I even knew their true name. My world had simultaneously expanded and contracted, allowing me greater freedom and responsibility as a technical officer, but somewhat less as an individual. The tradeoffs, for me, felt more than worthwhile; every day was an adventure full of twists and turns no one could foresee. I couldn't imagine living another life and certainly didn't want to.

———

Flying on India Airlines or Air India in this part of the world, you couldn't deny that the caste system in India, which had officially been eradicated in the Indian constitution in 1950, was still alive and well. Only privileged, educated, upper-caste Brahmin women were granted opportunities as flight attendants. Due to their high caste, however, these young women, who were always beautiful, could not perform most of the functions of a Western flight attendant. Upon your entering the aircraft, a stewardess would greet you with her hands respectfully folded in a silent, prayerful greeting. *Namaste.* After that, she could not help you with luggage, could not open the overhead compartments, or do much of anything. Her caste and refinement meant that she was allowed only to serve you tea.

Not long after setting foot in our new home, I boarded one of these flights. The goal of my trip was to test our team's exfiltration planning, which was part of our consistent focus on preparedness, which meant constantly assessing and anticipating future challenges and devising solutions to problems that could pop up urgently and when we least expected. A coup, a threat of exposure to one of our officers, an opportunity to wreak some havoc on one of America's adversaries, or a need to move an individual out of harm's way—all were potential challenges we perpetually tried to resolve in advance. We also always kept a watchful eye on opportunities to welcome a defector, or "volunteer," as we called them. You never knew when you might be approached by a foreign citizen seeking safe harbor, possibly in exchange for important and timely intelligence. We were mindful of Robert Baden-Powell's Boy Scout motto—*Be Prepared*!

OTS played an important role in these scenarios. In cases that required exfiltration, for example, we had the responsibility of moving people, even whole families, across various international borders around the globe. This trip would help us assess how safely we could move a subject across a particular border and onto neutral territory via airplane.

Today, in an adjoining country, the flight path was littered with peculiarities. Just boarding this international flight was a lesson in cross-border hostilities. These national airlines took great pains to needle each other. The most infuriating tactic they used in their silent wars was having passengers board flights and then creating interminable delays on the tarmac. On this flight, we sat in our seats, feeling like sardines roasting for hours on end, as the plane remained parked on the scorching runway. The dry, hot air felt so unbearable, my claustrophobia finally kicked in, forcing me to tell a flight attendant that I had to disembark and wait in the gate. Down the stairs I went.

Even just standing in the airport in this country, I could feel the gazes of men passing by. Women here were expected to cover themselves from the top of the neck down past their ankles, and their hair, too. Traveling as an unescorted woman was akin to wearing a flashing neon sign on my person. Not only did I stand out, I risked being harassed, or potentially worse. I realized then that our females would need to turn into men when on the street here to avoid unwanted attention. Fortunately, the typical attire for local men would be a forgiving disguise for a woman's shape. Our women would know how to play this game.

Attempting a short hop to a provincial city, we dodged heavy monsoon rains that forced us back twice, each time through strong winds and terrifyingly jarring lightning and thunder. After finally landing in the capital, we spent a couple of days hammering together an exfiltration scenario.

A few days later, after extended planning sessions, it was time to test our plan in real time. Brent, a local case officer, would play his part, and I would inhabit the role of the exfiltree, the person who needed to leave the country undetected. When it was time to begin our testing scenario, Brent and I approached the international airport. Under cover of early morning darkness, we separated. As planned, I headed directly out onto the tarmac, bypassing airport controls before stepping onto the aircraft. Thirty minutes later Brent joined me on the small plane. Once the pilot boarded, we would be off. They had both been processed through normal airport controls without raising suspicion or causing a delay. I had not. Would I be allowed to remain on the flight?

Or would they realize I hadn't gone through their regular channels? For an exfiltree, these moments would be harrowing. Being held or questioned might translate into imprisonment or worse, depending on the location and circumstances. While I, an official American, was less likely to encounter that level of threat, we knew our success or failure would have consequences for actual exfiltrees. Failure might mean a delay, and for many people who needed to leave their country unnoticed, each week, day, or even hour could put lives in peril. As I sat in my seat, awaiting takeoff, I tried to appear unfazed, but sporadically my pulse would quicken slightly and a small trickle of sweat would run down the side of my rib cage.

After takeoff a spectacular Kodachrome sunrise over the Himalayas finally appeared outside of the plane's windows, and Brent and I breathed a communal sigh of relief. All was proceeding according to plan, but the true challenge lay ahead of us: the last leg of our trip was crossing the border into the adjacent country. When we arrived at our transit city, I stayed on the plane as Brett and the pilot processed through immigration. Would I really get away with sidestepping the standard protocols on two consecutive flights? I did my best to remain as inconspicuous as possible. When that second flight finally took off and we soared up and out over the ocean, we all broke out in applause. Our test scenario had succeeded. We had made it.

Brent, an impeccable gourmet, promptly pulled out a picnic basket full of exotic French goodies from Fauchon, the legendary gourmet epicenter of Paris. As the flight neared our destination, we sipped chilled white wine and munched on French pâté, which made our clandestine flight feel less like an operation and more like a scene from a movie. In hindsight, though, I wondered if that basket would have been prepared for, much less offered to, one of the case officer's male colleagues.

Was it one of the more enchanting holdovers of chivalry? Memories can shapeshift over time, taking on context and meaning I didn't stop to calculate in the moment. If I didn't consider the role of my gender at the time, was it naivete or authenticity? Is what I see when I look back now born of experience or cynicism?

We eventually landed at our destination, spent the night, and then reboarded the plane for a short flight to meet with the Chief of Station. We were elated; a new international exfiltration route was officially in play.

On April 10, 1988, my colleague Jay and I were having a quick lunch in Islamabad. While planning future missions, a series of nearby explosions began. Instinctively, we ducked and looked around before making a beeline to the nearby office windows. Peering outside, we looked in horror at the fins of numerous missiles that were now sticking out of the ground. I could feel my heart thumping in my chest as my brain processed what I was seeing. Were we at war? We appeared to be under attack. Immediately reverting to our training as CIA officers, we proceeded as quickly as we could to the lower floors of the building, where we hunkered down, wondering if the worst was yet to come.

Unbeknownst to locals and most of the American intelligence community, me included, we were working near a massive trove of weaponry that was hidden in plain sight. The Ojhri ammo storage camp just outside of Islamabad was being used by our government as a depot for the Afghan mujahideen, who were fighting Soviet forces in Afghanistan. The site had been selected by the Pakistani government, and when the weapons stash ignited, the firestorm and rockets it propelled into the populated areas all around the city wounded over one thousand and killed more than a hundred people in Rawalpindi and Islamabad. It was later estimated that over ten thousand tons of rockets, mortars, small-arms ammunition, plastic explosives, and Stingers in storage were fired.

"A couple of 107 mm rockets hit the American International School in Islamabad, causing an understandable panic among the parents and students but no injuries," Milt Bearden, who was Chief of Station in Islamabad at the time, later wrote in his book, *The Main Enemy*.[*] "The people of Rawalpindi were less fortunate. The first major explosion flattened a shantytown that had built up outside the walls of Ojhri camp, killing dozens. As the explosions continued through the morning, with black clouds rising above Ojhri and drifting over Rawalpindi, many others were killed by falling ordnance and debris. At day's end, casualties were up to one hundred killed and one thousand injured." It wasn't the first time the American embassy in Islamabad had been thrown into chaos. In 1979 the embassy was attacked and nearly burned to the ground by a violent group of protesters.

Out the windows we could see stray shells spiraling in large hunks of shrapnel. White phosphorus rounds struck the auditorium of the American school, which was in full attendance, on the embassy grounds. There were no injuries at the embassy, or at the school, but the risk remained high as events unfolded. The wall surrounding the large US embassy was damaged, as was a building within the Chinese embassy. More than five hours after the initial blasts, small-arms ammunitions were still going off, cooking off in long bursts, simulating an unending infantry battle. Intermittently for the next two days, fear and uncertainty hovered over the city, all of us hunkering down, hoping we were in a safe place.

----

[*] Milt Bearden, *The Main Enemy* (New York: Ballantine Books, 2003), 325.

Throughout the attack I huddled with colleagues in the basement, still unsure what was happening or why. We were all shaken by the cacophony of sounds as munitions hit nearby; smoke and gasoline fumes and the sounds of war wafted in from the manicured lawns surrounding the building, now littered with bits and pieces of one of the largest weapons caches in the world.

CHAPTER 15

Good Intel Takes Its Toll

I was in my hotel room, seriously ill and pretty sure I was going to die, when the phone began to ring. It was Chaz, a Chief of Station I worked with at Langley, now on assignment abroad. A uniquely significant roll of film had come into his hands in the darkest hours of the night. He needed me to come into the office. Now.

I was on TDY in South Asia. I had been there before; by this point, the country was one of my favorite destinations. At the center of the country was a mountainous area that boasts enormous tea plantations. The site has a lush natural beauty that effortlessly enchants and inspires.

I had been working with Chaz for some time by this point. When we'd first met at headquarters, I could tell right away that he wasn't your typical, buttoned-up Directorate of Operations case officer. After taking in his blue jeans, denim shirt, and cowboy boots, my gaze had been immediately drawn to his shiny, bald head. How perfect, I thought. From a disguise standpoint, he was the ideal blank slate, a delight to my eager imagination. He also had a charisma that made you feel like a good friend within minutes of meeting him. It was an important attribute in pulling off the different personas that disguise often required.

From the start of our conversation about the various disguises we could try, he seemed to delight in the process. My idea was to give him something he would love—hair! Disguise was an additive process. You could make a person taller but not shorter, fatter but not slimmer, older but usually not younger. The custom-made hairpiece I designed for Chaz would need to fit him perfectly, of course. The process involved covering his head in Saran Wrap, then layering matte-finish Scotch Magic Tape over it. This created a close-fitting replica of his head. After carefully tailoring the edges, I drew the new hairline onto the form, indicating where the part would be, which direction the hair should lie in each area. Finally, I added color using a unique hair-specific palette. With the form complete, I then shipped it to our hair goods contractor in Los Angeles, which also produced hairpieces for Hollywood. Weeks later, Chaz's new wig arrived.

The plan was for his new disguise, wig included, to be his "new normal" throughout the assignment. When he needed a disguise, he would remove the wig and add a pair of slightly smoked wire-rimmed glasses, one of his European outfits, a particular cologne, and a gold chain. The transformation was simple yet effective. Within seconds he became a bald, vaguely European-looking man—perfectly nondescript, able to blend into his environment easily; he loved it.

On the night in question, I was in my hotel room, struck by what I assumed was food poisoning. When Chaz insisted that this was important, I hung up, got dressed, took some Advil, and drank a few shot-glass-size servings of Pepto Bismol. The film that Chaz needed me to develop might contain current photos of Carlos the Jackal, a terrorist being hunted by numerous intelligence organizations around the world. If that was the case, the next several hours could be big.

Most OTS officers were highly specialized, skilled in audio or disguise or photography. With my expertise in disguise, photography, and secret documents, I could straddle specialties that few others could. That sometimes allowed me to get more deeply involved in high-stakes cases, and this one was no exception.

Carlos was a Venezuelan who'd been working with the Popular Front for the Liberation of Palestine (PFLP) for years. He'd been involved in a high-profile 1975 raid on OPEC headquarters in Vienna that killed three French government officials, two of whom were counterintelligence agents. Following that, he'd participated in a string of attacks against other Western targets. His priority standing as one of the most-wanted fugitives in the world was well known and ongoing. In spy circles he was somewhat of a legend; catching him would be a considerable coup for any espionage team.

So sick I could barely stand, I slipped inside the car Chaz sent to pick me up. I felt dizzy and nauseated, but once inside the darkroom I had no time to bother with my symptoms. I developed and printed the film, methodically comparing the images on this new film to previous ones, first evaluating the usual physiological points of facial geometry. I started with the features and dimensions that couldn't be altered: the distance from the outer corner of the eye to the corner of the mouth and to the eyebrow; from the inner corner of the eye to the start of the brow; the positioning of the ears relative to the rest of the face. These were some of the measurements that typically helped to determine if the person in picture A was the same one who appeared in picture B. Often, however, the pictures themselves didn't allow for straightforward comparisons; their differences—partly out of focus, taken from different or odd angles, or blurred by movement—turned this work into an imperfect science.

Was this Carlos the Jackal? Did these faces match closely enough to make that determination? After several painstaking hours of measuring and examining, I couldn't make that call, so we arranged for an officer to hand carry the images to Langley the next morning. Years later, in 1994, Carlos the Jackal was captured in Sudan and taken to prison in France, where he is currently serving three consecutive lifetime sentences.

———

As my TDYs in the subcontinent steadily increased, I became enchanted by this part of the world. I was doing some of the best work of my career to date, and I could also feel a new part of me coming alive. At the same time, however, I was facing increased resistance from my new boss, Smallwood, who seemed to delight in grilling me each time I needed his approval for another trip. What would I be doing? Whom would I be working with? Was travel really necessary? Getting signoff was typically a quick and straightforward administrative requirement; my services had been requested, which meant his speedy approval was needed. However, Smallwood had his own agenda. Before becoming COS, he'd worked in the Office of Communications, which was notoriously macho and dominated exclusively by men. Each trip I took weakened his argument that I was unnecessary. Unfortunately for him, there were so many disguise requirements that I was as busy as most of the men in his office, a fact that was difficult to hide given my frequent trips. My extensive travel also qualified me for premium pay, which many of the men aspired to; the fact that I was steadily earning it without trying probably wasn't popular among my male colleagues, but I was usually too busy to notice. Still, every trip I took was a thorn in Smallwood's side, and every request I put in was an opportunity for him to get in my way. The longer I worked for him, the more determined he seemed to sabotage me. I was quickly realizing how right Tony had been; Smallwood absolutely was trouble, certainly where I was concerned.

———

When John and I suddenly had a simultaneous lull in our work and travel schedules, we joined the Chief of Station's secretary, Jean, and her husband on a vacation at Dal Lake in Srinagar, Kashmir. I had known Jean back at headquarters. The trip was taken on a whim, and she handled all the arrangements.

When we arrived, I was overwhelmed by the beauty of the place. The views from the houseboat where we were staying featured the snow-clad Himalayas, and the relatively cool breezes provided much-desired relief from the sweltering city we were now calling home. The houseboat dated back to the British Raj and was intricately carved out of cedar. As we delighted in our surroundings, a houseboy saw to our every need. From the outset the whole experience was bewitching.

In the evenings we glided across the lake on lavishly painted shikaras, which are light, flat-bottomed boats. With the vast mountains towering above us, their white caps barely glimmering through the night's darkness, the Kashmiri boatmen nestled small clay pots called kangri in their laps inside of their robes. As they gently paddled their boats, these pots, which were full of sand and slow-burning, glowing embers, acted as their personal portable heaters.

One afternoon Jean and I ventured off our boat, eager to explore this breathtaking location on foot. As we wandered through the open-air markets, our hair and limbs fully covered, the Muslim men kept asking us the same questions: "Where are your husbands? You have husbands, yes?" Even on vacation, hundreds of miles away from Small-wood, as a woman I felt stymied. This region I was coming to love so wholly put its deep-seated bias against women on display often and without reservation. Still, though, I reveled in every moment of the trip, which was so unlike the luxurious but boring Caribbean cruises John had long preferred during our vacations. I'd always been happiest when learning about history and culture, art and music; luxury for luxury's sake had never interested me. While I might always be viewed here as a wife, rather than a capable woman, I was too enraptured by the exotic sights, sounds, and scents to give it much thought.

The Himalayas, I later learned, had proven useful for more than relaxation. In many cases involving exfiltration, conventional air travel wasn't a viable option for moving individuals across borders, making other, more clandestine options, including travel by elephant, necessary. At one point, the COS told me, he had undertaken a trek to Nepal with an asset who was being sought by the KGB. Camping out together in those breathtaking but potentially perilous mountains, they successfully hid for an extended time.

On one hot and steamy night during that long stay in the Himalayas, the COS lay awake at their campsite and decided to take a dip in a local stream to cool off. He did this in complete darkness before slipping back inside his sleeping bag. After some time, he awoke feeling strange. And itchy. He got up and by the fire discovered in horror that his entire body was covered with leeches. They were on his chest, back, legs, and other, more tender places. He immediately called for the Sherpas, who gently pulled them off. His body was covered with welts, but he was probably lucky not to have contracted anything more from these bloodsucking organisms. For years after hearing this story I would occasionally have a nightmare about waking up covered with leeches, freaked out of my mind.

On another TDY, this time with my colleague Allen, I looked around a cavernous room inside the Peshawar bazaar, feeling vaguely haunted. We were surrounded by several dozen men, warriors sitting side by side in their dun-colored, desert-invisible dress, weighed down by bandoleers of ammunition with long guns slung over their shoulders. The sight briefly reminded me of a recent operation, where I'd been eye to eye with a terrorist in a hotel lobby. His bodyguards, too, carried these same weapons. This time, I didn't dare look around for too long; this was no place to be caught staring, especially as a woman. Even through my furtive glances, though, I could see the devastating aftereffects of their untold stories, the ghoulish remains of warfare and sacrifice flashing on their faces. Many of them were young, still catching their breath before returning to battle.

The Pakistani intelligence service, the ISI, trained mujahideen nearby and this area was a primary destination for resettled Afghans. As I sat there, wondering what these men had just been doing and what they were about to return to, I kept flashing back to the mujahid I had trained years earlier in DC. Was he nearby? Had he even survived? Had he and his uncle been caught trading their intelligence for lifesaving medicine?

Allen and I were there to assess how to move a defector out of Afghanistan. This time, there appeared to be a real possibility that a Soviet military officer could defect and require safe passage. We suspected that such a Soviet national, if he offered himself to the CIA, would appear in Kabul, where we had a heavily fortified embassy. What came next—getting him out of Afghanistan altogether—would be the difficult part.

The moment a Soviet walked into our embassy, word of his arrival would quickly spread. The Soviets would then set up surveillance around the embassy to prevent us from removing their citizen. That didn't worry us; we'd already worked with Hollywood's magic-building community, learning new and better ways to move an individual clandestinely. Invisibly. Our human-transport devices were already constructed with a variety of concealments that could be carted on a normal dolly, a simple hand truck like the ones found in almost any large building. Used to move office supplies, equipment, and consumables such as crates of foodstuffs, dollies were so commonplace that they were almost invisible.

Allen and I decided on a hand truck stacked with crates of clear, locally manufactured water bottles that could be wheeled anywhere. The apparent transparency and weight of that load could accommodate a human figure who would remain hidden in plain sight. Since the bottles of water would appear to be clear, the deception was especially convincing. A human body inside of a load of see-through water bottles? Impossible! The idea defied even the most discerning human imagination, which would enable us to get a defector out of the American embassy. The bigger question still loomed, though: How would we move him over the border?

There was a frequent stream of brightly painted Pakistani transport trucks that drove supplies from Pakistan into Afghanistan. The route included a long stretch on the Grand Trunk Road, which runs 1,700

miles from Bangladesh into Afghanistan. As we continued researching ways to move a defector out of Afghanistan, Allen and I became
especially interested in the piece of road that transits the Khyber Pass,
connecting the Pakistani city of Islamabad to Kabul.

As we proceeded along this stretch of road, we knew we were on
an out-of-the-ordinary journey. Many of the trucks that crossed this
pass every day were driven by smugglers and black-market dealers. We
planned to recruit several of these black-market drivers to move human
cargo for us. Security at the border was still relatively controlled since
the Pakistani tribes living nearby were paid by their government to
safeguard this priceless lifeline into Kabul.

The drive from Kabul to Peshawar, about 280 miles, would typically
take five hours, and our plan was for the Soviet defector to sit in the
passenger seat, next to the driver, wearing a burka, posing as the driver's
wife. The border guards would never ask a woman to lift her veil or even
ask her to speak. It was unimaginable. It would be a shooting offense.

We came away from this trip with a plan in place for moving a
"volunteer" clandestinely across the Afghanistan–Pakistan border to
Peshawar for transportation onward. Some years later, *Time* magazine
published an article about an incident at the Khyber Pass that brought
back memories of my road trip with Allen. According to the story, there
were two men in the front of a truck and about six women in burkas
sitting in the truck bed. Suddenly, something alarmed them. The truck
screeched to a halt, and the driver and passengers leapt out of the truck
and took off across the rocky ground. As they ran, you could see that
the "women" were wearing combat boots beneath their burkas; we may
not have been the only ones planning to use the burka for exfiltration,
but we left feeling satisfied that we could move someone out of the
country quickly and clandestinely if and when we needed to.

CHAPTER 16

Smallwood

I was almost a year into this overseas assignment when I walked into Smallwood's office, trying but largely failing to steel my nerves. I'd been trained to face any number of challenging, even dangerous situations without losing my cool, but this meeting scared me. My mother's warning about avoiding conflict was still deeply rooted inside me. Yet here I was, about to instigate a confrontation, and with my boss of all people.

It was still early morning, but already he was slouching on the sofa in his office, holding a coffee cup that had no coffee in it. I could smell Cointreau, its syrupy sweet, orange-like aroma wafting in the air between us. I knew I needed to get to the point; I wanted to talk to him while he was still sharp.

Dragging a wooden chair up to his desk, I proceeded to sit down. He then pulled himself up and off the sofa, ambled across the office, cup in hand, and slid into his chair. His faux British khaki drill uniform, a short-sleeved version, was already wrinkled.

"What's up?" he asked. I routinely avoided meeting with this man, so my deliberate entrance was piquing his curiosity. There was an ugly schism between Smallwood and me, freighted with overtones of misogyny and power. He was like a buzz saw, set on eviscerating my career.

"Tell me again, Tom," I said, making sure to slide my chair even closer, leaning forward and looking him in the eye, as John, a former polygraph officer trained in confrontation, had advised me to do the night before. "Say it again," I continued, staring at Smallwood. "I want to make sure that I got it, that I heard you correctly yesterday." I readied the small pad of paper and pen I held in my hands, making a show of my eagerness to jot down his feedback. As I spoke, I tried to keep my tone of voice firm and even, hoping to contain my anger well enough that he wouldn't notice that my body was stiff and tense.

Smallwood looked at me blankly, playing for time. The day before, he had boasted that on his recent trip to Langley, he had told Martin, my boss one level up at headquarters, that he wanted to send me back to DC short of tour. That would translate into a curtailed assignment, a failure, and a stain on my increasingly rock-solid reputation. Hearing him say those words, I'd been stunned yet also fairly sure he was drunk when he said them. Send me home? Short of tour? Was he kidding?

"Get as close to him as you can," John had advised me the night before. "Get right up in his grill." After hearing the story, John had been outraged at Smallwood's unprofessional behavior. He told me to challenge Smallwood as directly I could and see if he would repeat his veiled threat when he was a little more sober. John felt strongly that

Smallwood would back down. I wasn't so sure he would, but I knew I had to try. The only reason to send someone home short of tour would be for cause, and there was no cause here. I had received only accolades for my work in the subcontinent, and from all the stations and bases I visited. This was a clean case of professional misogyny, and it broke all the CIA's rules—at least all the official ones; whether misogyny was truly unacceptable to the agency, or to any American employer at that time, was a matter of debate.

This morning, up close and personal with him in his office, Smallwood suddenly seemed more butter knife than bludgeon. Keeping my gaze fixed on him, I enjoyed watching him stumble verbally, trying to rephrase what he had said, attempting to turn his words from the day before into something less than they had been. Perhaps he thought I was recording him. Possibly he was smart enough to worry about the damage I might do to his reputation if he carried out his threat. For whatever reason or reasons, he retreated, but only verbally and for a short period of time.

Smallwood and I had recently both taken part in a pretty spectacular operation in a neighboring country. After refusing to let me see the correspondence from headquarters outlining the op, which broke agency rules around operations preparedness, he'd offhandedly summarized the operation to me verbally. Not yet aware that his summary had been more misdirection than information, I showed up for our flight to the destination with all my photo gear, only later learning that the agent I was working with also required an elaborate disguise and false documents. Without my materials, I was forced to create a disguise and identifying papers out of thin air.

Tapping into my creative side, I asked the other CIA officers at the station to raid their wives' cosmetics shelves and then dug through the officers' own disguise kits. I devised a convincing disguise and then fabricated a fake identity card for our asset in his new disguise. To appear legit, the document needed an official stamp from the country we were in, which an officer at the local station arranged. Smallwood's apparent plan to sabotage my performance had failed. I had not.

When the operation was over, OTS sent a kudo cable and offered to put me in for an award. Smallwood declined their offer, saying that he would do that himself. Tellingly, I never did receive an award, not from him, and the stunning operational success was never mentioned in my yearly review. Praising and promoting me, a female Disguise officer, was beyond his capabilities.

Truthfully, this tour should have been my Waterloo, but even Tony's words of warning couldn't have prepared me for the realities of working with him. His dislike was visceral and unprofessional, bordering on childish. Smallwood seemed to have a personal vendetta against me. To him, an audio guy, the disciplines of disguise and certainly photography and manipulated documents were tangential, even unnecessary. The fact that I was a woman with all three of these specialties added insult to injury. His disdain for me oozed out of him, a slow drip of discord that routinely disrupted the morale of the office. It wasn't the first time I'd encountered a man who epitomized the label "too emotional to behave in a professional manner"; the first man of this kind had rolled a grenade at me. Smallwood was less brawny, preferring words and tactical maneuvers as his weapons of choice. More than once, his campaign to sabotage me placed me and others in danger. Determined to prevent that, I stayed alert, doubled down on my work, and ultimately developed a rather formidable backbone.

About halfway through my overseas assignment to the subcontinent, Rich, an old friend from headquarters, visited the station to gather information for the next promotion panel. John and I had always been fond of Rich. I was glad to see him and hoped to have some private time with him while he was there. However, Smallwood kept him so busy, during both office hours and the "guys only" evening events, that I had no possibility of sitting down with him one-on-one. This, of course, was Smallwood's plan. He knew that I would be only too happy to outline my current situation. As the week wore on and Smallwood's latest round of sabotage became clear to me, I recalled a TDY when another female, Judi, and I had been left out of the celebratory drinks the men had likely enjoyed after our encounter with a terrorist. My work spoke for itself, and back home in Washington I had considerable support. But if I didn't watch my back, men like Smallwood could still tarnish my reputation and risk putting my career on the eternal road to nowhere.

Unwilling to give up or give in, as the end of Rich's visit neared, I walked into the conference room during one of their promotion panel meetings, interrupting their deliberations, to hand Rich a note. I needed to speak with him alone, it said. At lunchtime we sat down, and I told him what was going on, reminding him that Smallwood controlled the communication channel, including sending private cables to headquarters about me that were untrue. I couldn't air my grievances because every communication would have to be signed and released by Smallwood himself. As I spoke, Rich sat back in his chair and listened. Then he leaned forward, putting his elbows on the table as he looked me straight in the eye.

"Go to the EEO people, Jonna," he advised me. "This is their bailiwick. File a complaint and take him on; go before their board. If your case has merit, they'll find in your favor."

I just looked at him, shocked and dispirited. He was letting me know I'd asked too much. He was washing his hands of me and the sticky situation I was in. Going to the EEO would be career suicide, I knew. Without clear, written proof to back up my claims, any deliberations would turn into a reputation-tarnishing game of "he said, she said" in a system designed by and for men. Even if I did win, my career would be over. I had seen that scenario play out with two female officers, both highly qualified technical professionals who won discrimination cases only to lose their careers. Neither was employed by the CIA anymore.

Smallwood's campaign to detonate my career would endure. All I had to do, I eventually realized, was survive this overseas tour with my reputation intact. The support I'd earned back at headquarters was considerable, but it, too, had its limits, as Rich had swiftly reminded me. There was no "old girls club" to protect me. This wasn't exclusive to the CIA, of course. I was rising to heights my mother never could have. The potential to succeed at these levels was finally real, but the climb upward was still littered with obfuscation and deceit.

At one point during my tour in the subcontinent I attended a party where a more senior CIA woman offered some unsolicited but useful advice. She advised me never to go into a man's office "just to chat" or vent, the way women often do with each other. Instead, present the problem you're having and propose a solution. Without one, men assume you're asking them to fix it, and that's more work for them. If you arrive with a solution in hand, they know you're prepared to do the work yourself. Once there's agreement around next steps, she added, leave their office; don't linger. It was sound advice that I've found useful in all parts of my life, but beneath her words was another equally important message—women still had to play by men's rules, not by our own. Fortunately, I soon discovered that I had one life raft back at headquarters: Tony Mendez. He became my mentor and bureaucratic muscle, helping to blunt Smallwood's maneuvers against me from his perch in Washington.

The standoff between Smallwood and me endured throughout the remainder of that tour; he kept trying to invent new ways to get rid of me, and I remained laser focused on watching my back and doing top-notch work. Ultimately, we both won: He succeeded at blocking my promotion in that round, and because I was unwilling to sacrifice my career, I did not file a discrimination suit. I survived with my reputation firmly in place, ultimately rising to levels that would have infuriated him.

Years later, the CIA's Glass Ceiling Study was published, and its contents perfectly mirrored my experience with Smallwood:

At a fundamental level, discomfort for women and minorities was caused by . . . harassment in the immediate work environment, which creates feelings of inferiority and powerlessness in those who are harassed. The feeling of powerlessness is exacerbated by employees' fear of creating additional problems for themselves should they use the EEO system and file a complaint. The general perception is that those who complain about such behavior are most likely creating career advancement problems for themselves.

There is a strong perception in the Agency's culture that it is not acceptable to complain. If an employee does complain, there is a perception that no real help is available and that such complaints are harmful to one's career.

Years after I worked for Smallwood, Rich told me that my reluctance to report my experiences to the EEO indicated to him that I had a weak case. That attitude was pervasive among men and as central to creating the problems women faced as men like Smallwood were.

CHAPTER 17

Parts Unknown

I had already traveled to Kathmandu, the so-called Roof of the World, many times. With Smallwood as my boss and so much travel in my agenda, I found it essential to sneak in whatever enjoyment I could manage, and Kathmandu always delivered. The city is one of the oldest continually inhabited places in the world, and it's situated alongside the tallest mountains on the planet. I'd long since discovered the perfect spot for viewing those breathtaking snow-topped peaks. It was easily reached by taxi, and the majesty of those mountains always inspired me.

With a new requirement in hand and eager to return, I went to Smallwood to obtain his signoff on the trip. Hoping to add extra value to my travel, I proposed flying a new route. Instead of flying directly to Kathmandu as I normally did, I would fly through Varanasi, India's holiest city and possibly its least-known international airport. Part of my overseas duties was to keep track of ports of entry into and out of the countries in our region of responsibility. A good part of our work involved crossing international borders, and the Graphics and Identity Transformation Group needed a continual flow of information on the idiosyncrasies of each airport. Varanasi had never made that list, and this trip would allow me to check out the logistical and procedural speed bumps involved if the airport was ever used in a quick exfiltration from India. I suggested to Smallwood that I take a short flight into the city and spend one night there before departing for Kathmandu the next day. It would be a quick in and out that would provide the agency with intel it didn't yet have. As Tony Mendez always said, "You can't do espionage from your armchair."

First Smallwood challenged me on whether Varanasi was an international airport. In another show of power and disrespect, he insisted on seeing proof of my claim as well as making a bet for a six-pack of beer that he was right and I was wrong. Silently fuming, I marched over to the local CIA station to retrieve the ten-pound Official Airline Guide. His doubt, in fact, *was* my point; nobody was using Varanasi for international flights. Very few people even knew the airport existed. That might make it an ideal spot to "disappear" a foreign agent. Once he was faced with proof that Varanasi was an international airport, he reluctantly signed off on my trip but insisted that I forfeit the six-pack of beer in return. He had lost our bet but secured the prize; given the circumstances, it seemed like a small price to pay.

Every religious Indian hopes to die in the holy city of Varanasi. Thousands travel there to live out their final days, many being wheeled around or carried by their families as they take their last breaths. According to Hindu lore, Varanasi is the gateway to salvation. Tens of thousands of widows, too, reside there; in Hindu culture, they are used goods, better off dead. With their short hair and white saris, they are hard to miss, although most live down narrow lanes, hidden in ashrams. Often the product of child marriages to older men, too many of these widows are in their twenties but abandoned by family and shunned by society the moment their elderly husbands die. For much of Indian history, the practice of sati, in which the wife of a deceased husband would climb up on the funeral pyre to be immolated alive with her departed spouse, remained prevalent. Sati was outlawed by the government in 1987, but the cultural stigma and devastating poverty forced upon these widows had outlived it.

While in Varanasi, I discovered that I'd done the one thing I continually advised my case officer brethren not to do: forgotten an extra battery for my camera. With my only battery dead, all I could do was pause and stare, capturing mental images I hoped to keep locked away inside my brain.

After spending a day exploring this holy city, I returned to the airport to depart. When I arrived at security, they asked to see my purse. The guard proceeded to remove every item in my bag, examining each one closely. My lipstick piqued their interest first as they twirled it up and then back down. My compact and mirror appeared equally delightful. Even my Cross pen seemed to fascinate. After my cigarette lighter was promptly handed around, I breathed a quiet sigh of relief; none of them had tried to light it. Curious about their wonderment, I stood back and watched as one then another of the guards examined my belongings with interest. The airport was emptier than most—most flights arrived and departed in the mornings—and these agents were bored. With so few Westerners coming and going from this airport, my presence was impossible to hide. I was an exotic traveler, a curiosity attracting attention.

The problem with using this route for an operation was immediately apparent. Seeing a Westerner was too memorable an experience for the airport staff. If the CIA ever tried to send or accompany a Russian fleeing from hostile pursuit, the airport staff would likely remember them. Seeing a Westerner in this airport was simply too rare for it to be safe, intel that gave my stop in Varanasi value.

———

Part of being a Disguise officer on overseas assignment was ensuring you always had the materials needed to do your job. This translated into periodic shopping expeditions. Being based in the subcontinent made it less costly and time-consuming to do that shopping in Hong Kong rather than the US or Europe. I would fly directly into the city's central Kai Tak Airport, approaching low and fast. Sitting in your seat, you were just above rooftop level in a densely populated city. You could see in the apartment windows that appeared to be a mere few feet below. Once the plane touched down on the runway it had only nine thousand or so feet to stop before we would slide into Kowloon Bay. Nobody slept through that landing.

When visiting, I was constantly aware of Hong Kong's Special Branch, the local intelligence service. It was a highly professional security apparatus numbering over a thousand officers on this relatively small piece of the British Commonwealth. Nobody wanted to tangle with them on their home turf or have one of our clandestine sources identified.

Hong Kong is a shopper's paradise, and an exceptional resource for custom and off-the-shelf hair goods. Many of the other tools I worked with—scissors, lab materials, and chemical compounds—were readily available there. Our wigmaker was a small company run by an amazing woman named Lin, who was also often contracted by headquarters directly. We would send her detailed patterns and specs for each design, and one week later we would receive our custom wigs, along with matching mustaches and beards when needed. She was an essential part of our supply chain, and visiting her office was a rare but welcome pleasure.

A ferry ride away from Kowloon Bay lay Tsim Sha Tsui, Hong Kong's shopping and nightlife district. There I might purchase three or four dozen pairs of eyeglasses. I needed so many and with such different yet specific prescriptions that I made sure to purchase them from multiple stores to avoid attracting too much attention. The frames typically needed to be American- or European-made, their lenses tinted in precisely this way or that.

These were not carefree shopping trips; every item had to meet specific criteria. After a couple of days of frantic shopping, standing cheek by jowl with noisy crowds in the day's oppressive heat, I would step into the sublimely air-conditioned lobby of the Intercontinental Hotel Hong Kong. After ordering an ice-cold martini, I would sit down to savor the lobby's singularly spectacular view of Victoria Harbor. These were always my favorite moments of my Hong Kong trips. At sunset, when the city lights glittered and the moon's reflection in Victoria Harbor shimmered just so, I would sip my martini and sink into the ethereal beauty all around me. For a few moments, the requirements of the operations I was working on would simply fall away, leaving me to my cocktail and a touch of lunar magic.

———

When an urgent clandestine photo operation came up, I was sent to the CIA station in Pakistan to handle sensitive darkroom work. This was a tightly compartmented activity in the region, and any intelligence product obtained from this highly visible op would go straight to the President of the United States.

A local asset was providing us with film from their highly classified files. The technology behind the operation was one of the CIA's proprietary subminiature film cameras. Only a few photo officers in the CIA could handle the film process for this operation.

Upon entering the station's photo lab, I quickly acquainted myself with the tools I would need. Slipping on the infrared goggles I would have to wear throughout the process, I then turned on the IR light source and positioned the tall, slender glass beakers in which this camera's tiny, unusual film would be developed. As I settled in to get started, I heard some loud noises outside the darkroom but ignored them, knowing I could not abandon this development process once it had begun. After removing the ultrathin, high-resolution Kodak film from its tiny metal cassette, which measured about one inch long, I checked the chemicals, ensuring they were mixed and at the proper temperature before continuing my work. Hearing more loud voices outside the darkened room, followed by other noises and more shouting, I went through the steps of the development process one at a time, ignoring the ruckus so I could concentrate on the delicate task at hand. As it grew quiet again, I proceeded through the final steps, producing a strip of film just over 3/16" wide and about 13 inches long that contained almost fifty black dots, each dot representing a photo of a full page of text.

Hoping the hardest part of the job was behind me, I quickly checked the images for text legibility and density before breathing a sigh of relief; the intelligence product was perfect. The agent who had taken these photos had risked his life to provide this film, a reality that always kept me focused and motivated to check and double-check each step.

Once I felt sure the finished product was viable, I stepped out of the darkroom, blinking to adjust my eyes to the blaring daylight. Surprised to find nobody in the office, I walked to the next office, but again, not a soul in sight. Continuing through the station, I proceeded into the hallway, but still, no one. Finally, I walked over to the windows that lined the hall, startled to see a long line of local armed Pakistani military officers guarding the adjacent facility from a sizable crowd of locals clamoring to get inside.

The American embassy was under siege. This was not the first time it had been attacked; in 1979 it had nearly been burned to the ground by a violent group of protestors. Four members of the embassy team were killed: two Americans and two Pakistani staff. To say that there was a very real sensitivity to security there would be putting it lightly. On this day, as soon as a clear threat had been established, all staff and personnel in the building had followed a carefully orchestrated, previously rehearsed protocol. The building I was in had also been evacuated; however, they had not factored into that plan the presence of a visitor who would be invisible and unable to leave at the time of an emergency.

Knowing I could not abandon the intelligence product, I returned to the darkroom and secured the film before heading down to the lobby. There I was met by two guards, who quickly found the CIA Security officer. He was mortified that I, his visitor, had been forgotten, literally left in the dark. It was a risk inherent in any field officer's job; safety was a goal, but never a guarantee.

———

Each TDY had its own set of goals and priorities, and invariably some included completing a hand carry, several of which included various brands of misadventure. One time after landing in a remote city in South Asia, I discovered that the bag I was scheduled to escort was being hauled across the tarmac with ten flats of chirping baby chickens stacked on top of it. I was lucky to spot it, catch up with it, and maintain control of it. Losing it would have been a firing offense!

On another trip to Latin America, we landed in a heavy downpour. I had difficulty in being the first off the plane, as required, and discovered that the bags were already on a baggage cart that was making its way from the plane to the airport terminal. I had to run to jump up onto the baggage cart. At the airport luggage entrance, the cart did not stop, heading directly through the rubber flaps. And so, bending down low in my stilettos to fit through that door with the flaps, I arrived inside the airport terminal via the luggage carousel. The officer who was to meet me had been delayed by the rain and arrived with great embarrassment. Standing on the carousel, dripping wet with my bag, I waved off his apologies, telling him that we now had another problem. I hadn't gone through immigration, which meant I was there illegally! The COS made a few calls to local officials and arranged for me to have a legal entry chop put into my passport. I departed without any fuss.

On a different trip to Kolkata, which I'd volunteered for thinking it would be a quick there and back, just after landing I was asked to wait with my bag in a long line at security. As people crowded around, growing increasingly restless, many began pushing. That was common in this region, where personal space wasn't a commonly recognized concept. For whatever reason on this day, irritated that I was in this line in the first place, I grew agitated and turned around to face the nearest woman pushing me.

"Stop pushing," I said, not bothering to mask my irritation. "And the rest of you, stop! We can't go any faster!" As soon as I turned back around, I froze, stunned by the realization that the woman I had just snapped at was petite, elderly, and wearing a white sari with a blue border. I'd just scolded Mother Teresa. Appalled, I was about to turn back around to apologize when I was approached by customs officers and escorted out of the line. On the other side of security, I noticed two young schoolgirls I had seen in line. I walked up to them.

"Did you see Mother Teresa?" I asked, hoping to find her and ask her to pardon my brusqueness.

"Oh yes, Auntie," the girls said, "Mother Teresa was taken to the VIP lounge." Knowing I couldn't simply march inside the VIP area uninvited, I thanked the girls and turned away, left to regret my rudeness for the rest of my life.

Later I relayed the story to a friend, who laughed. "She's there all the time," he told me. "You might keep your hand on your wallet if you see her," he added with a grin.

A frequent visitor to our American consulate, she was known for asking for donations to support her good works. I never did see her again, and since her canonization I've been haunted by my encounter with her in the Kolkata airport. To yell at a saint . . .

———

When my overseas tour ended, John and I began preparing to depart the subcontinent, feeling somewhat like veterans of this part of the world. From a geographic perspective, the Indian subcontinent consists of India, Pakistan, Nepal, Bhutan, Bangladesh, Sri Lanka, and the Maldives. From Dal Lake in the Himalayas to Peshawar in the west, Sri Lanka to the south, and Dhaka to the east, I had become well acquainted with this gigantic swath of land. Everything about this region—the buzzing of its cities, the enormity of its population, the religious and ethnic diversity of its people, its cuisine, and its landscape—had continued to fascinate me. All of it had helped to shape me, and in the process my perspective had shifted.

When I'd first arrived in central Europe years earlier, I'd had enormous admiration for Europeans, their mores, history, and cultures. By this point, however, I'd lived in East Asia and the subcontinent, too. I had loved all these experiences, but by now I could also feel a deeper appreciation taking root inside me. Throughout this last assignment in the subcontinent, where I'd wanted to live so badly and where I'd now stayed for several years, I'd been able to do a side-by-side comparison of two great democracies. While I always loved living overseas and was never in a hurry to get back home, I also found great comfort in knowing that the United States was where I would spend the bulk of my life.

America was no longer the default backdrop of my life, the stage set of my existence, but would always be a country I was proud to call my own. Seeing the differences between my native land and other parts of the world, I felt wholly dedicated to supporting the United States in every way I could.

CHAPTER 18

Disguise & CDC

When I finally returned to Langley—despite Smallwood's ongoing attempts to shorten my tour, as well as my career, I'd completed my full tour with my reputation intact—my female peers cheerfully greeted me as a survivor, which I was. In addition to Smallwood's long-standing reputation, word of his attempts to sabotage me had spread back at home. I gladly accepted their support. In the face of Smallwood's obstruction, I had gained valuable field experience, including disguising a Prime Minister among many others. I'd also grown wiser and more confident. Now, at long last, I could move on.

John and I had both had successful tours in the subcontinent, and we were both glad to be back home. During my time abroad, our office had moved nine miles down the George Washington Parkway, from our old historic buildings, which were directly across from the State Department, to the new CIA Headquarters campus at Langley. Initially, the Disguise labs were placed in a large bullpen in the basement level of our new building. We had no windows, no individual labs, no privacy or walls between us. This entirely open floor plan made it difficult for me to focus on clients when they paid us a visit. I struggled to concentrate, serially distracted by others' work.

Being surrounded by fellow Disguise officers had its advantages, though. No longer tied to one geographic region, my TDYs now took me to Africa and Latin America, among other places. Back in DC, working side by side with colleagues emphasized something I'd always known but had noticed less while working overseas: success nearly always required a team effort. Each op consisted of multiple smaller moments, all of them critical to the final outcome: training a foreign asset, adjusting technology, disguising a colleague, or performing a successful surveillance detection run. Every step of every operation mattered. And everyone played a role.

Even as this appreciation grew, I was aware of being the odd woman out. Prior to departing for my tour in the subcontinent in 1986, I had been in total-immersion disguise training for only a brief time. I must have looked like a dilettante to these seasoned disguise professionals, who had watched me speed through the learning curve too quickly and perhaps too casually. This was work they had been laboring over for years; I had zipped through it all in months. While my disguise skills and knowledge had been repeatedly field-tested abroad, I hadn't yet proven myself to the disguise careerists who were now my lab colleagues. It was time to buckle down and earn credibility here at home.

Unfortunately, the CIA overall wasn't having an easy time. Edward Lee Howard, a CIA officer, had betrayed us to the KGB, an incident that had led to a less favorable standing with Congress and the American voters. Budgets had been tightened, which had led to staff shortages and dampened morale. Fortunately, Tony Mendez was now Deputy Chief of the Graphics and Identity Transformation Group, which meant he oversaw the Disguise Branch along with its sister branch, Documents. When he approached me about working with him on the Moscow account, I knew it was a full-time job unto itself. However, with resources tight and an opportunity that was too good to pass up—I wanted to be in the middle of the fight, and Tony knew it—I agreed almost immediately. I would take over liaising duties for the Disguise Branch in denied-area operations. "Denied area" is an intelligence term describing an extremely hostile operational environment with heavy surveillance; in other words, among the hardest places on the planet for the CIA to run an operation.

Matching wits with Russia's KGB, East Germany's Stasi, Cuba's DGI, and China's MSS pushed us to a new level of problem-solving. Besides our regular working hours doing separate jobs, Tony and I began working long hours in the evening with the pipeliners, often married couples being trained for one of the most challenging but exciting cities for espionage—Moscow. Sending a man and woman abroad as a couple made them less conspicuous, especially in male-centric cultures like Russia. Tony and I would guide these new recruits through training simulations on the streets of Washington, DC, usually while being tailed by our OTS Special Surveillance Team. This often meant walking miles in a single evening as we honed their skills of observation and ability to complete a dead drop or put up a signal without attracting unwanted attention. By the time each couple was on the flight to Moscow, we'd worked with them extensively.

This comprehensive program required ongoing collaboration. Tony and I would sometimes meet for a walking lunch through Langley's trails, trading new ideas and tweaking our approach. We played off each other well. His creative mind fascinated me, and through our work, he became a sort of mentor to me. With him I felt respected and seen, free to share my thoughts and ideas.

One of our goals was to invent ways for our officers to slip away from surveillance when they knew they were being watched. It was important for them not to try to evade surveillance altogether, since that would effectively notify the enemy that their prying eyes had been detected, which could confirm that they were spies. We wanted to allow them to "disappear" using disguises that let them move around undetected for shorter periods of time. We first needed to assess conditions on the ground, and one of the locations on our radar was Cuba. Their intelligence service had been trained by Moscow, and since the government owned all the real estate and controlled everything, it was known as a place where there were eyes in the walls—cameras manned by live operators fixed on foreigners who dared to visit or reside there.

Upon landing in Cuba, officially I became Jennifer Calloway, a low-level American bureaucrat, there to determine cost of living for government employees being sent to work in Havana. Unofficially, I was there with John Winslow, one of our OTS surveillance guys, but per procedure we maintained a certain distance inside the airport. It was always best to get two individual accounts of arriving in a country rather than one.

My cover story was intentionally banal, designed to bore, yet almost as soon as I got off the plane, I noticed the long lens of a video camera aimed at me. Its operator, a man wearing a typical khaki uniform and black beret, mostly hid behind his long lens, but when he appeared again in the immigration area, his lens still pointed in my direction,

I knew we'd met the Cuban intelligence service, the DGI. Clearly my presence had been detected; what I didn't know was how.

Many years later I learned that Ana Belen Montes, an officer at the Defense Intelligence Agency, an intelligence agency of the Department of Defense, had spent years notifying the DGI of our officers' movements in Cuba. She later spent twenty years in prison and has only recently been released. She was likely the reason the DGI had been aware of our visit before we'd even landed in Havana. Despite my surveillance, I returned to DC with new ideas about how we could better prepare the pipeliners destined for Moscow.

One day back at headquarters, my new boss, Martin, called me into his office. I'd been chosen for an elite program designed to fast-track managers in the CIA's Directorate of Science and Technology. Being selected was an honor, he explained; only about fifteen people were chosen from thousands of candidates. This opportunity would mean stepping away from my job for three months to travel around the US visiting locations that supported the intelligence community.

Finally feeling settled in my new routine and work environment, I voiced my appreciation and my commitment to the work I was already doing. Could I pass on this training? Or at least postpone it? I'd been back in DC for about eighteen months and still felt that I needed to spend more time in Disguise establishing my bona fides and cementing important relationships. This was too important to pass up, Martin replied as he sat back, promptly overruling my resistance.

At the start of the Career Development Course (CDC) training, our class gathered inside a cluster of Tudor-style buildings that sat adjacent to gardens that had survived two world wars and the Great

Depression. Located in Virginia's famed Hunt Country, the site looked more like a country club than the girls' school it had once been.

I had attended numerous CIA trainings over the years, and for the first time, I wasn't one of only two or three women. Out of sixteen students, six of us were female. The women ranged from a classic Directorate of Operations officer to analysts to a member of the CIA's highly skilled and highly secret third-story unit. One woman was a Chinese linguist, another a chemist. The men, too, came from all parts of the CIA, representing an equally broad range of experience and skills. What we all shared was a sterling record of performance. We were all considered to be the top of our class and of our kind, destined for leadership.

From day one the instructors established a clear, unwavering expectation: this course would be life- and career-changing. We would see the broader picture of the intelligence community and learn about areas we might find interesting or challenging in the future. After completing this course, we would need to step out of our comparatively narrow career trajectories and broaden our horizons and overall contribution to the agency and its mission.

We began by introducing ourselves and our careers up to that point. Several of my fellow classmates seemed intrigued by my background in field work, as well as the extensive travel it had afforded me. I got the sense that my experience may have mirrored what they'd hoped for when they'd signed on the dotted line with the CIA. Meanwhile I was fascinated by another woman who'd taken part in clandestine-entry operations around the world. Almost immediately, the course felt like an auspicious new beginning, a leveling up that I hadn't been looking for, but that I suddenly yearned to explore.

Our travel over the following months took us on a zigzag tour of the United States. Early in our travels we flew to California, where we donned "clean suits" that looked like spacesuits to view the processes involved in building and launching the Space Shuttle. At the Los Alamos National Lab and the Trinity Bomb Site, where the first US nuclear bomb was tested, we got an impressive overview of the underground testing that was currently taking place.

Among our group, I was joined by several others who had a similar penchant for pranks, and together we had small brass plaques embossed with the CDC title and year of our class. We'd planned to distribute them strategically. After our first one was presented to the class Director at Los Alamos, he arranged to have it sent on an underground nuclear test. Our very first brass plaque was vaporized by a nuclear explosion! Excited to have such a spectacular beginning, we cheered.

In Miami we met "Fat Albert," a covert eye-in-the-sky balloon involved in America's drug interdiction program. During another trip to California, we saw the SR-71 Blackbird, which, leaking fuel in a dark hangar, looked like it was designed by Darth Vader. It's still the fastest plane in the world, and it eventually hosted our second plaque for three hours and twenty minutes at Mach 3.0. After inspecting the SR-71 we had lunch with the base commander and his staff. I was seated next to him and asked why there were no female pilots flying the SR-71. My question was followed by a mortifying silence at our table, where I was the sole female. There were difficulties arranging urination possibilities for female pilots, the commander explained. Stunned by the transparent flimsiness of his answer—adult diapers could have easily solved that problem—I looked at him, unable to think of an appropriate response. Several years later, in 1991 in fact, Marta Bohn-Meyer became the first female to fly the plane.

As we visited numerous sites, previewing technologies and capabilities most people never got to see, we had one-on-one conversations with pilots, leaders, and military commanders in many locations that remained inaccessible even to most of our CIA colleagues. During a tour at NASA in Florida, the bus driver turned to us out of the blue. "Who are you guys?" he inquired. "They don't even allow the families out here once the bird has been fueled." We were a private group being taken to the launchpad, up close and personal. The "bird" in question was the *Atlantis* Space Shuttle, ready to launch.

Before completing these tours, we made sure to find a home for our third plaque, which was surreptitiously attached underneath the conference table of a high-technology executive suite on the West Coast. I wonder if they ever found it.

After those three months away from my office, my colleagues and my regular workload indeed felt life-changing. I emerged from the CDC with a broader context in which to understand the CIA's mission and capabilities. Returning to Disguise Branch, I was humbled by the opportunity to preview this part of the agency's tremendous effort.

———

Not long after CDC, I was schooled in an entirely different way, this time by a much younger colleague, Pat. Her father had been a successful CIA officer, and she was one of a new breed in this relatively young organization: a second-generation employee. A chemist who worked in our Clandestine Communications Division laboratories, where I had worked previously, she had been the other female OTS officer in CDC.

One day we were walking down the hall laughing and chatting when we noticed Bill, one of our audio guys, approaching. He was a nice enough guy but had a bad habit of acting like a macho construction worker whenever pretty girls walked by. Like clockwork, he began his spiel as soon as we were close enough to hear him. "You two beautiful women," he said, "you know what I would like . . ."

"Bill," Pat said, never breaking stride as she glared straight at him, "FUCK . . . OFF!" It was the first time I'd heard this word used in "polite" office conversation. Startled by her ballsiness, I looked at Bill, whose face seemed temporarily frozen in shock.

I was impressed and considered myself duly mentored. We were highly respected officers who had earned our espionage stripes through years of hard work and dedication to our careers. It was high time that we, and all women at the agency, were treated with the respect we deserved. Up until that moment I'd thought of Bill's brand of everyday misogyny as a reflection of our broader culture at the time. I wasn't wrong about that, but I'd assumed it would change only once men changed. Hearing Pat's retort to his obviously inappropriate greeting opened my eyes to another possibility entirely—that younger women might force these cultural changes.

As Pat and I proceeded in the opposite direction from Bill, I felt sure he wouldn't bother Pat or me again. He never did.

———

Now aware that I was being groomed for more senior positions, I didn't hesitate to take advantage of my next training opportunity. Tony Mendez had created a new career trajectory for technical officers whereby you could be promoted without becoming a manager; my hope was to qualify for that. This next course was called Reality and Perception (RAP), and it was given to CIA women who were ascending to management positions. Developed for CIA women by a legendary CIA woman herself, Jinx Anderson, who had a degree in psychology, the goal was to teach us how to deal with the largely male infrastructure at the agency. It was billed as a hard and true look at men and how they handled professional women in their spheres of influence. Interestingly, the entire training was delivered, in two parts, by a Marine Corps Gunnery Sergeant whose name we never learned or used. We only called him "Sir."

Given the culture at the time, the course's premise made sense to me. It was (yet another) reflection of the male-centric culture that still dominated the CIA, as well as private industry and American culture overall. Unlike Pat's blatantly confrontational approach to Bill's inappropriate comment, the course focused more on helping women *fit in*, rather than setting out to change a culture that typically excused men's misogyny and discounted women's potential. I was grateful for the opportunities I was getting but continued to notice new and different ways the system worked against women, subtly pitting us as obstacles to our own success. It was not a coincidence that leadership was still largely reserved for men. The additional hurdles women faced were considerable, consistent, and no doubt for many women discouragingly immoveable. I was being given uncommon access; that wasn't the case for most women at the CIA.

On the first day of our RAP training about fifteen of us gathered around a long teak conference room table. The facilitator asked us to introduce ourselves. Then we went around the table another time, as instructed, describing ourselves, including weaknesses each of us wanted to address. Some claimed awkwardness, others mentioned a hesitation to confront a supervisor, or struggling when singled out for a mistake. I mentioned shyness and claustrophobia. Once the ice was broken, we learned that we would be traveling to Williamsburg, Virginia, where we would stay in a local motel for two weeks.

The next morning, we were startled awake at four thirty by pounding on our doors and a loud, male voice demanding that we assemble in the parking lot outside. It was still pitch black out and pouring rain, so we initially thought it was a joke. It was not. A Marine Corps Gunnery Sergeant was waiting for us out there in the maelstrom, and he was in a foul mood. His job, it appeared, was to instill some military discipline into this sorry group of wayward female intelligence professionals. After teaching us how to form an orderly line, he instructed us how to march—in the rain before sunrise, with him calling cadence throughout. This exercise continued every morning for the next two weeks in any weather.

The Gunny was short, cocky as a rooster, and wearing what he called his "lid" and what we called his "Smokey the Bear hat." We could never touch his lid, he told us, and he wasn't kidding. It was one of his most important rules. His other rules were: We were to wear no makeup. We were to wear no jewelry. No perfume. Just T-shirts and shorts. No distractions. Thankfully he let us keep our bras.

It soon became clear that he was trying to recreate Parris Island, the infamous Marine Corps training site in South Carolina, for the delicate flowers he assumed we were. He was there to school us in loyalty, honor, and integrity. Thanks to him—or so he assumed—we would finally learn about pushing ourselves beyond what we thought we were capable of. (Little did he know how much of that each of us had already done, simply to take our careers to this point.)

As he saw it, he would impart the *real* rules of success and leadership: men's rules. To him we were weak, like children, in need of discipline and rigor; as women, our characters were inherently lacking in these and other fundamental building blocks. The whole routine played out like a bad satire, but of course we had no cell phones to record the ridiculousness of it all.

One of his favorite tasks was giving us surprise challenges. At one point we were told to make him a chair out of pinecones, then to create electric light with a paper clip, some wire, a balloon, and a piece of cardboard. One of the women on my team was the daughter of the Deputy Director of my office, so we cheated and called him for advice. The winning team on that challenge received a personal lesson on playing five-card stud from the Gunny himself.

Outside male instructors also graced us with their presence, each detailing personal stories of working with professional women in their organizations and how they "dealt with" female problems. The Dean of the University at Sea program came in, along with very senior political and military officers, to tell us their stories, highlighting the fact that they were being paid to tell us *the unvarnished truth.* (Lucky us!) I still recall a tale from an Air Force general whose female line officer had a daughter who had been in a car accident. The girl suffered serious head injuries and brain injuries, and there was a real question about whether she would survive. The general sent a condolence card and flowers and gave the woman generous leave time. While she was away, he reassigned her to another position, a lateral assignment that was a dead end, career-wise. He said he knew that as a mom with a severely injured child, she would never be able to give her job the full-time attention that it required. He effectively truncated her career. "She never realized it," he said, clearly proud of his so-called leadership capabilities.

About a week into the course, I awoke before sunrise, feeling suddenly different, like I'd finally gotten it—the whole point of this course. After showering, I put my lipstick back on, added my hoop earrings and gold chain, and then spritzed myself with my favorite everyday scent, Chanel No. 5, before heading out in the dark to march at four thirty.

The Gunny never called me out on any of these rule-breaking choices. In fact, on our final march through the tourist-filled streets of

Williamsburg, in broad daylight, I was designated the leader, marching at the head of our formation and carrying the flag. On the last day we were quite proud of our ability to maneuver to his cadence without missing a beat. We were not the Rockettes, but we looked pretty good. I felt disappointed, though. Being at the front, I couldn't admire our precision. Had the Gunny sensed my disappointment, of course, he might have reassessed my worthiness. For him, aspiring to leadership *was* the point, the *only* point. That was success.

By the final day, we all felt we understood the men's point of view a little better. To this day I have the small gold number "6" pendant that the Gunny gave me when the class ended. It means "I've got your 6." *Your back.* I wear it, and my Wonder Woman solid-gold cuff bracelet from my sister Jennifer, the sister I lost to cancer, whenever it feels like I am going into battle.

Part of me wished I had taken this course before going overseas, before duking it out with Smallwood. I learned a lot about working with men, a subject that I had always felt, perhaps arrogantly, that I had covered. There were so many nuances, though, and there had never been a school to formalize them, to pass on the institutional kind of knowledge that can make a difference to women. While I was just one of many women in the RAP course, afterward I became more of a mentor. Advising the young women in my office came late to me. Thankfully, once I understood the importance of helping make a path, of laying a trail, I was able to pass along lessons to some of the young women I worked with.

Speak up and take control of your career. If you don't love what you do, change it. Be good at what you do, in fact, be the best, the one that others come to with questions. And don't fixate on the woman thing; use it. It may be your best friend. The soft power you can bring to this job is not to be undervalued. When you bring problems, also bring solutions.

All of that, I knew, was easier said than done.

—————

As soon as I'd secured my room key, the officer who'd accompanied me from the airport to my hotel turned to me. "There will be a car at the front entrance to the hotel at eight fifteen," he said. "They will wait for three minutes. If you don't show up during that time, they will leave, and you will have to call to arrange another pickup."

I looked at him incredulously. The streets in this city were so dangerous, he explained, that I would be transported to and from work each day on an irregular schedule by an armored car with a lead car and another following us, both full of men with guns. This was routine procedure for visitors working at our offices. There was reason to suspect that US officials were being targeted. The danger here was not from another intelligence service, I knew. It was from drug cartels.

I transited Mexico City briefly, after which I traveled farther south to Latin America. The CIA's Counter Terror Center had been formed in 1986, followed by the establishment of the Counter Narcotics Center in 1988. As the war on drugs became an increasingly urgent focus in certain parts of the world, disguise was becoming a form of body armor—critical and potentially lifesaving. In the war on drugs, the opposition was almost always armed and dangerous. There was unimaginable money involved. In some places just looking like a *nortamericano* could get you killed.

My requirement for this part of my trip was to make some of our men look less like gringos and more like locals. Darker hair and skin, even darker eyes (via plano contact lenses) did wonders once clothes and accessories and smokes were swapped out for local versions. It was not challenging work, but it would protect our colleagues from the very real and ever-present danger.

I should have done the same for myself.

I had been there for about a week and gotten more relaxed than I should have since that first armored car ride. Other than my daily commute, the city itself didn't seem that threatening. We ate out at restaurants and walked to the nearby kiosk to get whatever we needed. One evening—it was late but still relatively light out—I ran out of cigarettes. As I had done previously, I stepped out of the hotel and walked about a block to the local kiosk, bought a package of Marlboros, and began the short walk back to the hotel. Noticing a shortcut, I turned into a wide-open alley.

Bad idea.

As I began rounding a gradual curve, I saw a group of men, maybe a dozen, standing in a circle in front of me. A couple of them turned and looked at me. This is one of those moments the CIA trains you for: what to do (and not do) when you get into a potentially dangerous situation and there is no time to think. As I continued walking, my brain went into a frenzied overdrive. I knew I had two options. I could turn around and head back to where I came from, which would look suspicious in this highly charged town. That option, in fact, could invite a reaction, even incite violence. My other option was to walk through them.

My training instantaneously told me that I had to walk through them, which is what I did. As I got closer, they stopped talking and silently stepped back, stood aside, all of them watching my every step, my every move, studying my facial expressions. *Stay cool, be calm, keep walking.* I was scared shitless, but I kept going, making no noise and no eye contact, not a flinch or a grimace. Anything and everything could set these guys off.

As I passed by the line these men had formed in a matter of seconds, I knew they were likely armed, unlike me. I could also smell the beer on their breath. Once I reached the far end of the alley, I realized I was holding my breath and my eyes were tearing, but I made a point of keeping my pace steady. When I reached the sidewalk, about thirty feet from the entrance to my hotel, I finally exhaled.

Amazingly, miraculously, they had let me go. I, a highly trained and specialized CIA Disguise officer, had just offered myself as bait in this dangerous city, one of the drug capitals of the world. And I had done it in true face, without even a shred of disguise. The moment the hotel lobby door closed behind me, I fumbled with my cigarette package, pulling one out to light it. I stood there smoking, thinking about what could have just happened, all thanks to a few brief moments of overconfidence. I haven't done anything that foolish since.

Later it occurred to me that they might have wondered if I was Drug Enforcement Agency. They weren't worried about CIA, but they were very focused on who might be a DEA agent. But a female *gringo*? In the DEA? That surely didn't compute.

The next day, an American tourist, a female, was walking down a main street in that city when a guy on a motorcycle pulled up next to her and grabbed her large gold necklace. Refusing to let go, he dragged the owner down the busy street by her necklace, to her death.

Detecting unrest before it led to revolt had always been one of the CIA's goals. If certain groups within a regime were preparing to instigate revolution, the resulting instability and potential changes in power could have a significant impact on the agency's espionage efforts. Interestingly, during the years prior to 1990 a group *was* beginning to rebel, and yet again the impending upheaval was in the one place the agency's leadership still didn't think to look—inside its own walls. The senior leadership's long-standing disregard for CIA women was in fact the catalyst for these latest demands that women be heard.

This revolt became public in the early 1990s when Janine Brookner, a rare female Chief of Station, filed a claim of discrimination against the agency. A rising star among female officers in the covert operations directorate and one of the highest-ranking women in her division at the time, Brookner asserted that her male subordinates had made malicious accusations about her sexual behavior and drinking habits. This campaign against her had reportedly been launched by her male subordinates in 1992 after Brookner filed a complaint against her male Deputy Chief of Station in Latin America, who had beaten his wife and whose behavior, she contended, was affecting his work performance. Her case claimed that he and others in the CIA subsequently spread lies about her that had since sabotaged her reputation and her career. She charged that her experiences were symptomatic of "a pervasive culture of machismo and sexual discrimination receptive to accepting malicious and sexist allegations against women."

Brookner also pointed out that the promotion procedures within the agency were stacked against women. It wasn't until 1986, she emphasized, that the first woman reached the Senior Intelligence Service level. Although women made up 17 percent of the overall case officers, less than one half of 1 percent had been awarded an SIS rank. All of this was met with quiet but firm applause by women inside the agency, many of whom could relate to Brookner's story.

Women at the agency have always known that we make better operations officers. We are less threatening and, in many parts of the world, able to blend into the background precisely because we are dismissed as insignificant. This is hugely advantageous when, for example, making a clandestine meeting. Women also know how to flatter, are generally more observant, and tend to excel at reading body language. These are critical assets for ops officers, who must be able to walk into any environment and "get it" right away; it's a skill that can't be taught, and for many women, it doesn't need to be.

Brookner's case was covered in the media, which was how I learned about it. In 1994 the CIA settled, agreeing to pay Brookner $410,000 to resolve her complaint. It was a shamefully small amount of money. Seemingly determined to continue taking the agency to task on its bias against women, Brookner used the money to put herself through law school. After graduating, she specialized in representing women within the intelligence community. She never advertised, but they knew how to find her.

CHAPTER 19

Deputy Chief

Since taking the CDC training that had promised to expand my horizons, my responsibilities, experience, and dedication to my career had indeed shifted. I'd gained a deeper understanding of our efforts to counter Russia's influence in the world and been involved in an exfiltration in Latin America, among other ops. When I was suddenly promoted to Deputy Chief of Disguise, however, I was considerably less excited than expected. In fact, I initially resisted the promotion. I didn't thirst for leadership or victory, and I had no great desire to supervise or oversee staff or processes beyond those I was already handling. I wanted to continue doing what I loved—traveling the world, meeting with our foreign assets, and doing the hands-on work.

At OTS, which was composed of mostly men, this made me even more of an anomaly, an outlier for more reasons than gender. Everyone else seemed to be perpetually striving toward their next promotion. Oddly, my laissez-faire attitude around rising in the ranks worked like catnip on my superiors, who appeared to be intent, even insistent, on my ascent.

When I shared my predicament with John, he encouraged me to follow my instincts, even if voices inside me were telling me I didn't want a promotion that would take me away from hands-on work and into management. At the same time, I knew that turning down a move like this would be career suicide. Unwilling to risk my entire career to avoid a management role, I accepted the job. The upside was that this new role would pave the way for extensive travel to China and Russia, where I would be evaluating their current operational environments and helping to design disguise solutions for our officers on the street. That I was keen to do.

Now reporting directly to Martin, Chief of Disguise, I was charged with gathering a multitude of details for his budget proposals, staffing, and research and development. This was the part of management I abhorred. The budgeting and financial meetings proved especially onerous, but I jumped in anyway, reminding myself that the CIA had invested in me through extensive training over the years. This was another opportunity for me to give back.

Our disguise efforts spread across a wide variety of laboratories and studios, from Hollywood to New York City and down to Orlando, Florida. At the time we were focusing intently on mask technology. Our stunt-double masks were a strategy we'd learned from the magic community. The masks were cast from aluminum molds that John Chambers provided out of his studio, a small bungalow behind his home in Hollywood. They had proven to be a good solution for car meetings and low-light-level situations—any setting where a mask wouldn't be viewed up close, since these masks couldn't withstand close scrutiny.

We had also developed the semi-animated mask, or SAM, which was custom-made to create a natural appearance for each wearer. They were still always male—our officers remained predominantly men—and this mask ended just above the chin line, with the wearer's own lips being exposed. Except near the eyes and the lips, the material was fairly rigid, which meant it didn't animate well. We spent an inordinate amount of time trying to improve the animation. Unlike in Hollywood, we couldn't do a second take or rearrange the lighting. Our products had to perform perfectly when emerging from a dark parking garage, with no mirror. No mulligans.

Eventually it became apparent that we needed to focus on creating a new material that would animate better, which would allow the wearer to remain in disguise for longer periods of time without detection. The effort was ongoing, a group undertaking that couldn't have been accomplished without the talents of many, including Ben, our primary outside contractor, and Bill, whose exceptional talents with latex and pigments had made him our star. Together, they created a perfect team.

We would often perform tests in Georgetown to gauge how well a new mask technique or technology performed. One day I ventured out to test an early prototype of a new mask. This one turned me into a Black female. To soften the color transition immediately around my eyes, I wore medium-tinted glasses, but otherwise my disguise went on easily. I also wore a pair of gloves that went up to my elbows matching the pigment of the mask. The hair was longer than my own, casually styled. I thought I looked pretty good, which was something we never promised. I never met a woman who didn't want to improve her looks, but we seldom met that requirement in our labs.

The OTS Special Surveillance Team (SST) drove me to a residential area a few blocks east of Wisconsin Avenue. We synchronized our watches and confirmed the time and place of my pickup before they drove off. I was on my own, free to navigate this active, trendy waterfront neighborhood on foot. I had decided to wear a new pair of red stilettos. Together with a black dress and gold hoop earrings, I fit right into the neighborhood's hip crowd. Just as I was getting comfortable in my disguise, it started to rain. At first it was merely a drizzle. I considered opening the compact umbrella in my bag but ducked into a shop instead. Browsing the aisles of this men's clothing store, I was biding my time, hoping the rain would stop soon.

Before I'd even glanced at the store clerk, I could feel his eyes on me. Was he keeping a close eye on me because I looked like a Black woman? Or could he tell I was wearing a mask? Worried that my mask would be noticed, I slipped out the front door. By this time the rain was coming down faster and heavier, so I opened my umbrella as I stepped onto the sidewalk. I was almost at the corner of Wisconsin and M Streets when, as they say, the heavens opened. Rain began pouring down in sheets all around me, instantly fogging my glasses, making it impossible to see even a foot in front of me. Pausing under an awning, I removed my glasses to wipe them, knowing I couldn't duck into another shop. As I stood in the rain, slowly ruining my new shoes, a parking lot attendant across the street began waving. "Come on over here, honey!" he yelled, motioning me into his small parking lot attendant hut. I shook my head no. He stepped toward the curb, insisting. "My friends are on the way. They'll be here soon!" I replied, relieved when I noticed my SST guys in their van with the "Tony's Pizza" sign pulling up in front of me. Ruined, those high heels never saw the light of day again.

———

Nearly two decades into my intelligence career we were finally ready to launch a disguise concept that had been brewing inside my brain for years. At long last we would disguise a female officer and send her out in one of the highest-stakes cities in the world—Moscow. I felt confident it would be an effective strategy; the Russians didn't use women in the field, and I felt sure they wouldn't expect us to either. Still, this was a first and I wanted to be on the ground in Moscow when we rolled it out.

This was my inaugural trip as Deputy Chief, and I was looking forward to getting back out in the field. I could have easily sent one of our line Disguise officers to deal with the situation, but when I'd accepted the position, I'd insisted on remaining intimately involved with both our case officer customers and their specific problems. It was part of keeping my finger on the pulse of the operations directorate and providing solutions that would improve operations. I was a manager now, yes, but still a hands-on officer in many ways. That meant additional work, but it was work I still loved.

Before my departure, our SST team, which was composed of chemists, engineers, physicists, woodworkers, linguists, artists, and forensics experts, continued to plan and rehearse deception schemes on the streets of Washington, DC. To ensure our testing scenarios remained current, every case officer who returned from a Moscow assignment debriefed us on current techniques being deployed by the KGB.

We had always built our surveillance detection runs around the idea that we were being followed. However, most of our operational scenarios were based on the idea that the KGB would be responding to, not anticipating, us. Now it seemed that they had prior knowledge about our officers' destinations. We wondered if it wasn't due to their use of spy dust, a chemical compound named nitrophenyl pentadienal,

NPPD, or *metka* in Russian, which translated to "mark." Combined in a powder with luminol, it was a tagging material applied to car handles, doorknobs, and almost any other surface that our officers might touch. The KGB could then track anything else, or anyone else, that the CIA officers subsequently came in contact with. My hope was that by using a woman as our case officer, we would be able to address this problem. If the KGB overlooked the possibility that a woman could be a spy, they wouldn't bother to sprinkle the dust on surfaces she touched.

Putting a female officer out on the street also provided a multitude of disguise opportunities in a city like Moscow, which was crawling with suspicion. We might need to deceive a militia guy whose watchful eye was fixed on the embassy gate, blend in with an ethnically distinct population, or create a double of a known person. At other times, we might have to complete a dead drop or execute a car escape. Disguise could also be used to escape from *and then return to* the city's overwhelming daily surveillance. It was an active city where our officers always remained on high alert. Disguise was integral to our success there.

To ensure no parts of the female officer's disguise was tainted by spy dust, we used clothes and shoes that had been manufactured in Russia but never worn on Russian soil. We would disguise our officer as a babushka, one of the women who did janitorial work in the embassy every day. This disguise would give her an additional layer of invisibility, positioning her as someone without authority, special skills, or access.

The plan was for our disguised officer to join the throng of babushkas in the afternoon as they gathered to exit the building. They always left in a large group and went out the front gate together, past the militia man and onto the street. While their identification was checked as they entered the embassy grounds in the morning, there was no check as they departed. These women were regularly substituted and replaced, so a new face in the crowd was unlikely to draw attention from the other babushkas or from the militia. This would hopefully get our officer on the street without surveillance. If it worked, we intended to repeat this scenario over time.

When our officer walked back into the embassy hours later, she looked like the American she was, carrying a large bag from a hard currency shop as if she were just another employee returning from a shopping expedition. We were all slightly giddy with the success of our test run. We'd just added another weapon to our arsenal, and without arousing a drop of suspicion.

Sometime later we learned that spy dust wasn't our only enemy. A CIA officer named Aldrich Ames had been providing the Soviets with insider information about our Moscow operations. He was arrested in 1994, which was also when the KGB ceased to be able to anticipate our assets' every move in Moscow. Tragically, by that time most of our Soviet assets had been arrested and executed. Today Aldrich Ames is spending the rest of his life in prison. Somehow that doesn't seem sufficient, given the breadth and length of his treason and the number of Russian lives that were lost because of him.

———

As my professional life continued to thrum, my attention was unexpectedly diverted. In May 1989 I received a call; my dad had had a stroke. I flew home to Wichita, relieved to learn that he would survive. As he recovered, he seemed softer in his ways, a little less agitated. He was a different dad, a slightly more yielding one, but still dad. We thought the worst was over, but about a month later I got another call while on vacation in California with John. My oldest sister, Jennifer, who was forty-five years old, had collapsed one day while out picking up lunch for her boss and coworkers. Her doctors in Aspen had discovered a malignant brain tumor, a glioblastoma, that they deemed inoperable. Shocked and devastated by the news, I promptly flew to Aspen and accompanied her home to Wichita, where the doctors confirmed that, due to the location and nature of the tumor, surgery was out of the question.

Since she'd first left for Aspen at around twenty years old, we'd lived hundreds and then thousands of miles apart, sometimes separated by a vast ocean and at least one long airplane flight. She'd never married or had children, but she, too, had lived according to her own rules. Within the family, we'd always called her the blonde gypsy. She'd been one of the few family members who knew I was CIA, but most other details of my life I'd had to keep hidden. Throughout the years, however, we'd remained close. She was still an important part of who I was, and one of my very best friends in the world. She was too young to die, and I couldn't fathom my life without her.

Back in Wichita, determined to fight, I drove to Wesley Hospital, where I had once worked, and asked for the films and slides of her tumor. They opened the pathology lab, after hours, to provide the material. Once I had her records, I reached out to the Memorial Sloan Kettering Cancer Center in New York City. After examining Jennifer's slides and X-rays, they informed us that they did patient rounds on Tuesdays. Send us your sister, they said. We promptly packed for the trip, and I flew there with her in time to be seen that Tuesday. She was soon scheduled for surgery, which was later followed by a second procedure.

She was very sick, but she was still Jennifer. Before long, she'd charmed the hospital staff so well that they hung up a sign over the room number decal on her door. For the remainder of her stay, Room 132 became, simply, Jennifer's Room. Her neurosurgeon also got in the habit of buying her lunch at a restaurant across the street and bringing it to her. He'd sit in her room, and they'd eat and talk.

When she was released from Sloan Kettering, we flew her home to Wichita, where my parents could care for her. Even from a distance, I stayed involved in her care, ensuring she was getting the best medical treatment available and visiting as often as I could. They never could get the entire tumor, but the parts they did remove extended her life by about eighteen months. It was time we all cherished. None of us could imagine a world without her.

CHAPTER 20

Chief of Disguise

When the powers that be decided I should be elevated from Deputy Chief of Disguise to Chief of Disguise, I was once again the reluctant bride of our branch, being promoted when I still had no interest in overseeing the chaos intrinsic to that job. My dream of qualifying for promotion on technical merits alone required that I be truly exceptional in one specialty. I had three areas of expertise that I was very good at, but not exceptional; my only way up the ladder was through management.

The role was passed to me at a time of simultaneous expansion and contraction. Thanks in part to Tony Mendez's dedication when he was Chief of Disguise about ten years prior, Disguise had gained considerable visibility and respect within the agency. Once written off as a sort of mediocre wig and mustache dispensary, Disguise had since innovated lifesaving ways to protect officers in places like Russia, where disappearing was nearly impossible without the increasingly lifelike masks we were continually reinventing. Now that Disguise had proven its worth within the CIA, it, too, was promoted, transforming from a branch into a division. That meant greater visibility internally and a seat at the table, as an equal, with the other division Chiefs. There was also potential for a larger budget, although the agency was undergoing another protracted period of scrutiny from Congress and the American people. Budgets were tight—many were slashed and expenditures were closely watched, which meant hiring the new hands we desperately needed wasn't an option. Instead, we would have to do more with less.

Within the Disguise division, I faced additional hurdles. Several of my employees were relatively inexperienced and a couple of the older hands weren't interested in being team players. Our team was also geographically dispersed, with a full one-third of us located overseas. Requirements were growing and customer satisfaction needed attention. There was a lot of work to be done, and none of it would be easy. Nearly twenty years had passed since I'd first been told by David Chime in OTS Personnel that without a technical or engineering degree, my prospects within OTS were confined to the secretarial role. Yet here I was, stepping into leadership. Considerable challenges lay ahead of me—arguably the term "glass cliff" may have applied to my promotion to Chief of Disguise—but I felt honored and incredibly grateful. I had managed to stare down incredibly slim odds. I had been supported by most of my bosses, and the one who hadn't—here's looking at you, Smallwood—had made me sharper and better able to fend for myself. I would be the first person to hold the position when it became a full-fledged division. I certainly wasn't immune to the pressures of the job, but once I officially stepped into my new role, I relished the opportunity to contribute to the agency, and to the country I loved, at a higher level.

The honeymoon didn't last long, however. I soon began to hear rumblings that perhaps I'd benefited from favoritism. It was well known that Tony Mendez and I had worked together on the training programs for denied-area pipeliners. Tony was now reporting to Glen, who oversaw the Graphics and Identity Transformation Group, which we were part of. That meant Tony could have used his influence to help me. Knowing that I couldn't let those kinds of rumors fester, I went up one floor to visit Glen. Closing the door behind me, I told him what I'd been hearing. Before I could go any further, he shook his head. "Don't worry about it," he said. "I'm the one who nominated you for this job. If there's any question, I'll be sure that's made clear." I thanked him, relieved to hear the news myself.

Fairly soon after that meeting, the rumors seemed to die down. I was reminded of the criticism of Eloise Page, whom some had accused of moving "too fast." The men at the time attributed her rise to favoritism from her old boss, Bill Donovan, the original head of the OSS. Or perhaps I was targeted mainly because I was a woman heading up a technical division? It was certainly possible, and if so, undeniably hypocritical; throughout most of human history, men have unapologetically benefitted from the favoritism inherent in the "old boys club." However, in other ways I also understood why some may have initially felt ruffled by my promotion. I had spent recent years in Disguise but hadn't put in the lifelong commitment that many within the division had. I was a woman, yes, but I was also a relative newcomer. I would have to prove myself once again.

From day one it was clear that Disguise needed a salesperson who could tout its newest products within the agency and continue to increase awareness around their potential benefits. As I brainstormed creative ways to promote disguise to internal customers, I recalled the impact of my training experiences at the Farm, both as a student and as an instructor. Recognizing an important opportunity to spread awareness about disguise, I decided to do something that was virtually unheard of. Instead of filling my Deputy position, I assigned a disguise instructor to the Farm full-time. That would put a lot more work and pressure on me, but it would also likely lead to greater demand for disguise in the field, which would bode well for the division overall. Determined to do everything in my power to elevate disguise, I then zeroed in on two areas: improving our products and meeting customers' operational needs.

Almost immediately we set out to invent new ways for officers to transform into someone else instantly using a lifelike, animated mask they could slip on and off in almost any situation. The process began with an officer reclined in a barber's chair having their face, eyes, mouth, and ears completely covered with an alginate impressioning material, followed by a coating of plaster of paris. The staff who worked directly with customers were often female, whereas men still tended to dominate the technical side. Those tendencies reflected gender stereotypes—women acting as customer caretakers while the men worked with the technical "stuff"—yet the fact that more women were working in Disguise was progress unto itself. Both inside and outside of the CIA, women were still busy getting in the door. The work of infiltrating tech, science, and other typically "male" arenas—in government and the private sector—would inevitably fall to our children and grandchildren. Whether we liked it or not, women who'd managed to ascend in a technical field like me were still few and far between. Breaking down those barriers would take longer than I'd hoped.

To create more awareness around our customers' experience, I required all Disguise officers to undergo the mask impressioning process themselves. It was a detailed technique that could be traumatic, and I felt we all needed to better understand and empathize with our customer. The first time I had my own face impression made, I became so overwhelmed by my claustrophobia that I instinctively reached up and removed the material myself, ruining the attempt. Unwilling to be our department's failure story, I had them do it again and again until I could complete the process without hyperventilating or bolting from the chair. It was a humiliating but useful lesson.

As the frontline representative of Disguise, I was equally invested in finding creative ways to "sell" our innovations. When, in 1989, our fully animated ethnic- and gender-change mask was ready for the runway, I changed into a man's suit and donned the mask of a Black male, adding matching skintight latex gloves that were precisely painted with the same skin color, including veins. Exercises like this, if successful, provided proof of concept. Could I convincingly change my gender? What about skin color? Could I change both at the same time? I'd already disguised a Caucasian male field officer as an African student in a live operation, but this was new mask technology, and we were always testing new scenarios and pushing the proverbial envelope farther than we had previously.

Once I was in full disguise, I had someone accompany me to the office of Frank Anderson, our office Director. Upon entering, I was introduced as a new contractor. Nodding, I walked to his desk but said nothing, aware that I didn't sound like a man. Extending my hand, I shook his, which I knew would be the moment of my reveal. As soon as he felt the latex on my right hand, I peeled off the mask with my left. His eyes lit up as I transformed back into myself. He loved it and immediately insisted that we model it for the Director of Central Intelligence (that is, the Director of the CIA).

Judge William Webster.

A week later, as we entered Webster's suite of offices on the seventh floor of CIA Headquarters, I was more than a little nervous. Anderson had always been supportive of our disguise program, but I hadn't yet met Judge Webster, a former Director of the FBI. A tall, broad-shouldered executive, Anderson walked in first, followed by a 5'7" Black man wearing a suit and tie. "Sir," Frank said, "I would like to introduce you to . . ." His voice trailed off as I stuck out my hand. Once again wearing the latex gloves, I shook his hand, watching his face for a reaction.

As soon as I removed the full-face mask, Judge Webster's face lit up, briefly resembling that of an enthusiastic young boy. Astounded by the mask's ability to change ethnicity and gender, he and Frank decided then and there that we needed to show off this new capability to the President of the United States, George H. W. Bush.

I hesitated before speaking up but had to. "I don't think I can wear this to the White House," I said. "While it is lifelike and animates well, I can't walk or talk like a Black man. The Secret Service will take one look at me, ask me a question, and it will all be over."

Anderson and Judge Webster conceded my point; getting me through White House security as a Black man was too much of a stretch. We would present a female mask to the President, we decided. Promptly dismissed from their meeting, I returned to my office and the Disguise labs with a directive to prepare another mask. This wouldn't be just any mask, however. It would need to be the best mask we ever made.

Our first order of business was choosing a face. In the creation of every mask, the sculptor played a critical role. We specified gender, ethnicity, age range, sometimes even a specific identity, but ultimately the sculptor's hands shaped the final product. At this exact time one of our best sculptors, a young woman named Becky, was preparing to relocate to California. As my farewell gift and a bit of an inside joke, she decided to give me her face. She knew that her facial dimensions would easily fit over mine, and it was a perfect solution. Younger! Prettier! No woman in her right mind would turn that down.

A week later I walked into our contractor's lab and was immediately overwhelmed by the nauseating, pungent smell of burning rubber. The first version of my new face had melted into an ash heap. "Sorry about the fuckup," Ben, one of our contractor's most talented technicians, said. "The oven malfunctioned overnight, and I only discovered something was wrong when I arrived this morning." Dismayed, I nodded in agreement, silently hoping he'd be able to produce the next one quickly. Ben did, too, I knew. It was one of the few times I'd ever seen him lose his cool.

We were officially racing against the clock, and a lot was hinging on my meeting with the President. To put this new mask into production and into the field officers' hands, we needed additional funding. Getting support from the White House was critical, and the meeting date was fast approaching. Fortunately, we still had the mold that my "Becky" mask was made from. I promptly authorized overtime for Ben, who buckled down on crafting a new mask. Five days later he and I stood in our Disguise labs in Langley as he put the finishing touches on "Becky." The mask was a masterpiece. I sailed through the halls in disguise, popping in on several employees to show them the new product. I also modeled it for Frank Anderson, who applauded and whistled. Our meeting with the President was a go!

Two days later I waltzed into the White House, drafting through security behind Judge Webster. We got stuck, however, waiting in the President's outer office. His previous meeting was going long. John Sununu, Brent Scowcroft, Bob Gates, and others were already gathered there in a circle, laughing and cracking jokes. Judge Webster joined them as I tried to disappear into the woodwork, overcome by the usual paranoia I felt when wearing a mask publicly for the first time. This was a pretty high-level launch of a mask we'd never tested in the field, and I nervously chewed on the end of a pencil while pretending to study my notes. The delay seemed to stretch on endlessly. I worried that even if the mask didn't give me away, my nerves would. Confidence is everything, I reminded myself, impatiently awaiting the big moment.

When we were finally called to enter the Oval Office, we walked inside, where chairs were arranged in a horseshoe in front of the President's desk. Knowing that I would be the first one to speak, Judge Webster directed me to sit in the chair on the far right. As soon as we sat down, we went straight to business. Interestingly, this was always when my nerves abated. As soon as I could speak about a topic I knew a lot about, my jitters tended to fall away.

Webster promptly introduced me by my name and explained I was here to show the President some of the agency's new disguise capabilities. I pulled out the folder I'd brought, which contained photos of the President himself in disguise, from when he was Director of the CIA. After explaining that our disguise capabilities had improved immensely since his time at the agency, I began enumerating all the ways we could use them to evade the KGB. We could convincingly disguise an officer, even create a clone of an officer—a twin! We could change an officer's ethnicity or gender or "borrow" another person's identity if necessary.

This technology would change the way we were able to work against KGB harassment on the streets of Moscow.

As I was speaking, I noticed that the President was looking at the area by my feet, probably searching for a bag that contained our new disguises. When I told him I was wearing it, I raised a hand to begin removing it. Before I had touched my mask, he popped up from his chair. "Hold on. Just a minute, don't take it off yet," he said as he walked around me, peering at my face and neck. At this point, he knew I was wearing something fake. A false nose? A prosthesis? He tilted his head, no doubt looking for the seams of whatever I was wearing. When he seemed satisfied, I lifted my hand again and peeled off the mask.

I hadn't voted for the President, and I wasn't sure about his policies since he'd taken office, either. I'd always remarked that he seemed bored, flat, almost disinterested when I'd seen him on television. As soon as I took off my mask, though, his face came alive in a way I'd never witnessed. Suddenly charismatic and intensely curious, his eyes were almost sparkling as he asked me questions. At about the same moment, John Sununu, who had been working on his own notes during my presentation, looked up and over, almost falling out of his chair as soon as he saw my "new" (and true) face. While the President graced me with his attention, Dan Quayle tiptoed into the meeting, clearly not amused that he'd missed the moment of my big reveal. As my exchange with the President came to a close, it seemed clear we would get the support of the men in this room to roll out our new mask.

As I turned to leave—my presence at the remainder of the meeting was neither necessary nor sanctioned—I recalled the advice I'd received from Tony, who'd been in the Oval Office once himself. "Be sure to pay attention to the doors," he'd advised me, "especially the door you enter." One of the doors led to a hallway, one to a dining room, and another to a broom closet. Someone he knew had almost exited into the broom closet. I was hoping not to make that mistake, especially since I was only the third OTS officer ever to have been inside the Oval.

Once I'd successfully returned to the President's outer office, I was delighted to find a group of puppies, recently born to Millie, the Bushes' dog. Immediately seduced, I sank to my knees and began playing with them as the White House photographer exited the Oval Office and approached me from behind. She'd been in the meeting taking pictures, and as soon as I'd seen her in there, the photographer in me had mused silently, *Wouldn't that be a great job* . . . Now standing behind me in the outer office, she leaned down. "Excuse me," she said, "what did you do in there?"

"I thought you were taking pictures of it," I replied, still having fun with the pups.

"Well, I did, but what was that?"

"I can't talk about it," I said after a brief pause. "It's classified." I never sought out copies of those pictures, and I didn't receive them until ten years later. When I did, I wondered if my response had offended her. My package included a photograph of me wearing the mask and one of me talking while holding the mask in front of me, except the mask is airbrushed out of the second photo. That's the one I have hanging in my office. It looks like I'm lecturing the President, with my hand in the air, and when friends look at it and ask what I'm saying to him, I always reply the same way: "I can't talk about it," I tell them. "It's classified."

CHAPTER 21

The Heart of the Matter

By the end of my first year as Chief of Disguise, I'd lost 181 hours of paid leave. The job had proven so all-consuming that I'd skipped more than three weeks of paid time off that I could have spent refueling my tank. Those missed opportunities to refresh my psyche were perhaps a karmic distress signal I might have done well to heed earlier. During a recent work trip to China, my mind, heart, and soul had reconnected to each other, and what came out of that wasn't your typical vacation. A lot had changed during the four plus years since John and I had returned to Washington, DC, from the subcontinent. Still more needed to change.

During our tours abroad, including our most recent one in the sub-continent, John and I had spent long expanses of time traveling to different places for our respective jobs. We were accustomed to spending days, sometimes weeks, apart. When we were both at home we shared the same groups of friends, as well as a love of travel and exploration. But once we returned to our assignments in Washington, our lives had begun to split apart, at first slowly, but then in increasingly noticeable ways. We'd settled in a suburb near DC and built ourselves a lovely house that was great for entertaining, but somewhat tellingly, we'd done little to no hosting there. He spent his free time watching football I didn't care about, and I, reading books or attending cultural events that didn't interest him. He had his friends in Security, and I had mine in OTS. We both received regular invitations to events, dinners, and casual outings that the other had no interest in attending. This was hardly surprising for two introverts, but this pattern, which had played out during our previous home tour years earlier, felt different this time, more permanent.

Our marriage was still floating along, but many of the threads that had once connected us to each other were fraying before our eyes. Our lives were playing out in tandem, but not necessarily together, and we'd become more like indifferent siblings coexisting in a shared space than spouses building a life together. We didn't fight any more often than the typical couple, but the distance between us was widening. More than once we'd calmly acknowledged to each other that our union wasn't as enjoyable as it once had been. We'd also begun to casually "joke" about what we'd each take with us if we divorced. When we'd buy a new stereo, for example, one of us might "joke" that it was on "my" list. We didn't argue about it, but we both knew the growing chasm between us was becoming problematic.

Since accepting responsibility for denied-area operations two years prior, Tony Mendez and I had also developed an important working relationship. Through our many long nights walking the streets of DC training new recruits, we'd grown to trust, understand, and appreciate each other. We shared a commitment to the agency, to the work we were doing, and to the technology and artistry that it all required. About a week before a joint trip to Los Angeles, we'd had a long conversation about work and life that had ended with him giving me a friendly hug. Tony's first wife, Karen, had died years earlier, and he seemed to be contemplating the fixed yet changing nature of love. His hug had taken me by surprise, but by then it also felt somewhat natural. Our connection had always been professional, but we'd also grown closer in a gradual, organic way. Slowly but surely, over the course of our years working together, he'd become my friend, and I'd become his.

After that trip to Los Angeles, Tony and I had also spent a day in San Francisco, where he was visiting his brother and I was making a brief stop before flying to China. He knew that city at a level I had not imagined, and he spent the day showing me highlights like the Golden Gate Bridge as well as the ins and outs of the city's many neighborhoods. The next morning, he drove me to LAX in the convertible I'd rented, and when I got out of the car, our connection felt changed in ways that surprised me to some degree, but not entirely.

During the following weeks I spent in China, I navigated the busy streets photographing scenes that would help us disguise officers in Beijing and elsewhere on the mainland. Throughout that time, I found myself dwelling on many of the moments Tony and I had shared together. At night I made my way through a copy of *The Art of War* that he'd given me, and as the days piled onto one another, I began to admit that something significant had changed. I find travel has that effect on me at times, allowing me to clear away the everyday clatter of life and listen to that voice deep inside. It was clear that my feelings for Tony had expanded beyond the professional realm. Upon arriving back home in Washington, I knew what I had to do.

At the time, I was driving the only car I've ever truly loved. It was a Porsche 928 that an old friend had driven into my driveway a couple of years earlier. It was the most beautiful car I'd ever seen, like a siren seducing me. I told my friend then to call me if he ever wanted to sell it, and eventually he did. By the time I flew home from that trip to China, my 928 and I had logged some miles together already, but some of our more significant rides still lay ahead.

On my first night home from Beijing, I sat down with John and confessed, gently, that I hadn't missed him, hadn't even thought of him once during my long trip away. He wasn't surprised, nor was I, but we both knew it wasn't right or fair to either one of us. The next morning, I rolled up a few of the rugs I'd collected, packed a bunch of my books and clothes, stuffed them into my four-wheeled little beauty, and drove her about seven miles down the road to Shenanigan's Bar in Sterling, Virginia. I'd never been there in my life, but I got out of my 928, walked inside, found a phone, and called Tony.

"I just left John," I said, knowing that Tony and I had never had a "what's next" conversation or discussed any steps I might take in my marriage.

"I'll be right there," Tony replied without missing a beat. A dedicated artist in his "off" hours, he promptly put down the paintbrush he'd been using. Without even washing it off, he left his forty-acre property to come meet me. That night, he told his three adult children, who were staying with him at the time, to set out another place at the dinner table. There would be a guest in the house.

During the days and weeks that followed, his children enjoyed watching us navigate our new arrangement, bemusedly tsk-tsking us as they critiqued our "tradecraft" in concealing our burgeoning relationship. The arrangement was even more fraught because Tony's children were friendly with several younger CIA employees, who regularly frequented the house, which meant that I had to conceal my presence, including my car, at nearly all times. Fortunately, Tony was driving a Nissan Z—I always joked that his midlife crisis was way longer than mine—and had a car cover that we could drape over my 928.

Eventually, the situation became awkward enough that I rented a very cool, historic townhouse with a split staircase in Frederick, Maryland, where I then pretended to live. The landlord was a great guy, so Tony and I repainted the place simply to help him out.

"Are you ever going to bring furniture in?" the landlord asked me one day, many weeks after I'd signed a lease. I smiled and said something about not wanting to make any snap decisions.

Within a month after I left John, he and I were at an attorney's office. At the end of our twenty-three-year marriage, our split was as amicable as it could be, but the news hit my family hard. My sisters were especially heartbroken. Heidi, my youngest sister, had lived with us during our time in Frankfurt. A high school senior at the International School back then, she'd grown to love John as a kind of paternal protector. When she'd occasionally missed her curfew, he would question her about where she'd been and why. When she learned that John was a Security officer at the CIA, she remarked how serious his demeanor had always been during those conversations. "That was the polygraph officer in him, the professional part of him you weren't supposed to meet," I explained. Holly, too, had grown close to John over the years, and as they all digested the shock of my news, Jennifer continued to fade, her brain tumor once again taking hold.

As we navigated the heartbreak and turmoil of her illness, Tony was fast becoming an integral part of my life and our family. Our romance was enchanting, but the weight of the loss my family and I knew was coming cast a shadow that was impossible to ignore. A few years earlier, before she'd gotten sick, I'd written Jennifer about this "great guy" I thought she should meet. "I think you'd like him," I'd told her. "His name is Tony Mendez." Now I was visiting her with him at my side.

As Jennifer's energy and lucidity seeped out of her, she expressed a desire to contribute to the causes Tony and I had spent decades supporting through our work. "I'm a ticking time bomb," she would say. "Tell the CIA I'm here. They can parachute me in, anywhere in the world." She was only half kidding.

We were in New York with Jennifer following her second surgery. Driving home, I almost collapsed in the passenger seat, erupting in a flow of tears that was hard to stop. Tony, without a word, pulled off the New Jersey Turnpike and into the parking lot of a liquor store, emerging with a huge cup of ice and a bottle of bourbon. He poured a gigantic drink for me, gave me a long, long hug, and pulled back onto the road. I don't really remember the rest of the drive . . .

———

Soon after I began living at his house, Tony asked to see my photographs. I was surprised, and a bit hesitant. John had never expressed any interest in them, and I wasn't sure if they'd have any appeal. Still, I unearthed the large collection of photos I'd taken through all my years of travel. Tony loved them, and promptly asked if I'd be interested in selling any at his art shows. The thought had never occurred to me, but it sounded like fun, so I agreed. That was how so much of our life would unfold—naturally, through moments that felt like serendipity and turned into much more. With Tony, I felt like a fuller, truer version of myself, a fellow creative and an espionage professional, a woman and a Chief of Disguise, a lifelong traveler and a bookworm. We connected on a level that can't be explained by any one characteristic or shared interest. We were soulmates, and we felt it.

As my relationship with Tony became increasingly serious, we knew something needed to change. We were going to great lengths to hide our union, but inside of OTS I was still in his chain of command, which meant that one of us would have to move. Tony began looking for alternate positions that would constitute lateral moves within the agency. However, after so many years working inside OTS, his experience and skills were too specific to translate into equivalent positions inside other offices or directorates. When the agency began downsizing in 1990, it unexpectedly announced that employees who were at least fifty years old and who met a long list of criteria could retire earlier than planned with full benefits. Tony was exactly fifty years old and one of the relatively few who qualified. Recognizing what a beneficial offer it was, he decided it was time to leave.

There had been a time when the average OTS employee would die eighteen months after retiring. Tony had always said that working at OTS was like "drinking from a fire hose" and retiring like "jumping off a moving train." The job wasn't a career; it was an entire lifestyle that consumed you, body, mind, and soul. Most of us had few, if any, friends or community outside of the agency, and our work was our passion. Without those elements, perhaps those who retired simply lost the will to live and their bodies soon followed suit.

When the opportunity for Tony to retire arrived out of the blue, it came with a caveat—a two-week window during which those who qualified could accept the offer or let it pass them by, perhaps never to return. When I voiced my concern that if our relationship didn't last and he'd given up his career, he would hate me forever, he was unfazed. "You have more runway ahead of you," he explained to justify why he should retire rather than I.

Fortunately, Tony's retirement wouldn't be like most at OTS. His secondary career as an artist had been patiently waiting in the wings for a long time, and he was ready to bring it to center stage. His three passions had been espionage, art, and golf; he would now have two of those three, which he knew would still constitute a rich and rewarding life, especially, he said, with me at his side. At fifty years old he would embark on an entirely new chapter. Instead of waking up early to drive to DC, he began waking up at the same hour to take his morning coffee to his studio on the forty acres where he'd lived for years, and which I, too, now called home.

Still committed to my career, I joked that I would stay at the agency until they dragged me out in my heels. However, some parts of my weekly routine would change in ways that were less enjoyable. The nearly hour-long commute from his house to my office was now a trip I made alone, rather than with Tony. Upon arriving home each evening, I also initially discovered that he and his adult kids seemed to be waiting for my arrival. Realizing that they were thinking I might arrive home and cook dinner, I promptly announced that I wouldn't be cooking. It was a promise I kept for the following year. After working a full day, I needed about a half hour by myself, preferably with a drink and newspaper, to decompress, I explained to Tony, after which I would be ready to join the group. Dinner would have to be made by someone else.

That autumn, as Tony and I were driving home to our house in the woods on a beautiful evening, proceeding down a small country road sandwiched by pumpkin fields, he suddenly pulled over. On each side of the road were dozens of carved pumpkins, each one lit from within. As I looked out the window, enjoying the magic of the twinkling jack-o'-lanterns around us, Tony proposed. I think we both knew my answer before I'd even spoken. Our lives had fused quickly and seamlessly, and our love for one another was undeniable. Truthfully, I had known for months that I was going to marry him.

That night we celebrated over a fabulous dinner at the South Mountain Inn feeling the many promises of our new life together expanding before us. At one point he asked me what worried me. I didn't want to be bored, I said. "That won't be a problem," he replied immediately with a long, slow look. I didn't yet know what he meant, but his confidence was comforting. Over the many years that followed, I would learn that it was well-founded, too.

On December 23, 1990, nineteen years to the day that Tony and I had first met at the CIA station Christmas party in the Far East, he met me in Berlin on my way back from an operational trip to Moscow. Early the next morning we walked to Brandenburg Gate, where in November of the year before, we, along with the rest of the free world, had watched the first breach in the wall. The West Germans had danced on the wall during that first night, holding umbrellas to protect themselves from the pressure washers the East Germans were aiming at them. Watching the wall forcibly crumble before our eyes had felt surreal, an event we'd all hoped for but never imagined happening. As

Tony and I recalled our memories of those momentous days, we bought memorabilia from starving Russian Red Army members, who were selling their uniforms and medals for the price of a German breakfast. I remembered visiting East Berlin over the years and marveling at the unrestored, crumbling infrastructure left from the war, at the lack of creature comforts and the absence of commercial activity. It had been left behind in a time warp. Now that would all change, and in some small way we had helped to make it possible.

Soon after, we took a deep breath and stepped through the wall, still amazed that we could safely walk down the east side. Arriving at Checkpoint Charlie, or Checkpoint C, which had been the best-known crossing point between East and West Berlin since the Berlin Wall was erected in 1961, we marveled at the new symbolism of this spot that had played an iconic role in the Cold War. Later that day we drove to Munich and spent Christmas Eve midnight mass surrounded by the cacophony of bells from the cathedrals on the central square of the city. That night we stayed at an exquisite and cozy hotel, a renovated mill inside of the Englischer Garten, that became a favorite place we returned to over the years.

On July 13, 1991, our wedding day, Tony and I gathered in an old redbrick church in the Blue Ridge Mountains of Maryland with exactly one hundred friends and former colleagues. It was a beautiful day, and my mother and sister Heidi, neither of whom had been able to attend my first wedding, traveled to the area to join us. Jennifer had also come all that way, but on the morning of the wedding was too sick to leave the hotel room. My dear mother, who must have felt terribly conflicted, came to the ceremony before returning to the hotel to care for her. The shadow of Jennifer's illness was palpable, but we all made it as happy a day as possible.

After the ceremony we were to host our one hundred guests to a sit-down dinner at our show pavilion. Led by our dapper female driver, who wore a tuxedo and pink cummerbund, Tony and I rode home in a horse-drawn carriage, waving to our guests as they sped by in their cars and we sipped Russian champagne that Tony had procured years before. When we were nearly to the house, however, our progress ground to a halt. To get to the property you had to cross a narrow bridge, about ten feet wide, that spanned Israel Creek. When we got to that point, our magnificent draft horse, Chessie, stopped short and refused to continue. Betty, the pastor's wife, who was riding in the car behind us, jumped out of their car, insisting that she could fix this. Quickly slipping off the half-slip she was wearing underneath her dress, she slid it over the horse's head, expecting that his inability to see the bridge ahead of him would do the trick. Chessie, however, didn't fall for the deception. I then jumped out of our carriage, hoping to direct "traffic," but again, Chessie had no intention of falling for such trickery.

Finally, Tony asked his son Toby and some guests to fetch moving blankets from the garage at the house. They then covered the bridge, the surface of which was made of a kind of see-through metal mesh, with blankets. After they broke off tree branches and laid them on both sides of the blankets, Chessie finally decided to comply, dutifully carrying us over the bridge and to our wedding reception. A new life I'd only begun to imagine during my trip to China the year before was officially beginning, but our biggest surprises lay ahead.

CHAPTER 22

Life's Best Surprises

About a month after becoming Mrs. Tony Mendez, I was scheduled to attend a leadership training in San Diego, California, for Directorate of Science and Technology managers, many of
whom were from OTS. During the weeks leading up to the course
we'd been overwhelmed by course preparation paperwork. From
all sides—supervisors above us, peers alongside us, and employees
reporting to us—our performance was subjected to a 360-degree
evaluation that would inform our training. All the feedback was provided under the cover of secrecy, in the hope that everyone would
share honestly and openly.

Almost as soon as we began the training, we learned new and raw information about how we were perceived. We were also given psychological test results. This onslaught of data and feedback proved painful. We all heard frank appraisals from our colleagues, both good and bad. I felt somewhat dismayed to learn that my peers and supervisors thought better of my management style than my employees, who felt I wasn't spending enough time or energy supporting and training them. It was indispensably useful and humbling feedback that helped me reevaluate how to approach my job as Chief.

Early on, we were asked to line up in a long row across the classroom in an order that was neither alphabetical nor by office. In fact, the order initially made no sense to me. Once we were all in place, the instructors explained that our position in the row illuminated our personality type. Larry, as the most extroverted, was at the far-left end of the row, and on the opposite end was our most introverted. I was amazed to find myself standing fourth from the right, knee deep among the introverts. I objected to this positioning privately with my counselor, wondering how I could be placed there when my forte was public speaking and dealing with high-level domestic and international government officials, as well as working with all kinds of people around the world. My communication skills were strong. I could talk to anybody, and I did, often.

My counselor agreed with each of my points. Then he asked me a series of questions. "What do you do at the end of a day that has not gone well?" he began. "How do you react to a personal setback? Do you call your five best friends to hash it over? Or do you grab a trowel and go into your garden and dig?"

"Dig," I responded. I didn't have five best friends. My counselor just smiled. By the end of our time in San Diego, I'd had a uniquely eye-opening opportunity to look at myself from multiple different perspectives.

On the last day of the course, we attended a celebratory dinner for our entire class, which was made up of three or so women and maybe seventeen men. Overwhelmingly the vote was that we would head down the street to the nearest club, a strip club, for a few drinks. Without hesitation I joined the guys, many of whom were my colleagues and some now friends too. We settled at a long table and watched some rather beautiful women perform for an almost entirely male audience. I briefly flashed back to the *Caligula* episode years earlier but was too caught up in the conversation, banter, and drinks to think twice.

Decades earlier, I had entered the CIA as a quiet young woman with a longing to do something that mattered. By this point, a lot had changed. I had spent my career transforming others through disguise and other methods, and in the process, I, too, had been transformed. I no longer needed to become one of the guys; I was their equal now, a respected expert in my field and a manager among peers. Without anything to prove, I didn't feel bothered by the mostly male crowd or all-female strippers in my midst. I had proven my mettle—to others and to myself—and I no longer needed to question my worth. The odds had been steep, but I'd made it here, and that milestone deserved celebration.

The CIA, and the country it was protecting, was still steeped in misogyny. In ways that were sometimes overt and sometimes subtler, men were still testing us as women leaders, often thoughtlessly or from some vague curiosity about if we would resort to emotional displays that might later discredit us. I was a veteran by now, and I knew better than to take that bait. Getting more women into leadership was the goal and the only way that true change would occur. We, as women, were playing the long game, making as much incremental progress as we could in each generation. If that meant enduring another strip club, then I was ready and willing. My hope was that future generations of women would get more say than I had, and that their daughters would then have more sway than they'd had. Each generation had its role to play, and I had worked hard to play mine and had no intention of stopping now.

———

During my drive home one day, I was doing about 80 mph on a Maryland interstate, half-heartedly listening to NPR. I was barefoot; my stilettos were lying on the passenger seat, and I was looking forward to exiting the interstate and pulling into a nearby McDonald's for a soda when the radio program caught my attention. On the air two women were discussing a new book about the role of women in American history. The interviewer paused as the other woman, a commentator, mentioned that there was one person in the book that she *certainly* wouldn't want to introduce her daughter to. Who was that? the interviewer inquired. "That Civil War female spy," she replied primly. Women who did that kind of work were unfit for polite society, she added.

Feeling the heat rushing to my cheeks, I swerved over to the shoulder, narrowly avoiding a rear-end collision as the evening rush hour traffic thundered by. "No Stopping/Standing on Shoulder Except for Emergency," the sign in front of me stated as I slammed my gearshift into park. Well, this *was* an emergency. I pulled out my cell phone, waiting for the invitation for listeners to call the station. When it came, I punched the number into my Nokia and pasted it to my ear, impatiently navigating the station's cascading telephone directory as I wrestled off my suit jacket. Finally, I was confronted not with a person but with a beep. I delivered my message at full tilt:

"Thousands of women are going to be offended by your words," I began, "and the female professionals in espionage are going to be writing letters to the editor around the country protesting your characterization of female spies." I paused for breath, fixing a concerned eye on my rearview mirror. "Women have been performing patriotically and professionally in the field of intelligence for centuries. Women have been some of the best spies this nation has ever seen, and they have done their work without public acclaim and with little else to show for it. They should be honored, not insulted."

When I finally pulled up to the garage at the end of our unpaved, mile-long road, Tony met me outside. "How was your day?" he asked. "My day was great," I replied, still furious, "until I turned on the radio." Even now I bristle when I remember that misogynistic slight. As a woman I'd faced plenty of resistance within the agency. Over decades, I'd been condescended to and excluded by male intelligence officers and then judged and slighted. Throughout, however, I'd felt a certain solidarity with women, including the masses I'd never meet outside the agency. But to be spurned by women civilians? There were days when my community felt like the smallest club in the world.

Some months later, just as I was settling into my solo commute, I raced to Wichita as Jennifer's cancer finally overtook her. She died at our home in Wichita, where my mother had cared for her until the end. We were grateful for the additional months that her surgeries had given her and us, but no less heartbroken to lose the sister, daughter, and friend we all loved. She never did serve the CIA, but her light still shines brightly for those of us who knew and loved her.

One of the hardest parts of losing her was that she never did learn the biggest and best surprise of this phase of my life. From our early days as a couple Tony and I had mused more than once about the children we could have had. In so many ways we felt like twentysomethings building an entirely new life together, but we were realists, too, and I was forty-seven years old. Then one day I got a copy of the latest *Time* magazine. The cover showed a picture of a tree whose leaves were on the ground and a bold headline about menopause. It seemed like a sad and borderline insulting commentary on me and all women of a "certain age." When I brought the issue to Tony, he looked at it, and then at me.

"You're pregnant," he said with a big smile.

"You're crazy," I replied. "I'm forty-seven."

He was undeterred, so I called a close friend, who said she agreed with Tony. Neither one could explain why they each felt so sure; they just knew, they said. Surprised by their joint conviction, I drove to CVS, got the test, and waited patiently. When we got the news that the test was positive, I was stunned, and we were overjoyed. Soon afterward I went to my OB/GYN and told him I'd make him famous.

"You're not the oldest," he replied immediately, "so I doubt that." He gave me a clean bill of health and praised me for my years of running, which he said probably explained my robust health. "Having the baby won't be an issue," he continued, "but by the time he turns eighteen, you might be getting tired."

The news of my pregnancy was received differently at the office. Certainly, people were happy for us, but above all, I think, shocked by the news. It wasn't just my age that took them by surprise, it was the singular dedication I'd always exhibited around my job. Most of my colleagues had simply never envisioned me as a mother. Now I would become a working mother with a leadership position at the CIA. It wasn't a life I'd imagined for myself either, but I'd never felt happier.

As my belly steadily grew, I remained as committed to my job as ever, but the impending arrival of our new family member also occupied larger parts of my attention. In the Disguise labs we stayed busy, and I continued to try to imagine keeping up this intensity with a newborn at home. Tony was painting full-time in his studio, and somehow we would make it work.

In the Disguise labs I always made sure we were maintaining a display for the elite members of the White House, Pentagon, and Congress who would occasionally arrive for a tour, often with relatively short notice. At one point Lawrence Eagleburger, the sixty-second Secretary of State, stopped by. As I presented our newest innovations, I picked up a new walking cane we were developing that broke down into a small pile of sticks that could be easily concealed.

"Does yours have whiskey in it?" he asked, leaning somewhat on his own elaborately carved cane.

"No, sir, it doesn't," I replied.

"Well, mine does."

Eagleburger officially held his position from December 8, 1992, to January 20, 1993, earning him the title of shortest-serving Secretary of State in our history. Perhaps his secret whiskey stash had something to do with it.

When Colin Powell, the sixty-fifth US Secretary of State, visited, many employees from the Disguise division lined the halls, peering inside for a sighting. As soon as I saw him, I was struck by his commanding presence. "If he ever ran for office, I would vote for him," I remarked immediately to Frank Anderson, the OTS Director. As I demonstrated our newest technologies during my briefing, he confirmed my first impression. He seemed built for leadership. It's a shame he never got the chance to rise to the highest office.

In December I gave birth to our healthy baby boy, Jesse Lee Mendez, and rather predictably, in a matter of hours our lives changed forever. Like most first-time mothers, I was terrified. How should I hold him? Feed him? Get him to sleep? Every part of our new routine felt intimidating during those first weeks and months. As my maternity leave ended, my confidence as a mother began to take root, but I still needed to figure out how to be Chief of Disguise and a mom. Having Tony, who was already a seasoned dad, working from home would be enormously helpful, I reasoned, but how would I balance a career and personal life that each demanded my full attention?

Once I returned to the office, I began adjusting to working motherhood. With Tony in his home studio painting all day, I didn't have to worry, but I did feel the inevitable longing to be home with them. While I was at work, Tony would put Jesse in a playpen he'd erected in his studio, where he'd invent creative distractions to amuse him while he painted. At one point, I arrived home after a long day to discover a row of painted broom handles Tony had attached to a series of faces that he'd painted on pieces of cardboard. As Tony walked by, he could roll the broom handles, giving Jesse a new set of imaginary friends that could be animated at will. Each time I was reminded of all the fun they were having in my absence, I felt grateful, but torn. I loved my job, but life at home was offering a kind of domestic joy I had never experienced, and it felt too good to pass up.

Several months after Jesse's birth the CIA launched another initiative to downsize, opening another unexpected but brief window during which employees who met certain criteria could retire early. Knowing it was an opportunity that might never arrive again, I went home that night and discussed it with Tony. He voiced his support for my decision regardless of what I chose but was clearly excited about the idea of us all being home together.

Wanting to do my due diligence before making a final decision, I began meeting with all kinds of people inside the agency, letting them know I was considering accepting the offer. Over and over, people advised me to consider how it would feel to become an outsider.

"You'll wake up and see stories in the papers, knowing you're only getting a small slice of what actually happened," they reminded me. "You're going to hate that. You're going to miss this. You'll be back."

As much as I yearned to spend more time with Jesse and Tony, they had a point. Being a spy was who I was, a role that had defined my purpose and given my life meaning. In that regard I was very much like the men I worked with. I had developed a set of unique skills, applied them to the best of my ability, and found great personal satisfaction in that. If someone had asked me back then to describe myself, I would have said, "I'm an intelligence officer." Now that would be over, and that person gone. Who would I be if all the trappings of my career in espionage were stripped away? I didn't know. Ultimately, I realized it was a question I needed to answer for myself. Being Chief of Disguise demanded my full attention, and that was something I could no longer give.

Looking back on my decision to retire at forty-eight, my choice was arguably more controversial than I realized at the time. Women in leadership, especially in technical fields, were far more of an anomaly in 1993 than now. However, the truth was undeniable—my heart wasn't in being Chief the way it had been prepregnancy. I hoped my achievements would help the women who would come after me, but it was still my life. Living life on my terms had gotten me to this point, and whatever new adventures awaited me, I trusted they would take me where I needed to go next. I'd been given a golden opportunity to retire early, and I took it.

At my retirement luncheon, held at a long table in a Chinese restaurant we all frequented on occasion, Jesse, who was still a baby, sat in a high chair at the end of the table, a first for the CIA. The mood was jovial and high-spirited. The people who had cautioned me that I'd dislike being an "outsider" had meant well, and everyone seemed to understand that I'd made the decision with my eyes wide open. Privately I'm sure some people were amazed by my departure, but also I sensed that Tony and I were showing people a new option for their postretirement life. Rather than disappearing into a vacuum, perhaps their post-CIA years could constitute a kind of second life.

Unlike most who retired from the agency, I didn't feel that I'd be severing ties with everyone I'd worked with. I knew that whoever didn't personally visit the house would eventually show up at one of Tony's twice-yearly art shows. The proverbial door that was about to clang shut behind me might not reopen to let me back in, but it would allow many of those still inside to come to us. Those opportunities to maintain contact with at least some of my colleagues were rare among agency retirees.

Still, after twenty-seven years at the CIA I was keenly aware that the course of my life and my career was at yet another inflection point. Tony and I had had several conversations about what my retirement would mean for us. We had met and ultimately fallen in love as two CIA officers. As two civilians, who would we be as a couple? The question was equal parts daunting and thrilling. How would our relationship change? Would we feel untethered? Or unburdened? There were no guarantees, we knew. For me, the lesson has always been to move forward, without hesitation, when the future summons you and life or your heart demands a response. And so, when I walked across the CIA seal embedded in the marble floor of the huge lobby for the last time, and past that pulsating, breathing Wall of Stars, what might have unspooled into the end of a somewhat dramatic and hectic career suddenly became a portal into the world of motherhood and a host of other opportunities I couldn't yet imagine.

CHAPTER 23

Civilian Life

I settled quickly into a new routine with Tony and Jesse at our heavily wooded oasis in the foothills of the Blue Ridge Mountains. Tony had bought these woodland acres, which were about thirty miles outside of DC, years earlier after one of his overseas tours. He had since spent many years building and refining a home and family compound there. A native of the arid landscape in Nevada, he loved the lush green expanse that surrounded us, and I soon discovered that I did too. Since his first wife, Karen, died, the original log cabin that he had constructed had been occupied by his daughter, Amanda, and her husband. The art-studio-cum-showroom that Tony shared with his son Toby, a celebrated sculptor, dwarfed our small post-and-beam house.

Knowing that our limited square footage would feel cramped as Jesse grew older, we made plans to expand our house. I had sold my Porsche 928 and was now driving a Pathfinder, which seemed a more fitting choice for a new mom. The road leading to our house was private, unpaved, and one mile long. I had always longed for a quiet place, and initially I thought this might be it, but I was wrong. It was a beehive of activity, literally buzzing with art and music and people, and I loved it more than any place I had ever been.

Occasionally I would call my friends, who were all my age, and ask what to do when Jesse was doing something puzzling. They would hesitate, trying to remember what they'd done decades earlier when their children were this young. "I don't remember," they would reply with a shrug. As I navigated my way through the maze of motherhood, I discovered that my friends had been right all along. I hadn't known what I'd been missing all those years, but then, I hadn't wanted to be a mother before now. Nothing could compare to parenting, I discovered again and again. While I hadn't spent much time with children as an adult, Jennifer and I had been part-time caretakers to Holly and Heidi after they were born. What I didn't yet have in experience, I could make up for in love and maternal instincts. With each new age came new capabilities and new activities—story time, playgrounds, art, music, piano and karate lessons—and I dove into all of it headfirst. Being a mother, it seemed, was the most natural thing in the world. I loved every second of it.

As Jesse grew into a toddler, Tony began to suggest that I pick up my camera again. When we traveled, which we still did often, he would paint and I would take photos, often of the same view at the same time. It was fascinating to see what he saw, and he enjoyed my perspective as well, sometimes painting directly from my photos. We were fellow creatives, carving out an atypical life, a "retirement" that was incredibly active, varied, and rewarding. I didn't miss my job or the CIA, and our marriage didn't seem to need the CIA, either. Our life had changed enormously, but it was at least as exciting, unpredictable, and rewarding as it had been before we'd retired.

Each quarter, we would host one of Tony and Toby's art shows. I was thrilled by the idea of including my photographs, but also aware that I didn't have the money to contribute what would be my share of each event's considerable up-front expenses. Instead, I offered to be the event planner for the shows, and just like that, our three-way partnership was born.

———

One morning as I sat down with my coffee and opened the *New York Times*, I could almost peer above the tree line at our home and see the proverbial fireworks going off at the CIA. A civil suit had been filed alleging that hundreds of women working in the agency's Directorate of Operations had been denied promotions and power by what some in the media were calling "one of Washington's classic 'old boys' networks."* No longer an insider, I looked out and raised my mug, silently cheering on the brave women of the DO, which is the agency's heart and soul, the operations division that keeps the agency going.

Years before I retired, OTS, historically a part of the DO, was moved to the Directorate of Science and Technology, mainly due to OTS's increasing budgetary needs. Even after that move, however, OTS partnered closely with the DO, where most of our internal customers worked. OTS's roots in the DO had left a cultural imprint that

---

* Eric Schmitt, "9 Women Object to Settlement of Bias Complaint at C.I.A.," *New York Times*, June 6, 1995, www.nytimes.com/1995/06/06/us/9-women-object-to-settlement-of-bias-complaint-at-cia.html.

OTS women felt clearly and often. Left to their own devices, the CIA men would have "allowed" women to stay behind, at home in Washington, tending to the paperwork. They would probably also continue to "allow" women to do some analysis. Women with technical degrees might even be continually permitted to work in the research and development labs. In operations, however, where the agency's "real" work occurred, men ruled the roost. This was especially true for the most interesting assignments, which were typically abroad. Smallwood, my former boss and OTS Chief in the subcontinent, was among the better known of his ilk, but hardly one of a kind.

The women of the DO eventually won the suit, which resulted in a series of retroactive promotions and pay raises and a $940,000 settlement, a sum that, when spread across dozens of women, amounted to little. Throughout, I read about the case with avid interest, aware that I'd been one of the fortunate ones, gaining access to leadership in a technical area of field operations where women weren't "supposed to" rise above a certain level. Far too many of my former colleagues had been kept out of the more-senior roles they deserved. This wasn't news, of course. The Glass Ceiling Study, as well as the findings of the Petticoat Panel and others, had underscored the agency's gender bias for decades. But those findings had all remained under lock and key, tucked away under the guise of necessary secrecy. Now these same findings were part of the public record. With yet another suit being filed, would the agency finally learn its lesson and grant women the same opportunity and access as men? I certainly hoped so.

CHAPTER 24

Forever Changed

As I set up my camera to capture some shots of Notre-Dame cathedral in Paris, I had a feeling that I was not alone. Still vigilant in noticing my surroundings, I made a quick mental note of my suspicion and went on with my day. It was the summer of 2001, and Tony and Jesse had gifted me with a solo trip to Paris, where my camera and I were excited to explore and have a little fun. Later that morning, as I continued walking down the river in the direction of the Musée d'Orsay, I confirmed my hunch. I was being followed on foot by two men. Initially surprised that the DGSE, the French intelligence service, had come out to see me, I soon remembered a call I'd made to the American embassy upon my arrival. Would the embassy gates be open for American tourists on July fourth? I'd asked. No, they wouldn't, I'd been told, unaware that the call was being intercepted. I didn't yet know that there was a credible bomb threat against the US embassy in Paris at the time, so I was amazed that the DGSE was interested in me. I had visited Paris many times, but this was my first time as Jonna Mendez, not Jonna Goeser.

Deciding to shake them off, I stepped off the sidewalk and set down my tripod as they walked down the opposite sidewalk toward me. Unable to step out of my camera angle without being obvious, they disappeared shortly afterward, knowing they'd been seen. They were promptly replaced by two other men, so again I used my espionage skills and photographed them in the foreground with the Pont Neuf and Sainte-Chapelle behind them. Feeling like I'd had enough for the day, I then turned left around the side of the Musée d'Orsay, toward Saint-Germain. On the sidewalk straight ahead of me I saw the original two men, only this time one of them had his cell phone to his ear. He saw me as I saw him, but neither of us could stop walking, so we silently passed within ten feet of each other. During the five additional days I spent in Paris, I didn't see them again. They'd clearly sent a junior team to check me out; a seasoned team would have been more challenging to detect. What struck me, though, was how innate my detection skills still were. Even after so many years as a civilian, I'd effortlessly shifted into my old routines, prepared to outsmart surveillance.

———

Two months later, Tony and I, along with countless others, watched aghast at and deeply saddened by the lives lost at the hands of the terrorists who flew four planes full of passengers to their untimely end: two into the World Trade Center in New York, one into the Pentagon, and a fourth, which may have been intended for the White House or the US Capitol, into an empty field in Shanksville, Pennsylvania.*

Soon afterward the CIA issued an all-points bulletin calling on former employees who wanted to return to duty. Tony and I considered it, even drafting several memorandums to our former office suggesting ideas for tracking down Osama bin Laden and protecting our officers. We reminded them that with our masks we could create more than one bin Laden and position him around the world in situations and locations he should not be seen in—bars, strip clubs, China, etc.—to discredit him. Tony had organized a deception operation during the Iranian Revolution, creating not one but two doubles of the Shah of Iran. We also devised several scenarios designed to sow dissent among the ranks of the al Qaeda faithful, creating doubt from within about who was leaking what, who could be trusted, who was an infiltrator.

In the end, we didn't send any of our memos. We had given our all to the CIA for many years, but many years had passed since we'd each retired. The current generation now doing the work was more than up to the task, we realized, and our suggestions from the sidelines might be more irritating and distracting than helpful.

———

At the tail end of the 1990s Tony was approached by our good friend Keith Melton at the behest of Milton Maltz, who was in the process of founding what would become the International Spy Museum in Washington, DC. During the Korean War, Maltz had worked at the NSA, but he had never

———

* Katherine Huiskes, "Remembering the September 11 Terrorist Attacks," University of Virginia Miller Center, https://millercenter.org/remembering-september-11/september-11-terrorist-attacks.

been a spy. When he asked us to assist him and his staff plan the content and flow of the exhibits and programming, we were delighted.

For three years prior to the museum's opening in 2002, we had a great time helping them. At one point in the process, we were all in Cleveland, Ohio, where Maltz lived and had supported the opening of the Rock and Roll Hall of Fame. Over cocktails I mentioned to him that the museum was missing an important piece—a library. Museum staff, speakers, and sponsoring organizations would all want a place to access books about espionage. We briefly discussed the expense of adding one. When he asked who would take charge of that part of the project, I immediately volunteered. That library has remained a vital part of the museum to this day, and the museum overall has gone on to great success. Tony and I became increasingly involved in its activities as speaking, teaching, and planning exhibits there opened new opportunities. Eventually the museum outgrew its real estate and moved to a new, purpose-designed building perched next to the Wharf, in Washington, DC. A new venue for telling the story of the intelligence community to the public, this museum became our second family and significantly changed our lives.

During the years that followed, we also made several on-camera appearances. In addition to acting as technical advisors on *The Agency*, a television series, we were also featured on "Hounds and Hares," which was part of the PBS *Innovation* series. The premise was that we would demonstrate to the public how we worked with the FBI in honing their and our surveillance and surveillance-detection skills. We met with the film crew at the Mayflower Hotel in DC, where we were given cameras and microphones—one in Tony's tie, the other in my purse. We were on a "mission" to meet with a terrorist and pass him or her a written document. The FBI's highly regarded surveillance team, known as the "Gs," would tail us as we moved on foot through DC. Their goal was to witness our illegal handoff to these foreign nationals. Our goal was to "win" this televised competition by eluding their surveillance, but we knew that wouldn't be easily accomplished.

Feeling excited and nervous, as soon as the "chase" began Tony and I split up, which forced the Gs to make a quick, possibly unexpected decision—would they follow Tony? Or me? Or both of us? They chose Tony, which allowed me to follow the plan that Tony and I had devised in advance.

The entire episode lasted about thirty minutes. I changed my appearance twice, first turning into an old woman walking a large poodle and then morphing into an old man walking rather gingerly and smoking a huge cigar. The FBI was not happy when I successfully passed my faux document to the terrorist, a young woman who resembled a Georgetown college student.

The taping was great fun, the piece was well received on PBS, plus we enjoyed having drinks with the FBI team afterward. It was also another great example of one of the themes that had dominated my espionage career. Being chronically underestimated by men was an advantage that women could and should use to their advantage. That, in fact, was precisely what Tony and I did that day, when we planned in advance for me to be the one to pass the intel to the faux terrorist. We'd bet on the FBI assuming that he, the man, would perform the "real" work, which allowed me, in my different disguises, to proceed undetected. It was a strategy we'd used before in many parts of the world, in real-life espionage operations. For better or worse, in the twenty-first century it still proved just as effective.

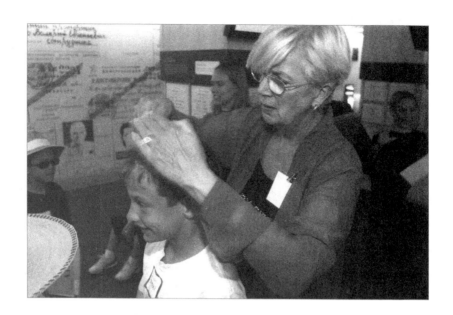

CHAPTER 25

Emerging from the Shadows

During Tony's time as Chief of Disguise in the 1970s, he had spent time on set in Los Angeles standing next to Hollywood makeup artist John Chambers to study his craftsmanship. When in 1979 the Canadian Caper, aka Argo—the rescue of six American diplomats during the Iran hostage crisis—began, Tony had called on Chambers again. Together they created the fake film company that allowed Tony, and the diplomats he was accompanying, to escape capture. It was a momentous achievement born of a partnership that continued throughout the remainder of Chambers's life.

At one point Tony and I visited Chambers, who lived in an apartment inside the Motion Picture Country House, a retirement facility on Mulholland Drive in Los Angeles, where Hollywood retirees often lived in later life. He gave us a brief tour from his wheelchair. One of his walls was covered with photos of him with all kinds of famous names in Hollywood alongside awards and other honors he'd earned. Wheeling toward that wall, he pointed to the mostly blank space in the middle, where a single framed medal was hung.

"See where it is?" he asked, pointing to that medal. "See how I can reach it? If this place ever burns down, that's the one thing I'm grabbing."

That "thing" was the first award the CIA had ever given to a civilian, the Intelligence Medal of Merit. Over the years it had remained Chambers's most cherished possession.

The mastery Tony had gained decades earlier during his time with Chambers had helped to transform the art and science of disguise in the CIA, paving the way for innovations that earned Disguise a new level of respect and significance within the agency. Together they had changed each other's lives and those of six American diplomats in Tehran. Little did we know that their partnership hadn't yet run its course. The work Tony and Chambers did together would continue to ripple through our lives, and the lives of many others, in ways that would shock and delight us.

———

Upon retiring from the CIA, Tony and I had each signed documents pledging to keep our espionage work secret. When each of us walked out of the agency for the last time, we'd been walking into a life of utter anonymity. There would be no reminiscing about the operation in Africa or that mishap in the Middle East or the close call in Western Europe—not with friends, not with family, in fact, not even with each other. We kept that promise, focusing entirely on the new life we were building. If 1997 hadn't played out the way it did, we would have been known as a painter and a photographer who married late in life and had a son at ages when most people no longer could.

The very things we never expected—public visibility and acclaim—first arrived at our home in an overnight envelope addressed to Tony and slipped under our screen door. It was a letter signed by George Tenet, then Director of the CIA. To commemorate the agency's fiftieth anniversary, the agency was "recognizing fifty agency officers, from our earliest days to the present, who by their actions, example, innovations or initiative have taken the CIA in important new directions and helped shape our history." This was the first time the CIA had ever given its officers public recognition of any kind. Being one of the original fifty Trailblazers was a tremendous honor. Six of the fifty were women, and one of them was my personal idol, Eloise Page, whose work alongside Bill Donovan during WWII and for years afterward had helped our country as well as the agency and women's roles within it. For Tony to be named alongside Eloise was a real honor.

Shortly after we learned about Tony's Trailblazer Award, *60 Minutes*, one of our favorite television shows, decided to film a segment on him. Since the filming would coincide with our autumn art show, they decided to tape the segment at our art studio in the Blue Ridge Mountains when the fall leaves were at peak color. Excited about this unexpected opportunity, we also knew the risk this posed and dutifully called all our CIA friends who might attend to warn them that the media would be in attendance.

To our astonishment, my old friend Liz arrived at that art show unannounced from New York. When the *60 Minutes* producer asked her about her longtime friend Jonna's career as a spy, Liz was flabbergasted. Until that moment, she'd had no clue about the true nature of my career. Those interviews never aired, but it was my first lesson in mending fences over the lies I'd had to tell, even to people I cared about deeply. Understandably, it took months for her to process all the half-truths I'd had to tell her over the many years of our friendship.

Shortly after the Trailblazer ceremony, we got another surprise, this time in the form of a call to Tony from George Tenet. He wanted Tony to do something even more shocking.

"This is a moment when the world is kind of quiet," he said. "It's a chance for the CIA to put out one good story. It's never been done before, and we'd like that story to be Argo."

Up to this point, the Argo story had remained classified. The internal CIA magazine, *Studies in Intelligence*, had wanted to publish the details of the operation years before, but the agency had vetoed the idea, saying it was still too sensitive to tell, even to its own. Suddenly the Argo story (otherwise known as the Canadian Caper) would be made available to the mass media. Telling the story in such a public way went against Tony's grain, but somewhat reluctantly he agreed to sit down with the *New York Times*.

Soon after the article came out Tony was contacted by a literary agent, and within a couple of years his first book, *The Master of Disguise*, was published, and the true tale of the Argo operation featured in its own chapter. In the space of a few short years, we went from total anonymity to being publicly known as retired CIA officers, and Tony as an author, too.

By this time Tony and I were also teaching across the multitude of agencies that form the intelligence community: the CIA, DIA, NSA, and more. We were proud to be able to pass on some lessons learned, and I found teaching cathartic, perhaps because it allowed me to integrate my "old" life with my new one. The cluster of courses we were teaching was also broader and reached many more people than any of the talks I'd done at the Farm in the years before my retirement. I marveled at the growing number of young women in our classes, excited that I was helping young versions of me to step into espionage careers that had once been exclusively reserved for men.

———

With growing public interest in CIA women and Tony's and my new public status as retired intelligence officers, the doctor who'd delivered Jesse reached out to me. As head of one of the medical communities in Washington, DC, he asked me to come talk to a group about my experience with childbirth and about my career in the CIA. It was the first time I spoke publicly on my own about my career. It was also the moment I realized how interested people were in the espionage work I'd done. From that point onward I began getting requests from groups around the country who wanted to hear about my career.

Since retiring from the CIA to be a wife and mother, I was as surprised as anyone to find myself now working as a teacher, photographer, public speaker, and event planner/Vice President for a nonprofit music foundation Tony and I had gotten involved in entirely by happenstance. Before long I would be an author, too. Unlike so many CIA employees who retired and returned with a "green badge" to work as consultants or contractors for the agency, Tony and I had created hybrid "second act" careers that were anything but the norm at the time. So much of our new life had unfolded organically in ways that often surprised us, but as the years rolled on, we found ourselves having more fun than even we'd imagined.

In the summer of 2006, a journalist named Joshuah Bearman pitched the story of Argo to *Wired* magazine.* At the time, each story pitch was given a score from zero to six. Argo earned a 4.0 grade that day, which put it in fifth place out of twelve stories under consideration. The Editor in Chief liked the story but felt that it wasn't a fit for *Wired*, which was about optimism and the future. The Argo story was in the running but struggling to make the cut.

When Bearman reached out to Tony, I suggested that they both sign documents that protected Tony; Hollywood's reputation for taking ownership of other people's stories was the industry's worst-kept secret. Then Tony began telling his Argo story to Bearman. The final piece was published in 2007 and laid out in cartoonlike image blocks, like a visual storyboard, a classic screenwriting beat sheet destined for the big screen. The story, in fact, was bait for Hollywood, which evidently conducted its own version of espionage. One night before the article had even come out, our phone rang. Smokehouse, George Clooney's production company, was interested in buying the rights to the story. Later that night the phone rang a second time; Brad Pitt's production company was also interested. Rather than rely solely on Hollywood, which was prone to embellishment, Tony decided to write the true tale of Argo in book form. We worked on it together for months, collaborating with a writer.

As this newer, more public version of our lives began to blossom, I noticed a slight change in Tony. At our quarterly art shows he was his typical, gregarious self, engaging with our guests as usual, except for

* Nicholas Thompson, "The *Wired* Origins of 'Argo,'" *New Yorker*, February 21, 2013, www.newyorker.com/culture/culture-desk/the-wired-origins-of-argo.

one difference. Instead of looking them in the eyes, his gaze would drift slightly off to one side. His oldest son, Toby, the sculptor, approached me at around this same time in 2009. "Have you noticed that thing Dad's been doing with his pinky finger?" he asked me. I had not, but we resolved to schedule Tony for a checkup. The local doctor we saw asked him to walk and make a certain movement with his elbow, among other vaguely odd requests. "I'm afraid you have Parkinson's disease," she said when she sat us down at the end of his exam. We were both shocked, but neither of us knew enough about the disease to understand quite what she was telling us. Knowing we needed real answers, I found a Parkinson's specialist at Johns Hopkins and made an appointment. To our deep disappointment and dismay, he, too, confirmed the diagnosis. Parkinson's disease is a progressive disorder involving the nervous system, but no one could tell us how quickly it would progress or how long Tony had left.

Rather than losing myself in despair, I did what I'd learned with Jennifer and leaned on my leadership and management skills. Together, Tony and I had always made a formidable team, and this time was no exception. After sharing the news with his children and closest family members, we sought out top specialists and developed a long-lasting relationship with his new doctor, a Parkinson's expert. Thanks in part to the excellent care he was getting, Tony's disease was progressing slowly. He was still in the early throes. He was growing slower, but that was noticeable only to those who had known him for a long time. We agreed that the wider world didn't need to know, at least not yet. He and I had always traveled together, and that certainly wouldn't change, but from that point onward, I would make a point of remaining nearby, just in case.

For a period of years, the Argo movie project sat in George Clooney's project queue. Eventually, someone sent a screenwriter out to our home to talk to us. The day after he arrived, however, we discovered him fast asleep on our porch. He suffered from narcolepsy, we were later told. Eventually, Smokehouse sent Chris Terrio to see us. *Argo* was the first movie he'd written, but we couldn't have asked for a better partner. Over time we became friends, and Tony began jokingly calling him our "penetration agent." Later Ben Affleck stepped in for George Clooney, who had gotten stuck in postproduction on another project. As we heard the story, Ben was at Warner Bros. one day and noticed the project. When he asked who was doing it, they replied, "You are."

During filming we were invited on set and flew to Los Angeles for a couple of days, where we were promptly driven to an abandoned VA hospital where they were filming the movie's early scenes inside the Tehran embassy. When we drove up to the site, all six of the actors who played the "houseguests" Tony had helped to rescue were standing outside the building, still in full character makeup and wardrobe, taking a break from the shoot. "Look," he said, pointing at them one by one as we drove up to the building. "There are the Staffords and there's Cora." The real-life versions of these characters had all stayed in Tony's life over the years, including visiting him at our home for a picnic and badminton. Seeing their Hollywood likenesses felt almost like seeing them.

On set between takes, Tony and I struck up a conversation with the actor who was playing the COS in the movie. "I was so pissed at you," Tony began, shaking his head. "Why did you have those [fake] passports in your desk?" We all laughed, amused that the taping felt so real to Tony that he was admonishing the actor for what the real-life person had done. Excited to witness more of the filming, we wanted to travel to Istanbul to watch some of the overseas filming, but Ben was concerned that the streets were so narrow and crowded we'd have no place to stand. Later in the process he graciously shared how the overseas filming had gone. The blue mosque they'd used in the movie had been a site of particular focus. In the movie there's this beautiful, ethereal glow coming from multiple chandeliers that hang from the ceiling there. That glow had resulted from the four thousand lightbulbs the film crew had methodically replaced, one by one, to create that precisely perfect lighting temperature. Tony and I smiled knowingly. Just as the camera needed a perfectly calibrated Kelvin score, various kinds of masks had also required different kinds of light to be effective.

Throughout this period, Ben Affleck was a continual presence in our lives. Ben and Tony did several interviews and photo shoots together. I always went to these events, poised in the background with my Nikon F3 camera. By this point, Tony's disease had turned him into a quieter man and, of course, that was the version of Tony that Ben played—the Tony Mendez he had met.

As filming continued, we became aware that some parts of Tony's story had been changed, but we didn't have details; all we'd seen were pieces of the early filming and an early partial draft of the script. Once the movie was finished, we received an invitation to an exclusive screening, just for us and one Warner Bros. representative. Together at a small, private theater in Washington, DC, before it was available to the public, the three of us watched *Argo* on the big screen. From start to finish, as Tony and I sat there watching, we were stunned. They'd turned this chapter of Tony's life and career into an incredible movie. We loved it.

In the movie version, they'd altered details of Tony's personal life and the operation itself. Tony was never separated from his first wife, Karen, who is in the movie but with whom in real life he'd had a wonderful marriage until her untimely passing years after Argo took place. He's also portrayed as the father of one child in the film when he had three, which I think briefly left two of his children, Toby and Amanda, wondering why they'd been cut. Tony also hadn't traveled to Tehran on his own. He'd been accompanied by a linguist, who was helpful in translating the documents that got them home safely and without whom they probably all would have been caught. Nobody was ever chased down a runway with a gun, either, but as Chris Terrio told us, "My job is to get the audience sitting at the edge of their seats, and you're telling me you're terrified as you sit on a plane and stare out a tiny window?" Understandably, they'd added some drama to the final climax. From our first viewing, that chase scene remained Tony's favorite scene in the entire film.

From that day forward, to a far greater degree than ever before, Tony became "the guy in *Argo*" and I, a novelty—a female spy who'd risen in the ranks in the CIA. For a while our life was filled with Hollywood parties and film award ceremonies that we flew all around the country to attend. At one of George Clooney's parties, we met John Goodman, who played John Chambers in the movie.

"Did you know John Chambers?" we asked him, amazed by the accuracy of his portrayal; Chambers had passed away in 2001. No, Goodman told us. He'd never met him, hadn't even known who Chambers was before seeing the script. It was a brilliant casting decision that had been acted and directed to a T. In addition to the other actors, we met Maz Siam, who had played the aggressive guard at the airport. He'd portrayed the meanest, scariest character in the movie, but he was one of the kindest, sweetest men I'd ever encountered.

We first met Bryan Cranston during filming at Dulles Airport while sitting in makeup chairs being prepared for our walk-on roles in the movie. A man came in and sat in the chair between us. He began telling jokes, and we were all laughing when Tony realized who he was. I had no idea that Bryan Cranston was a famous movie star. We met him as a friendly, funny, and colorful raconteur. Jennifer Garner was also on-site at the Dulles filming, pregnant and glowing.

Our favorite memento from the movie was the director's chairs they had made for us. Our names were printed on the fronts and the CIA seal on the backs. For years we kept them in the studio, and after each art show, inevitably some of our CIA friends would come over and quietly ask how they could get their own chair. Unfortunately, we didn't have any covert insider agency contact to offer, only a host of great memories from a Hollywood experience that couldn't be easily duplicated.

Prior to the film's official release on October 12, 2012, it was shown in Telluride in September, where it was extremely well received. Later that same month, Tony and I flew to the Toronto International Film Festival. There were so many other great movies that year—*Life of Pi*, *Zero Dark Thirty*, and *Lincoln*, to name a few. When they showed *Argo*, everyone stood up and cheered. "If this keeps up, the film might have a shot at the Oscar," Tony remarked to me later.

Amazed by the overwhelming response, I turned to Tony at one point and said, "But they know how it ends, don't they? It's history. They know they're going to get away, right?" It was a lesson in the power of good storytelling. Even CIA insiders were swept away. When we watched it at the Canadian embassy, seated between the Canadian ambassador and David Petraeus, who was briefly the Director of the CIA, they, too, stood up and cheered. Everywhere we went the movie was received with a standing ovation.

In February of 2013, our third book, *Argo*, was released, elevating our visibility yet again. When the film version was nominated for an

Academy Award, we were surprised to learn that our invitations weren't a given. The long list of Hollywood elite, cast, and studio execs who needed to attend occupied most, if not all, of the available seats. Getting on that list was a competitive sport. We were in the running, but in no way guaranteed to make the cut.

About a week before the big night, we got the call. We'd made it onto the list. Excited by the news I quickly picked up the phone and called a friend who had far more experience attending galas and other big social events than I. She agreed to accompany me on a shopping expedition. When we walked onto the appropriate floor of Bloomingdale's in New York City, she pointed to a pale floor-length gown I never would have picked for myself. "I don't wear pastels," I told her. Ignoring my comment, she insisted I try it on, along with a few others. To my surprise, her first pick—a light peach gown with a shawl collar and shimmering brocade skirt—was perfect.

We stayed at the Four Seasons in Beverly Hills, and on the morning of the ceremony a team of professionals arrived to get us Oscar ready, which meant hair, makeup, manicures, and pedicures for us both. We had never been pampered like that before and never were again. On the red carpet we encountered Hollywood's best and brightest, although not always in ideal ways. At one point Tony stepped on Amy Adams's huge ballgown, and I mistakenly reversed Channing Tatum's name and called him "Tatum Channing." As we walked across the lobby toward the auditorium, people would whisper "Argo" as they passed by. The entire evening was a blur of glamorous faces and encounters, the likes of which we'd never experience again.

From that point onward, we got used to being recognized in public. In hotel lobbies and other places, people would pass Tony and mutter "Argo" without missing a step.

Our increased visibility also led to additional speaking opportunities. When we went to the Air Force Academy in Colorado, the entire audience stood up and cheered for Tony as we walked into the auditorium, before he had even spoken. One day as we settled into our seats on a domestic flight, the pilot emerged from the cockpit, kneeled by Tony's aisle seat, and congratulated him on the movie. We experienced these kinds of receptions and responses repeatedly. It was an incredible way to finish a career.

CHAPTER 26

The Adventure Continues

On December 30, 2017, Jennifer Lynne Matthews, Chief of CIA Forward Operating Base Chapman, was standing in a line alongside Elizabeth Hanson, a female CIA analyst, and five CIA men. They were in a remote valley in Afghanistan awaiting the arrival of a potential defector with invaluable intelligence. Seconds after the man's car drove up, the driver got out and opened his vest, revealing his true purpose. His body was encased in explosives; he, an al Qaeda faithful, was a human bomb.

The massacre that immediately followed killed all seven CIA officers. Jennifer Lynne Matthews was a mother of three working in an active war zone as one of the CIA's top al Qaeda experts. Thirty-year-old Elizabeth Hanson had often provided intelligence that led to successful drone strikes against key terrorists. Their deaths highlighted a generational change that I always knew was coming. There could be no more comparing genders; Jennifer and Elizabeth had done the work of men, going toe-to-toe with some of the world's most ruthless terrorists. They had also died as many CIA men had—tragically and suddenly, for a country and a cause they'd sacrificed everything for. That day they joined more than 130 CIA officers for whom stars are chiseled into our marble walls. I only wish I had known them.

Jennifer and Elizabeth were descendants of every CIA woman who came before them—a long and storied tale that survives their tragic deaths, even today. Eloise Page led the charge in World War II, proving her worth in our fight against the Nazis. She was perhaps the highest-ranking of that early generation of female spies, but she was not alone. Virginia Hall and analysts like Adelaide Hawkins and thousands of young women were also recruited and trained by the OSS, the predecessor to the CIA, and other military intelligence agencies as code breakers.* When the men returned home after the war, many women who had worked as analysts and a few as field officers were again relegated to clerical jobs. However, the seed had been planted, the potential unearthed: women possessed the talents, abilities, and daring required of any good espionage officer. For a time that knowledge simmered beneath the surface, percolating inside our hearts and our minds.

By the late 1970s, the women's liberation movement could no longer be denied, and Deputy Director E. Henry Knoche wrote in an internal memo: "What kind of careers do you want for [your daughters]? Do you want to see their opportunities limited to the GS-07 or GS-08 level where the majority of women in the Agency remain today?" Finally, he invoked the Equal Employment Opportunity Act of 1972:

---

* A. J. Baime, "The History of Female Spies in the CIA," History Channel, www.history.com/news/cia-women-spy-leaders.

"Women's lib is open to debate, the law of the land is not."* Much like in the private sector, however, these changes would be gradual.

After arriving at the CIA, some of us became determined to leave the typewriters and file folders behind and do the real work—the "men's work." Slowly but surely, we used our unique abilities to rise as far and high as we could. Somewhat ironically, that upward trajectory into management was my path but never my goal. Those among us who did reach new heights for women remained the undeniable minority, of course. Still, we oversaw critical operations and attended meetings where few, if any, other women were permitted. That reminded us, our peers, and our bosses and direct reports what was always plainly obvious to me: women make great spies.

In 2011, a journalist at the *Washington Post* wrote of my generation: "CIA veterans said the gender gap is closing largely because of the persistence of a group of women who joined the agency in the 1970s and 80s and made their way into its upper ranks." As Mary Margaret Graham, one of the first women to hold a senior position at the Directorate of Operations, expressed it, "It is a generational thing . . . They proved they were ready for bigger and more important jobs."† I'm proud to be part of that generation, but I retired knowing how much progress for women still lay ahead.

Throughout my CIA career nearly all my bosses and superiors were men. Most of them supported my work and my rise within OTS, but the three who didn't stand out. First there was David, the head of OTS Personnel, who told me during my early days as a branch secretary that I couldn't qualify for a nonsecretarial job in OTS without an

---

* Tasneem Raja, "The Secret History of CIA Women," *Mother Jones*, November 4, 2013, www.motherjones .com/politics/2013/11/women-cia-history-sexism.
† Greg Miller, "At CIA, the Glass Ceiling Shows Its Cracks," *Washington Post*, November 10, 2011, www.washingtonpost.com/blogs/checkpoint-washington/post/at-cia-the-glass-ceiling-shows-it-cracks /2011/11/10/gIQAjEm38M_blog.html.

advanced technical degree. Years later I would encounter Henry, who rolled that physically harmless but terrifying grenade at my feet during OTS's Career Development Program. Finally, my greatest challenge appeared in the form of Tom Smallwood, my Chief in the subcontinent, who worked hard but ultimately unsuccessfully to sabotage my reputation and my performance. Each of these men taught me a lot. I'm grateful for those lessons, but I don't wish them on any woman. Jumping through the hoops of men's misogyny shouldn't be part of our job descriptions.

As a twenty-one-year-old "contract wife" who first entered the CIA through the typing pool, I certainly didn't have a life plan, or even clearly defined goals. What I did have was a deep-seated desire to do work that mattered. Over the years that followed, I encountered any number of roadblocks in my path, but never quite believed they applied to me. However "impossible" each new goal I set seemed—to become a technical officer even though I didn't have the required degree or experience, to attend the Career Development Program that few women had ever been chosen for, to expand my skills into disguise in order to qualify for the overseas assignment I wanted—I knew I would find a way forward. You could call it fearlessness, or you could call it blind determination. Whatever it was, it propelled me forward time and time again.

Without a doubt my experience at the CIA was atypical. Years before Tony and I worked together on denied-area operations, and even longer before we became friends and then a couple, he seemed to be insulating me from the potential impact of Smallwood's obfuscation and deceit. I didn't have a mentor, per se, and I certainly had to earn my way up the so-called food chain, but I did have a branch of the "boys club" advocating for my hard-earned reputation. Too few women can say as much.

Nora Slatkin, who served as Executive Director of the CIA from 1995 to 1998, famously said:

> We have had problems at CIA, and some women have left the agency in frustration. But for every woman who left there were hundreds more who stayed, excelled, and changed the agency in the process. These are women who have traveled the world, dined with ambassadors, briefed princes and presidents, run clandestine operations, and pioneered new technologies.

In 2018, nearly twenty years after Slatkin's departure, journalist and CIA historian Tim Weiner stated that "apart from the Marines, there is no branch of service in the United States government as hostile to women as the clandestine services of the CIA." Having never worked in other parts of the government, I can't definitively agree or disagree with that statement, but my hunch is that since its inception, the CIA has reflected American attitudes toward women in the workplace and positions of leadership. In some ways, CIA women have fared comparatively better. Even in 1953, the CIA had 14 percent more female employees than other federal agencies; their average GS grade was GS-05, compared to GS-03 in other sectors of government.[*] By 2012, 43 percent of the CIA's GS-14 officers and 37 percent of its GS-15s were female. However, the leadership pipeline for women reportedly still narrowed once women reached GS-13.[†] Throughout the agency's history, it seems women have also been denied critical roles where they

---

[*] Martina Uková, "Women in CIA: From Typists to Trailblazers?," (PhD diss., Univerzita Karlova, 2016), www.academia.edu/27677085/Women_in_CIA_From_Typists_to_Trailblazers.
[†] Brent Durbin, "Addressing 'This Woeful Imbalance': Efforts to Improve Women's Representation at CIA, 1947–2013," in CIA, *From Typist to Trailblazer: The Evolving View of Women in the CIA's Workforce*, October 30, 2013, https://scholarworks.smith.edu/gov_facpubs/20.

count most—in field operations, where I was fortunate to carve out a fulfilling career.

In more recent years, considerable progress seems to have been made, although that, too, has been imperfect. As the number of women in the field seemed to increase, Valerie Plame was publicly outed by the Bush administration in 2003, arguably misused as a political scape-goat. In her best-selling book, *Fair Game* (2007), she highlights the lack of mentoring that was available to CIA women, as well as what I observed—that promotion panels were historically composed exclu-sively of men.* Echoing these gender imbalances, national security expert Amy Zegart was quoted in 2009 as saying, "It's pretty remark-able that we've had three women Secretaries of State, but no woman at the head of the FBI or CIA."[†]

Yet additional, flawed progress for CIA women continued, includ-ing at Alec Station, the group that gathered the intelligence that led to the killing of Osama bin Laden in 2011. One CIA operative recalled the patronizing attitude toward the team and their leader, Michael Scheuer. "What's his staff? It's all female. It was just widely discussed at the time that it's a bunch of chicks. So, the perspective was frankly condescending and dismissive. And Scheuer (and his staff) essentially were saying 'You guys need to listen to us; this is really serious. This is a big deal, and people are going to die.' And of course, they were right."[‡]

However challenging the trajectory for CIA women may be, progress appears to persist. In 2018 Gina Haspel, a career clandestine operations officer, became the first female Director of Central Intelligence. During her

---

* Valerie Plame Wilson, *Fair Game* (New York: Simon & Schuster, 2007), 56–57.

† Michael Scherer, "Is America Ready for a Spymistress?," *Time*, December 16, 2009, https://swampland.time.com/2009/12/16/is-america-ready-for-a-spymistress.

‡ Peter Bergen, "A Feminist Film Epic and the Real Women of the CIA," CNN, December 13, 2012, www.cnn.com/2012/12/13/opinion/bergen-feminist-epic/index.html.

tenure, women headed most of the agency's primary components. Haspel certainly had her hands full navigating the political climate. From day one she undoubtedly used all her clandestine skills and operational savvy to walk the walk against the stiff wind of President Trump's displeasure with the intelligence community generally and the CIA in particular.

When in May 2019 the President announced that he was stripping retired CIA Director John Brennan of his security clearances due to his criticisms of the President, sixty former CIA officers issued a statement protesting the removal of those clearances. It was published in the *Washington Post*, where more names were added, including Tony's and mine. In this tense environment Haspel was forced to walk a thin line, staying faithful to her mission at the CIA while inventing new ways to stay as far out of politics as her job allowed.

I thought a lot about Haspel throughout that time. Would she make it through the dangerous terrain she was forced to travel? Or were there too many proverbial trip wires hidden along her path? Most of the criticisms I heard around Haspel's conduct came from a male-centric point of view, which is often how we evaluate female leaders. I would like to offer an alternative interpretation. Haspel was a veteran intelligence officer known for her fierce loyalty to the agency. Her operational antennae were finely tuned, as was her ability to focus on her target. She spoke in public only a few times during her tenure, wisely maintaining a low profile. Multiple CIA insiders expressed appreciation for her performance; during a politically fraught time in the agency's history, she built morale, boosted recruitment, and insulated the CIA's workforce. She used her power as Director, and as a woman. In the end her softer, gentler interpersonal style may have saved her and the agency too. Her loyalty, above all, remained with the CIA and the work to which she'd devoted her career.

I have always thought that women make better operations officers than most men, occupying leadership for the sake of the larger whole rather than for themselves and a small cadre of cohorts. Gina Haspel personified that. Most importantly, she held on to her seat long enough to ensure that the next Director of the CIA, William Burns, arrived to find the agency still intact.

———

During the years that have passed since my retirement from the CIA, a lot has changed for me as well. In January 2019 Tony's battle with Parkinson's ended. He left us all with a lifetime of memories, hearts bursting with love and gratitude, and me with a mission to continue the work he and I had begun upon retiring from the CIA. I miss him every day, yet I also feel his presence in my life in so much of what I now do—speaking to groups around the world, appearing in documentaries and on podcasts, contributing to the Spy Museum's programs and events, and of course, writing books. This book.

I have been a full-fledged civilian for over twenty years, yet the CIA remains at the center of so much of what I do. While writing this book, I was honored to be the author in residence at the Hemingway House in Ketchum, Idaho. Hemingway, too, once worked for the CIA. I can almost envision him navigating the Caribbean waters on his boat, the *Pilar*, sipping mojitos while hunting German U-boats. Past and present, the CIA always seems to be by my side.

Some of my most gratifying moments now come from some of my youngest audience members. They appear each summer when I speak to groups of high school students that come to Washington, DC. They comment online and approach me at the Spy Museum to tell me that they have read my books and heard my talks. It somehow still surprises me, being known in this public way. I like to think it helps all younger people, especially girls and women, to see that there is no such thing as "men's work" and "women's work," that those old ways of thinking were never based in fact. Most importantly, I hope my story reminds everyone that when we discover work that adds meaning and purpose to our lives, it could be our willingness to go for it, despite whatever steep odds we may face, that counts most in the end. It worked for me, and I hope will for many more of today's girls and women too.

In the summer of 2020, I was reminded again of the power of women's contributions when I attended a performance at the Kennedy Center. While I was sitting with my friend Tracy at a small round table in the members-only Russian Lounge, her eyes lit up as a small group began moving slowly across the floor. Ruth Bader Ginsburg, accompanied by NPR radio host and friend Nina Totenberg, was being seated at a nearby table. Leaning slightly forward, Tracy whispered, "No photos, Jonna." I nodded, smiling knowingly, even as the CIA photo operative inside me moved my sequined bag onto the tabletop. After opening it, I subtly positioned my phone on its side, still inside the bag, leaning against the hinge of my purse, with the viewfinder facing RBG. I couldn't check the angle of my camera; all I had was my instinct. When Nina returned to the table with RBG's tea, I snapped a photo of an icon and role model who had inspired me and countless other women.

Moments later, the chimes rang, prompting us all to enter the auditorium and take our seats. As the lights lowered, the vast space grew quiet and we awaited the first notes from the orchestra pit. Then the lights slowly began to come back up. Instinctively, I looked over my shoulder. The tiny yet formidable RBG herself was proceeding down the aisle, escorted on each side by uniformed staff. Immediately, the entire audience of the opera house stood, erupting in a standing ovation. I doubt I was the only woman in that room covered in goosebumps as RBG took her seat and we all sat down. The lights then dimmed again, and the opera began. This apparently happened every time she attended a performance, but for me it was a first and a memory I will always cherish.

This woman. This brilliant woman who had to fight the good fight before the glass ceiling even had a name. The Supreme Court Justice who, on many levels, represented women in America and their struggle for equal treatment in the workplace. This powerful, petite woman made me tear up that night. I felt moved by her and Eloise Page and Janine Brookner and the thousands of others who carved a path for the rest of us. I'm so grateful for my place on that path, and for all the others who walk it behind me.

ACKNOWLEDGMENTS

This book, like those Tony and I once worked on together, has its own story of twists and turns. Born during the strange and isolating days of the Covid-19 pandemic, when so many of us were stuck in lockdown, it began as a straightforward memoir about my life and career. From one week to the next, the pages I wrote became a sort of companion, helping me to focus on something other than everything I temporarily couldn't do—traveling around the world to speak to groups and working on-site as a founding board member of the Spy Museum in Washington, DC, among other things. Eventually, I shared my pages with Christy Fletcher, who turned to me and asked, "But what was it *really* like rising into leadership as a woman in the CIA?" *Oh*, I thought, *I suppose that is an important part of my story.*

I was born into a generation of women who dared to break the mold. In our own ways, both subtle and overt, many of us stood up and demanded to be considered for opportunities that had been inaccessible to our own mothers. Some among us rose to new heights. Nearly all of us were mocked and disrespected along the way. The path wasn't always obstructed, though. Telling that story, *my* story as a woman working my way toward leadership in a notoriously male-dominated environment, soon became the mission of this book. In the process,

I reached out to many people I'd once known and met others who became integral to the book as it stands now, in your hands.

Upon first sitting down with Wyndham Wood, I thought I was presenting her with a finished book that might require some polishing. What took place instead was her closer, more intimate look at my career, placing it in the larger context of women in the CIA and, indeed, women in the American workplace. It became clear that I could not tell my story without alluding to theirs. Wyndham didn't just polish this manuscript, she helped me structure it in a way that tells two stories— one in the world of espionage, the other in the world of women. I will be forever grateful for her input. And her friendship.

The many other helping hands who enabled and supported this book have proven indispensable. Gráinne Fox, my agent, has been a steady hand throughout, as well as a delightfully fun-loving plus-one during at least one fabulous event! Maddy Hernick has also been instrumental in keeping the process moving forward, and Kristina Moore, in working to spread my story far and wide through other media. I am fortunate to have them, as well as Christy Fletcher, on my team, always available to provide guidance.

My editor, Ben Adams, and the entire team at PublicAffairs and beyond—Katie Adams, Kelly Lenkevich, Emily Andrukaitis, Sheryl Kober, Emily Baker, and Pete Garceau—polished and designed the inside and outside. Each of your contributions has helped make this book a reality. Thank you.

To my son, Jesse Mendez, whose long workdays were not infrequently disrupted by my questions and need for tech support, I love you and am forever grateful for you. For your dad and for me, life changed in the most enduringly beautiful ways the moment we learned you were on the way.

The many people within the CIA who supported me during my decades inside those hallowed walls are mentioned in these pages, but I have no doubt that there were also some invisible hands steering the careers of women like me. Those who were known to me, most especially my late husband, Tony Mendez, will remain forever in my heart. Those who attempted to barricade my path, I owe you, too, a deep bow of gratitude. At times your sheer determination to push me down may have been what inspired me most.

I continue to be amazed and delighted by the opportunities and people who now cross my path. Speaking to audiences around the world, of all ages, creeds, and origins, I am humbled by the curiosity and interest they express. Retiring from the CIA to discover an entirely new world filled with the exciting roads I now travel down has been one of the most surprising developments of my life and career. I feel incredibly fortunate to do this work I do, and by telling my story, I hope I encourage other young girls and women to pursue the life they most desire. Together, forever, we remain invincible.

INDEX

JONNA MENDEZ is a former Chief of Disguise with over twenty-five years of experience as a CIA officer working in Moscow and other sensitive areas. With her late husband, Tony Mendez, she is the best-selling coauthor of *Argo*, *The Moscow Rules*, and *Spy Dust*.